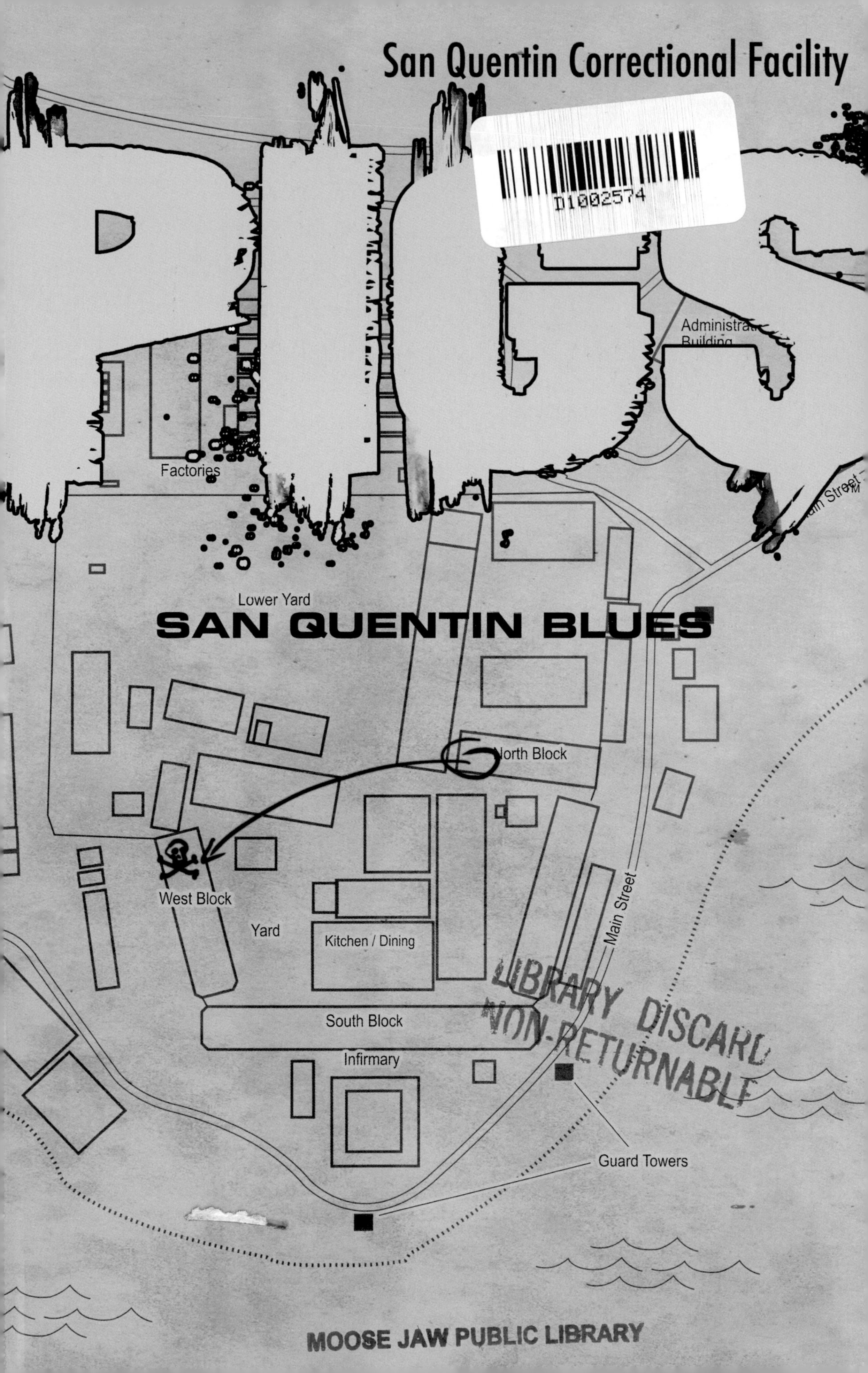
San Quentin Correctional Facility
PIGS
SAN QUENTIN BLUES
Factories
Lower Yard
Administra
Building
Main Street
North Block
West Block
Yard
Kitchen / Dining
Main Street
South Block
Infirmary
Guard Towers

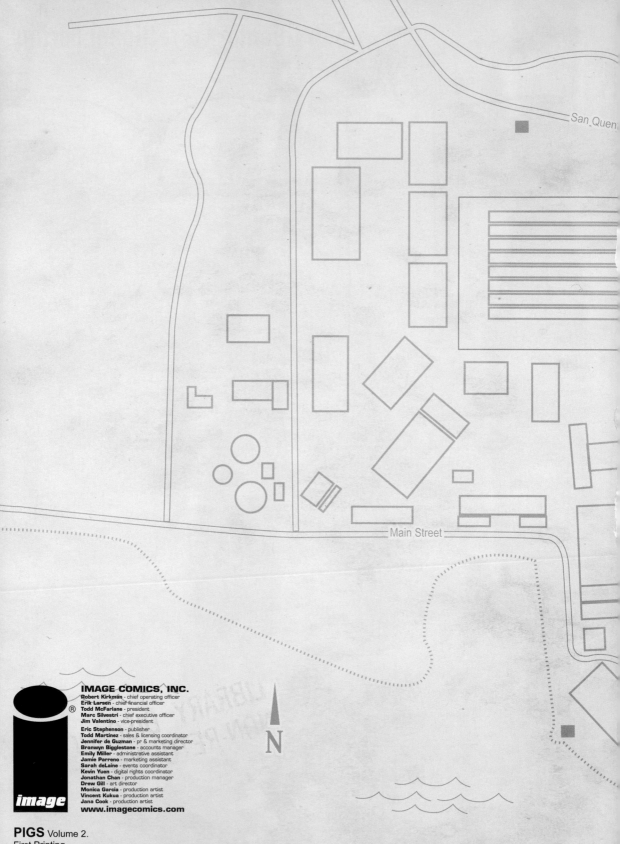

San Quen...

Main Street

N

IMAGE COMICS, INC.
Robert Kirkman - chief operating officer
Erik Larsen - chief financial officer
Todd McFarlane - president
Marc Silvestri - chief executive officer
Jim Valentino - vice-president

Eric Stephenson - publisher
Todd Martinez - sales & licensing coordinator
Jennifer de Guzman - pr & marketing director
Branwyn Bigglestone - accounts manager
Emily Miller - administrative assistant
Jamie Parreno - marketing assistant
Sarah deLaine - events coordinator
Kevin Yuen - digital rights coordinator
Jonathan Chan - production manager
Drew Gill - art director
Monica Garcia - production artist
Vincent Kukua - production artist
Jana Cook - production artist
www.imagecomics.com

PIGS Volume 2.
First Printing
ISBN: 978-1-60706-554-8

For International and Foreign Rights contact: foreignlicensing@imageomics.com

PIGS™

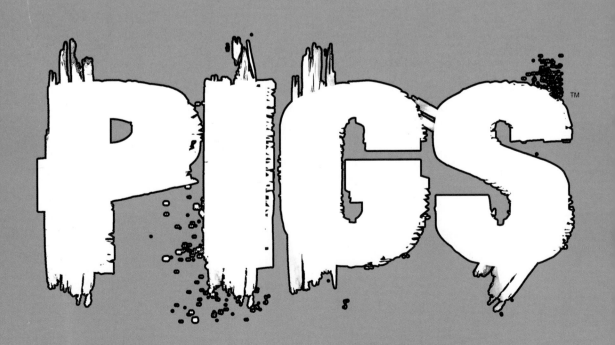

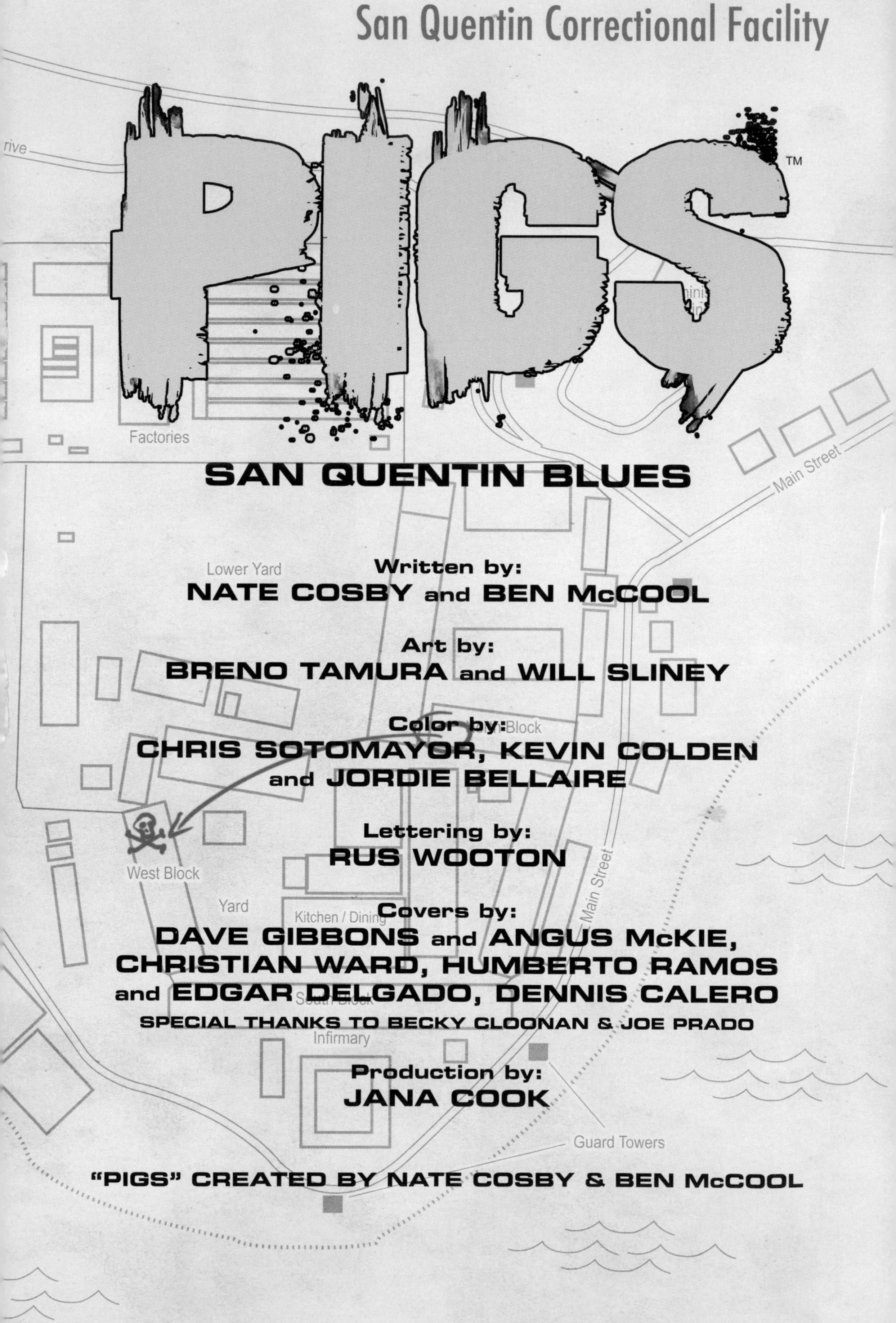
San Quentin Correctional Facility
rive
Factories
Main Street
Lower Yard
West Block
Yard
Kitchen / Dining
Main Street
South Block
Infirmary
Guard Towers

PIGS™

SAN QUENTIN BLUES

Written by:
NATE COSBY and BEN McCOOL

Art by:
BRENO TAMURA and WILL SLINEY

Color by:
CHRIS SOTOMAYOR, KEVIN COLDEN and JORDIE BELLAIRE

Lettering by:
RUS WOOTON

Covers by:
DAVE GIBBONS and ANGUS McKIE, CHRISTIAN WARD, HUMBERTO RAMOS and EDGAR DELGADO, DENNIS CALERO

SPECIAL THANKS TO BECKY CLOONAN & JOE PRADO

Production by:
JANA COOK

"PIGS" CREATED BY NATE COSBY & BEN McCOOL

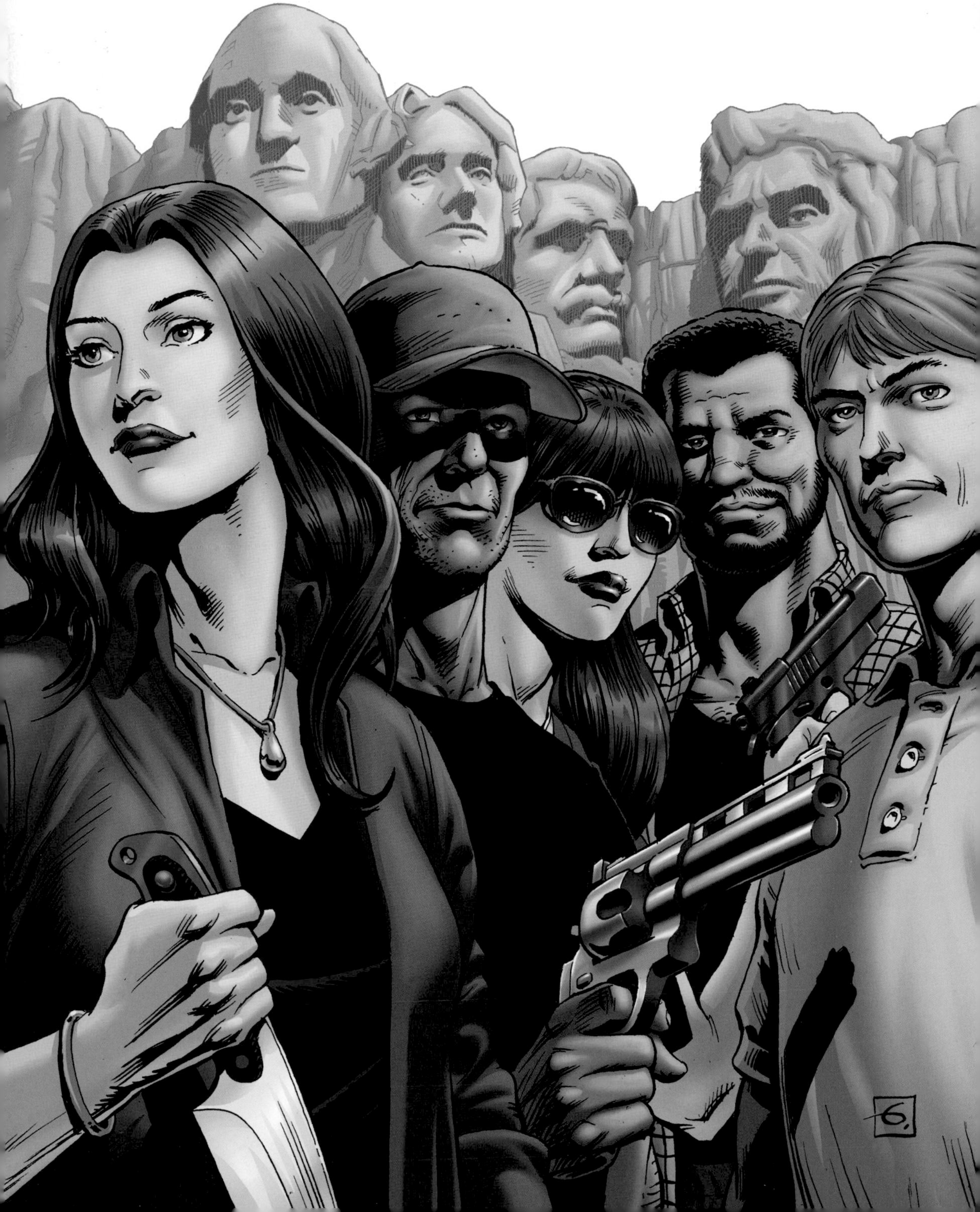

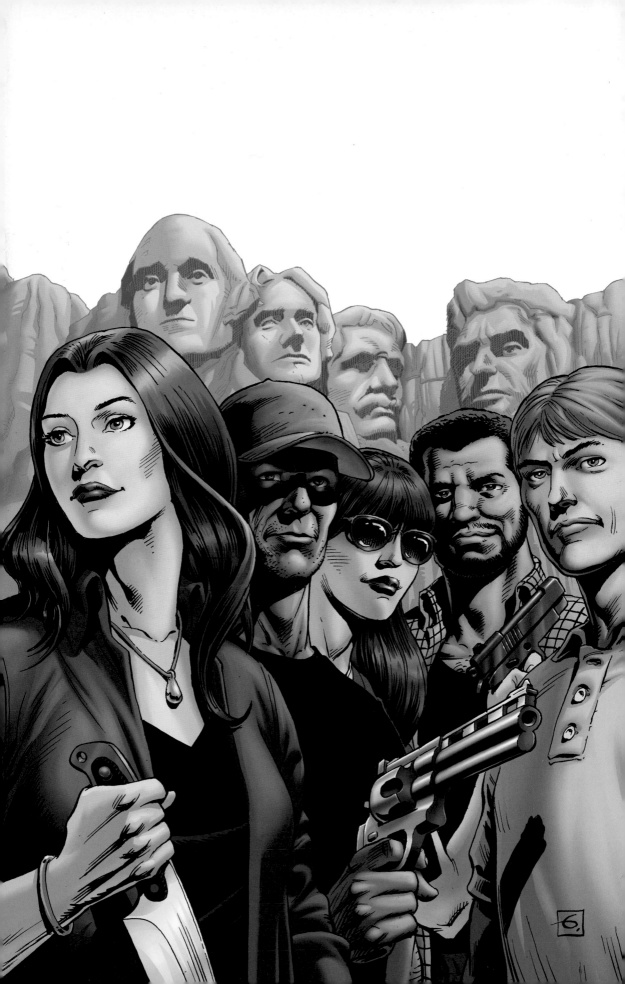

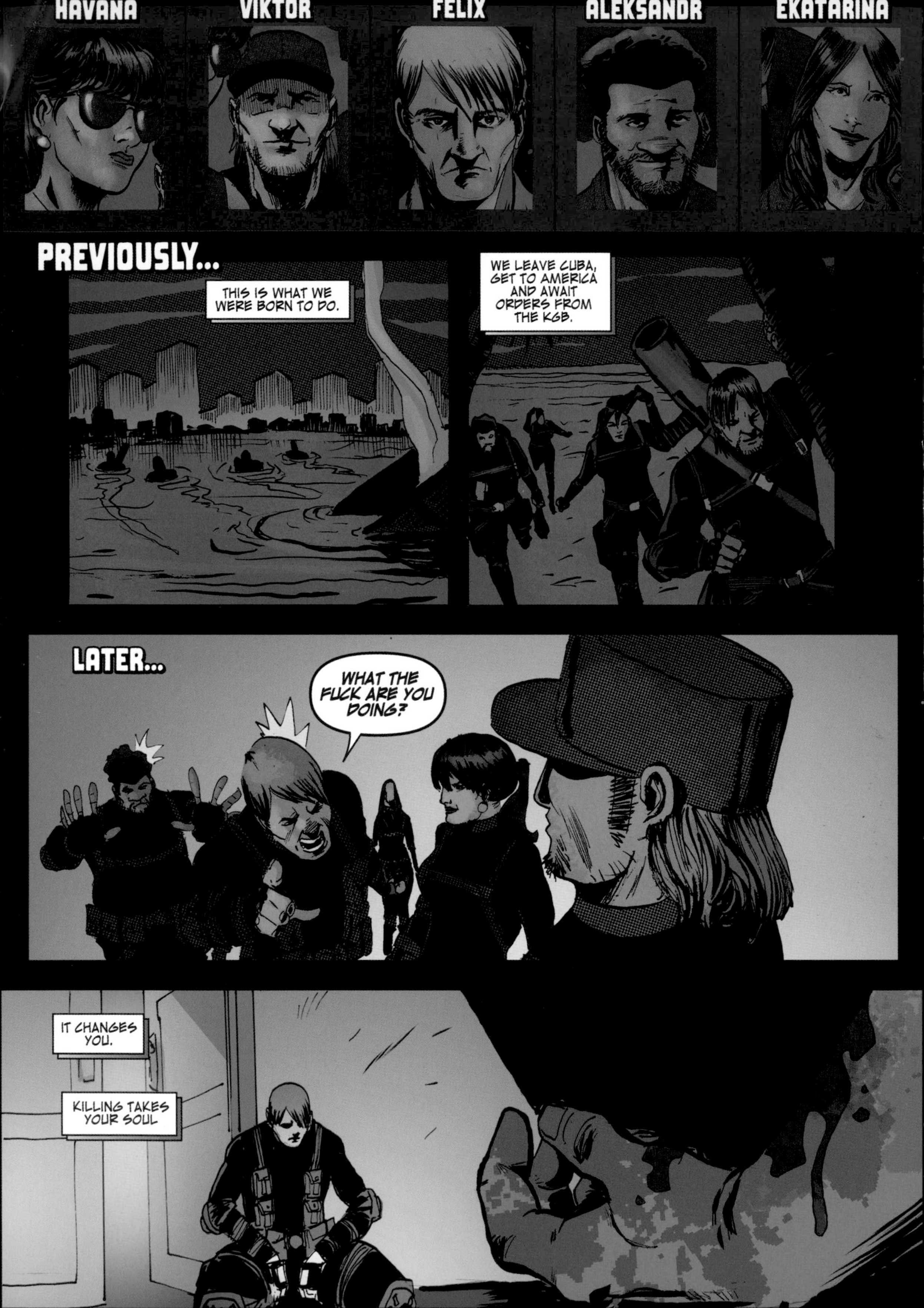
HAVANA
VIKTOR
FELIX
ALEKSANDR
EKATARINA
PREVIOUSLY...
THIS IS WHAT WE WERE BORN TO DO.
WE LEAVE CUBA, GET TO AMERICA AND AWAIT ORDERS FROM THE KGB.
LATER...
WHAT THE FUCK ARE YOU DOING?
IT CHANGES YOU.
KILLING TAKES YOUR SOUL

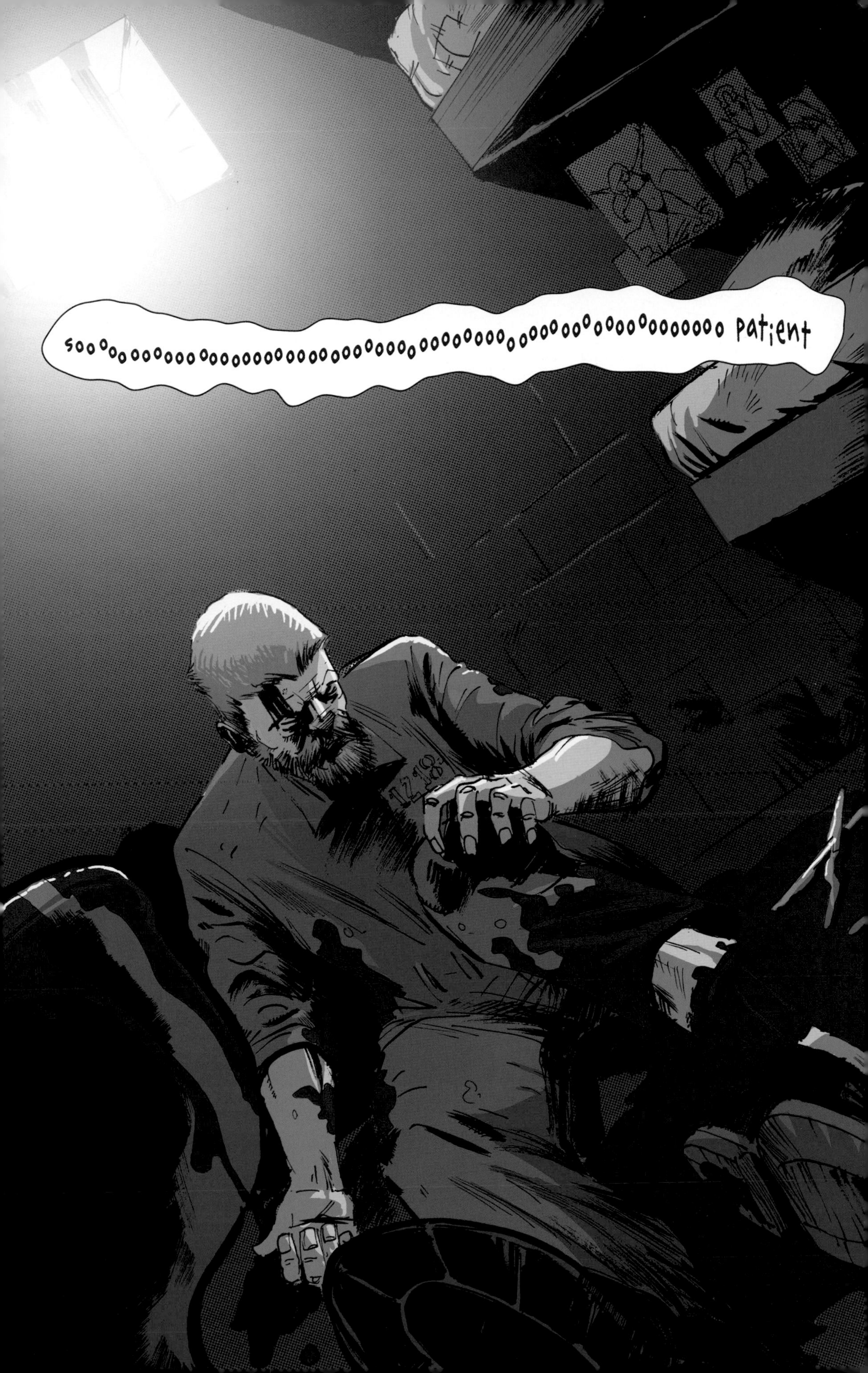
sooooooooooooooooooooooooooooooooooooooooooooooooooooooooooooooo patient

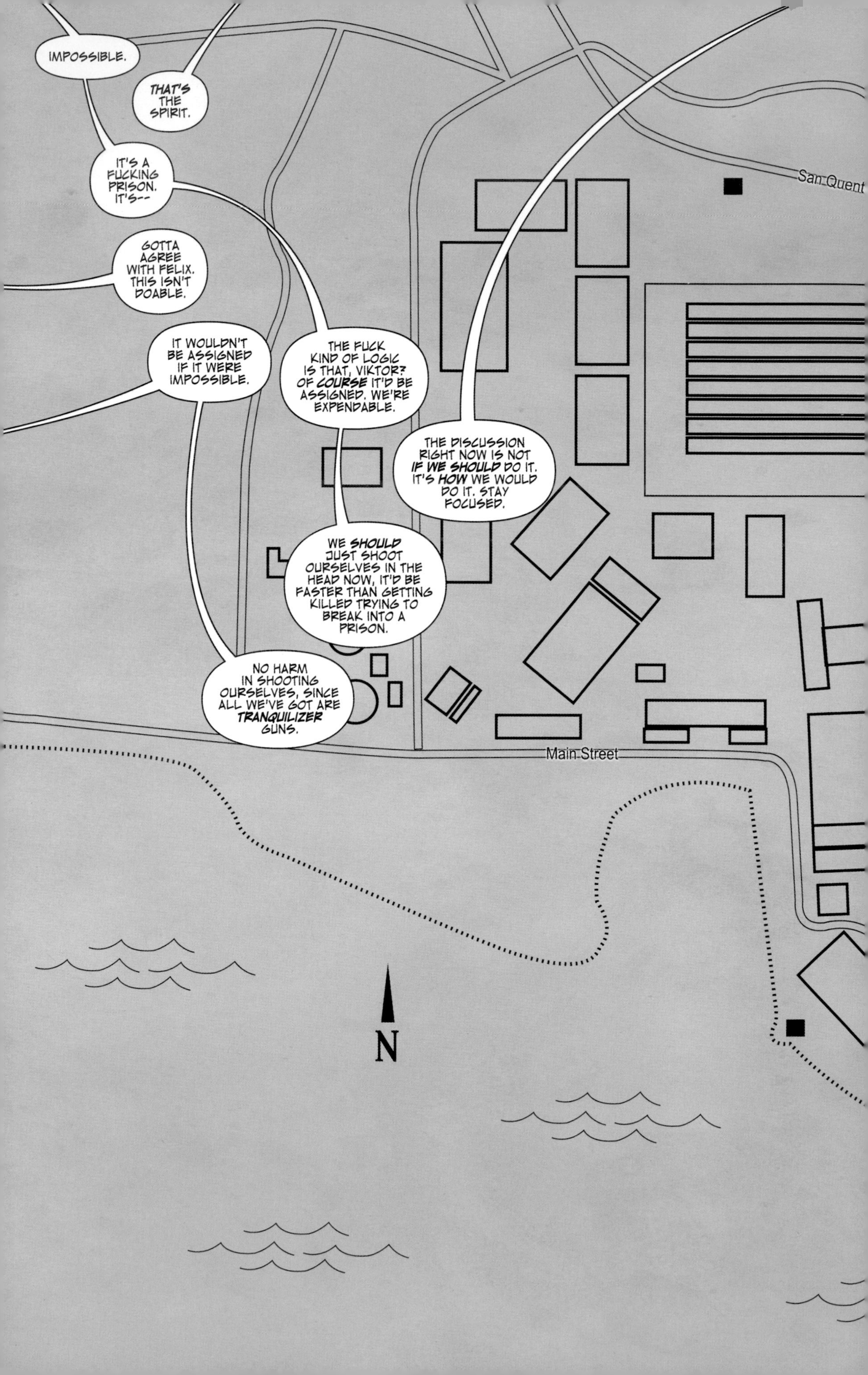
IMPOSSIBLE.
THAT'S THE SPIRIT.
IT'S A FUCKING PRISON. IT'S--
GOTTA AGREE WITH FELIX. THIS ISN'T DOABLE.
IT WOULDN'T BE ASSIGNED IF IT WERE IMPOSSIBLE.
THE FUCK KIND OF LOGIC IS THAT, VIKTOR? OF COURSE IT'D BE ASSIGNED. WE'RE EXPENDABLE.
THE DISCUSSION RIGHT NOW IS NOT IF WE SHOULD DO IT. IT'S HOW WE WOULD DO IT. STAY FOCUSED.
WE SHOULD JUST SHOOT OURSELVES IN THE HEAD NOW, IT'D BE FASTER THAN GETTING KILLED TRYING TO BREAK INTO A PRISON.
NO HARM IN SHOOTING OURSELVES, SINCE ALL WE'VE GOT ARE TRANQUILIZER GUNS.
San Quent
Main Street
N

San Quentin Correctional Facility

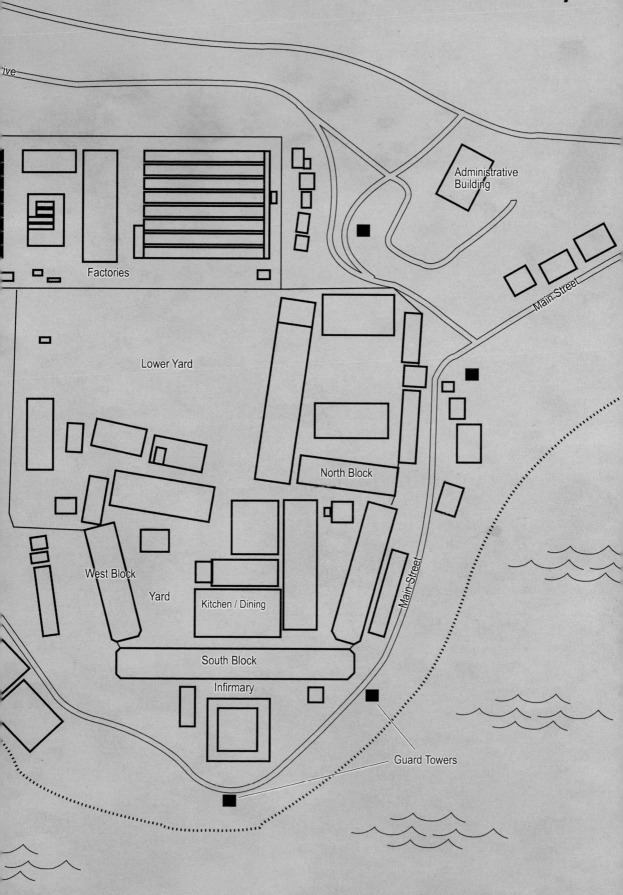

Administrative Building

Main Street

Factories

Lower Yard

North Block

Main Street

West Block

Yard

Kitchen / Dining

South Block

Infirmary

Guard Towers

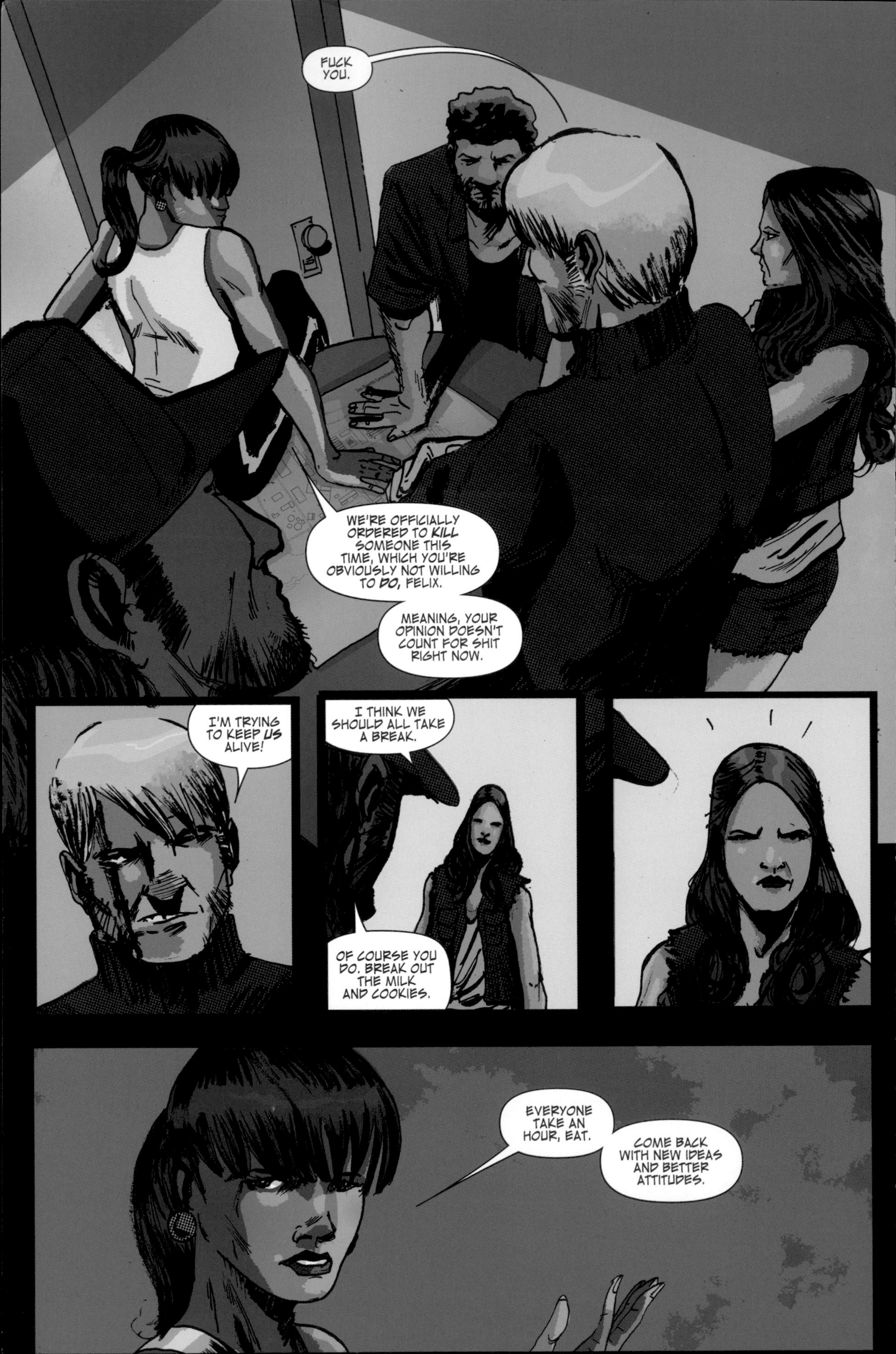
FUCK YOU.
WE'RE OFFICIALLY ORDERED TO KILL SOMEONE THIS TIME, WHICH YOU'RE OBVIOUSLY NOT WILLING TO DO, FELIX.
MEANING, YOUR OPINION DOESN'T COUNT FOR SHIT RIGHT NOW.
I'M TRYING TO KEEP US ALIVE!
I THINK WE SHOULD ALL TAKE A BREAK.
OF COURSE YOU DO. BREAK OUT THE MILK AND COOKIES.
EVERYONE TAKE AN HOUR, EAT.
COME BACK WITH NEW IDEAS AND BETTER ATTITUDES.

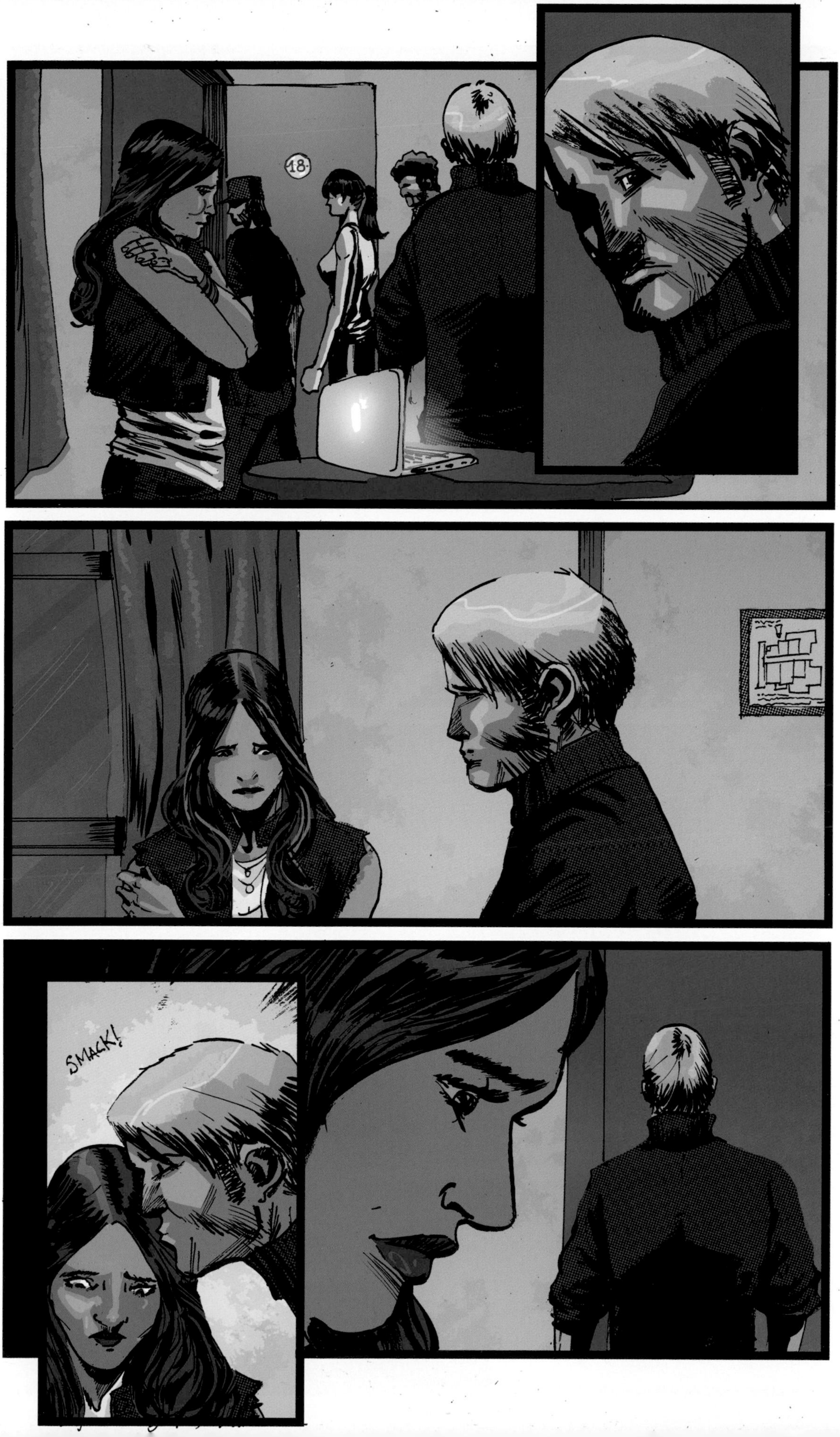
18
SMACK!

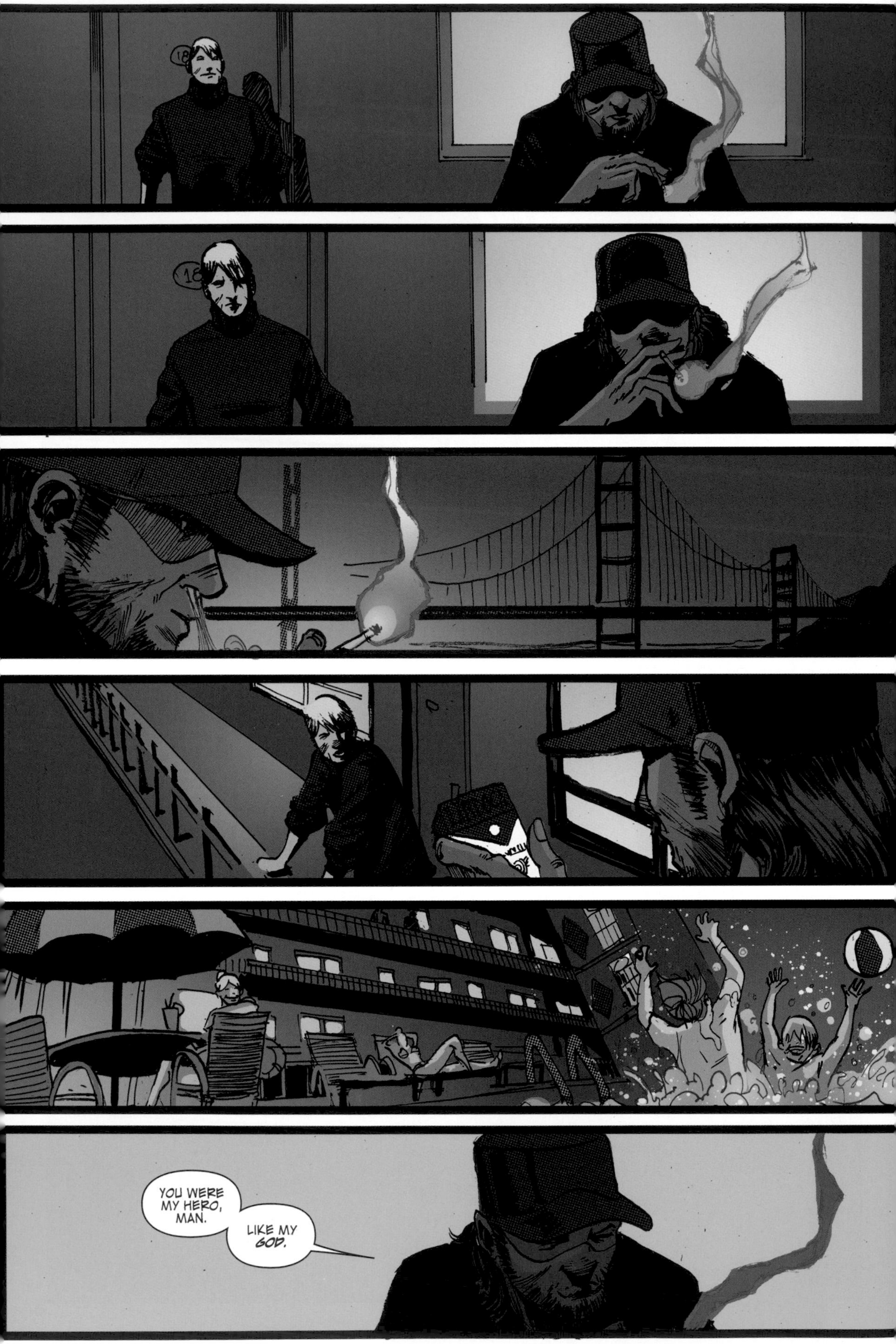
YOU WERE MY HERO, MAN.
LIKE MY GOD.

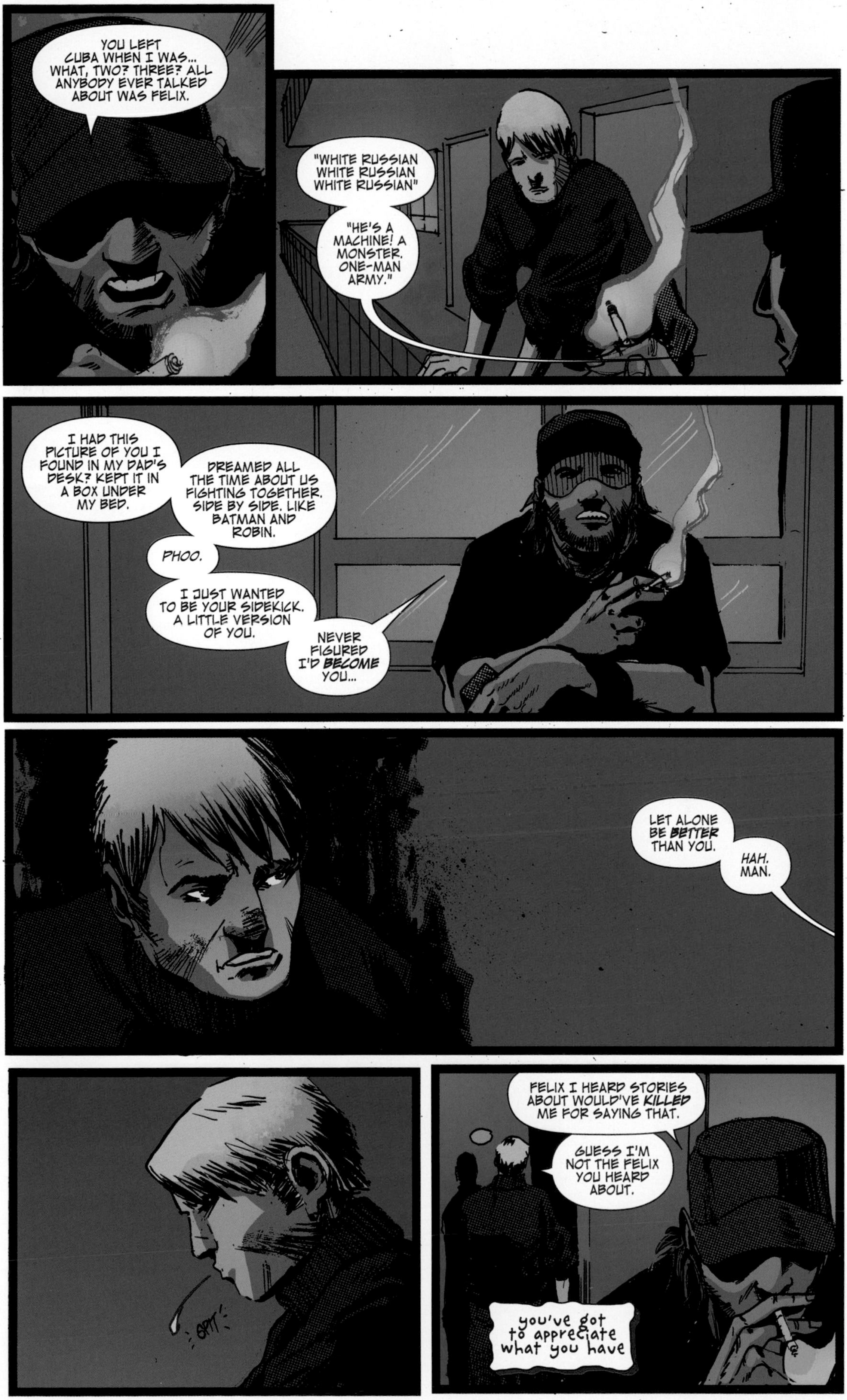
YOU LEFT CUBA WHEN I WAS... WHAT, TWO? THREE? ALL ANYBODY EVER TALKED ABOUT WAS FELIX.
"WHITE RUSSIAN WHITE RUSSIAN WHITE RUSSIAN"
"HE'S A MACHINE! A MONSTER. ONE-MAN ARMY."
I HAD THIS PICTURE OF YOU I FOUND IN MY DAD'S DESK? KEPT IT IN A BOX UNDER MY BED.
DREAMED ALL THE TIME ABOUT US FIGHTING TOGETHER. SIDE BY SIDE. LIKE BATMAN AND ROBIN.
PHOO.
I JUST WANTED TO BE YOUR SIDEKICK. A LITTLE VERSION OF YOU.
NEVER FIGURED I'D BECOME YOU...
LET ALONE BE BETTER THAN YOU.
HAH. MAN.
SPIT
FELIX I HEARD STORIES ABOUT WOULD'VE KILLED ME FOR SAYING THAT.
GUESS I'M NOT THE FELIX YOU HEARD ABOUT.
you've got to appreciate what you have

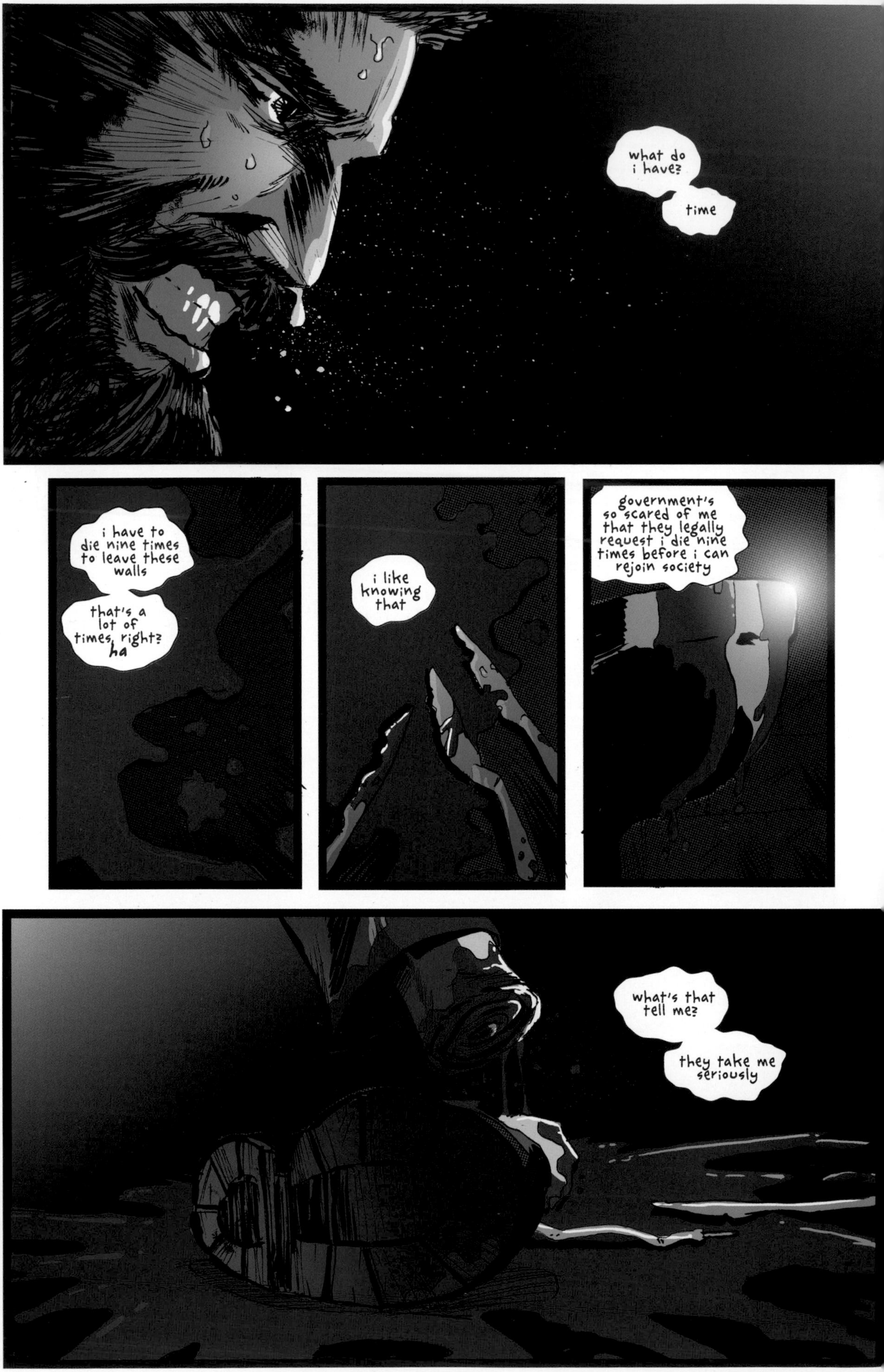
what do i have?
time
i have to die nine times to leave these walls
that's a lot of times, right? ha
i like knowing that
government's so scared of me that they legally request i die nine times before i can rejoin society
what's that tell me?
they take me seriously

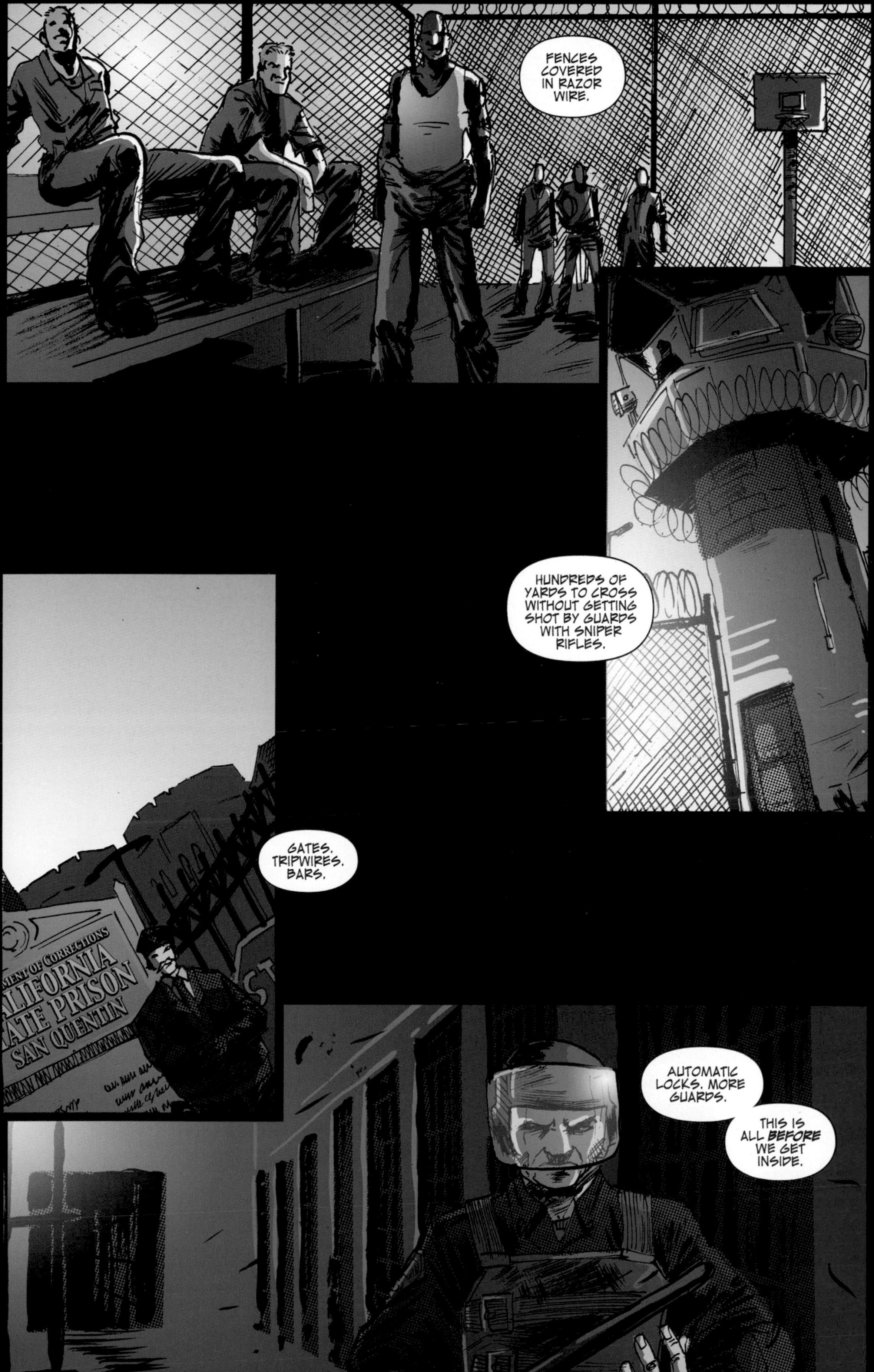
FENCES COVERED IN RAZOR WIRE.
HUNDREDS OF YARDS TO CROSS WITHOUT GETTING SHOT BY GUARDS WITH SNIPER RIFLES.
GATES. TRIPWIRES. BARS.
CALIFORNIA STATE PRISON SAN QUENTIN
AUTOMATIC LOCKS. MORE GUARDS.
THIS IS ALL BEFORE WE GET INSIDE.

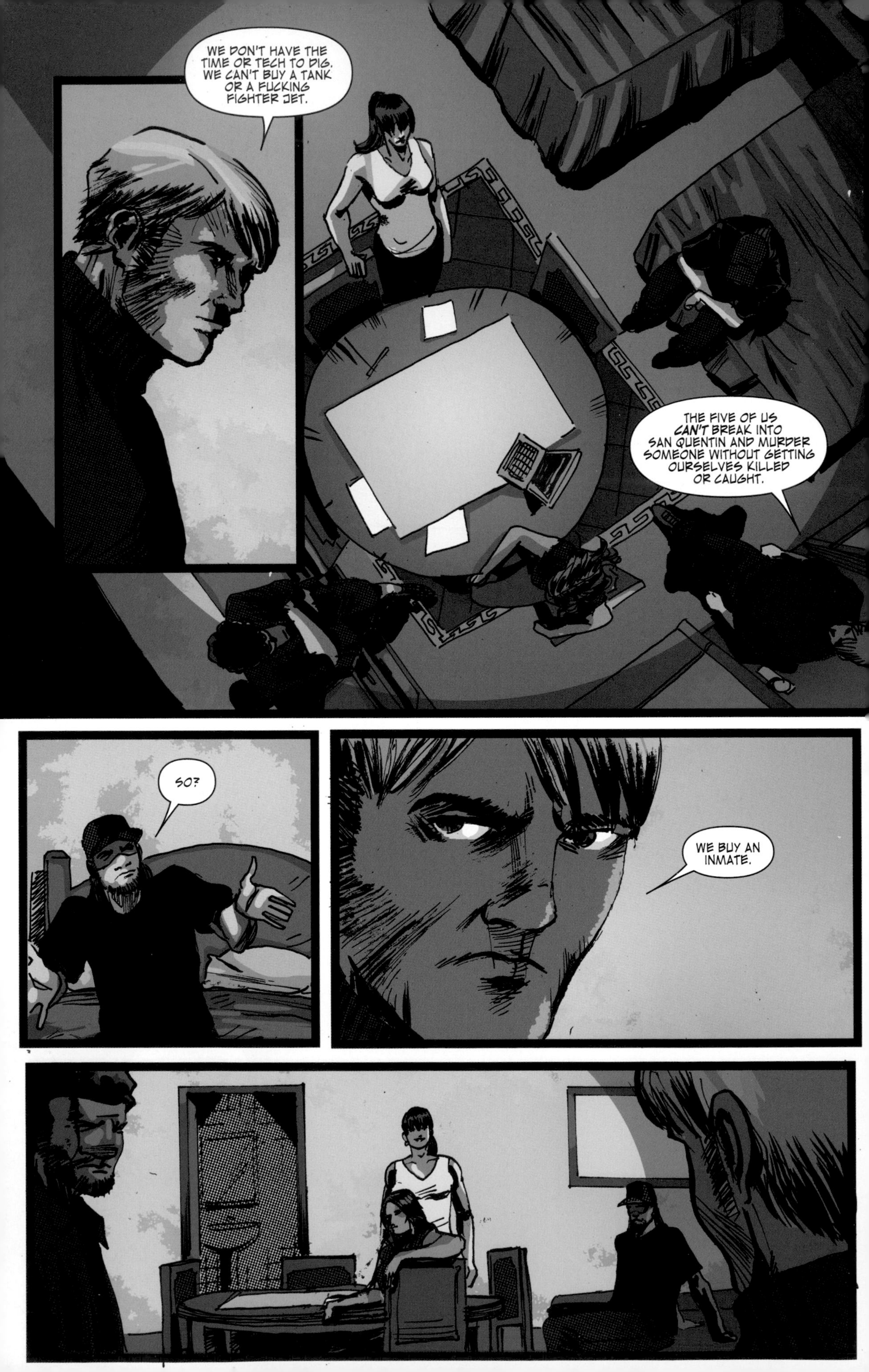
WE DON'T HAVE THE TIME OR TECH TO DIG. WE CAN'T BUY A TANK OR A FUCKING FIGHTER JET.
THE FIVE OF US *CAN'T* BREAK INTO SAN QUENTIN AND MURDER SOMEONE WITHOUT GETTING OURSELVES KILLED OR CAUGHT.
SO?
WE BUY AN INMATE.

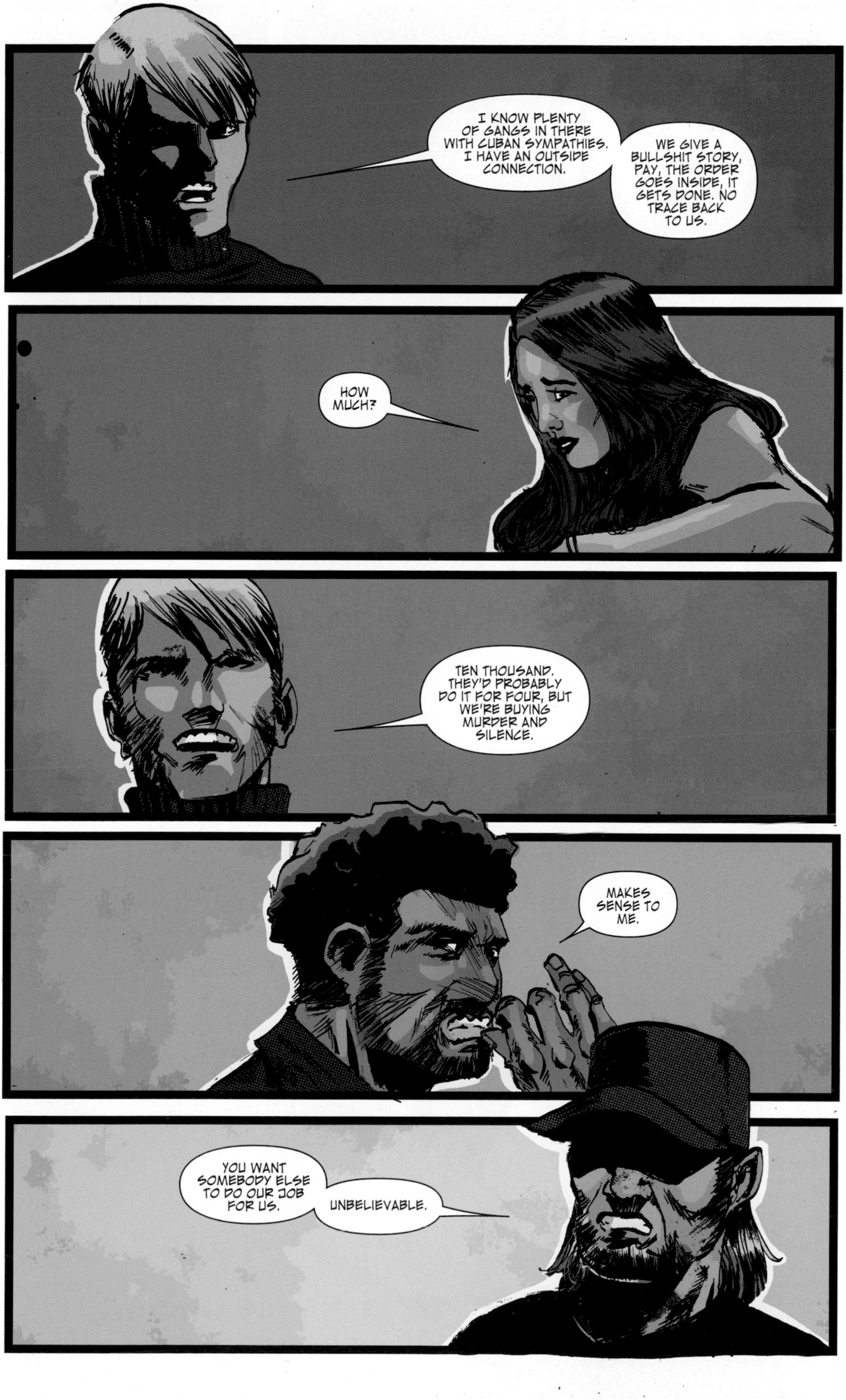
I KNOW PLENTY OF GANGS IN THERE WITH CUBAN SYMPATHIES. I HAVE AN OUTSIDE CONNECTION.
WE GIVE A BULLSHIT STORY, PAY, THE ORDER GOES INSIDE, IT GETS DONE. NO TRACE BACK TO US.
HOW MUCH?
TEN THOUSAND. THEY'D PROBABLY DO IT FOR FOUR, BUT WE'RE BUYING MURDER AND SILENCE.
MAKES SENSE TO ME.
YOU WANT SOMEBODY ELSE TO DO OUR JOB FOR US.
UNBELIEVABLE.

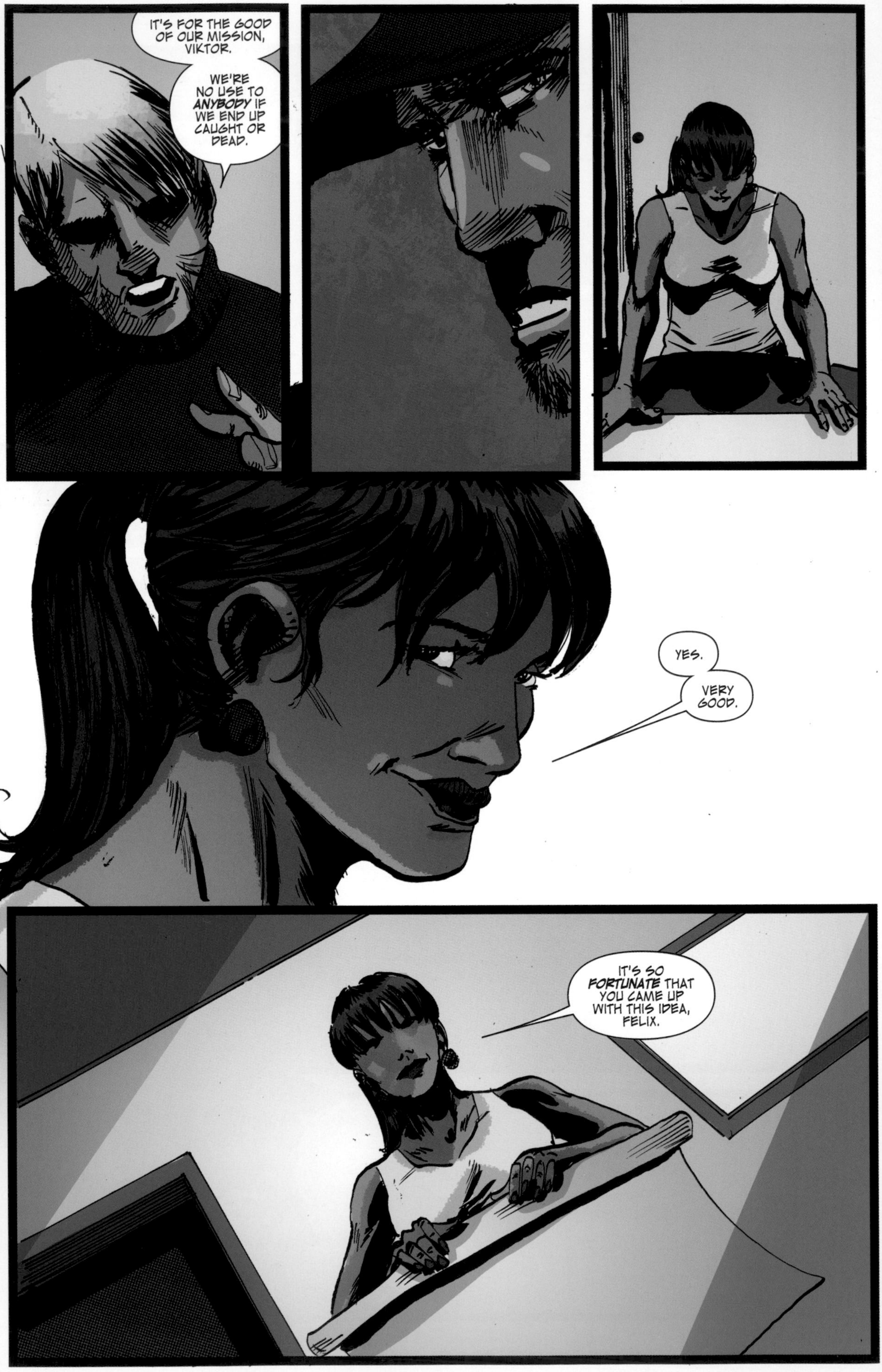
IT'S FOR THE GOOD OF OUR MISSION, VIKTOR.
WE'RE NO USE TO ANYBODY IF WE END UP CAUGHT OR DEAD.
YES.
VERY GOOD.
IT'S SO FORTUNATE THAT YOU CAME UP WITH THIS IDEA, FELIX.

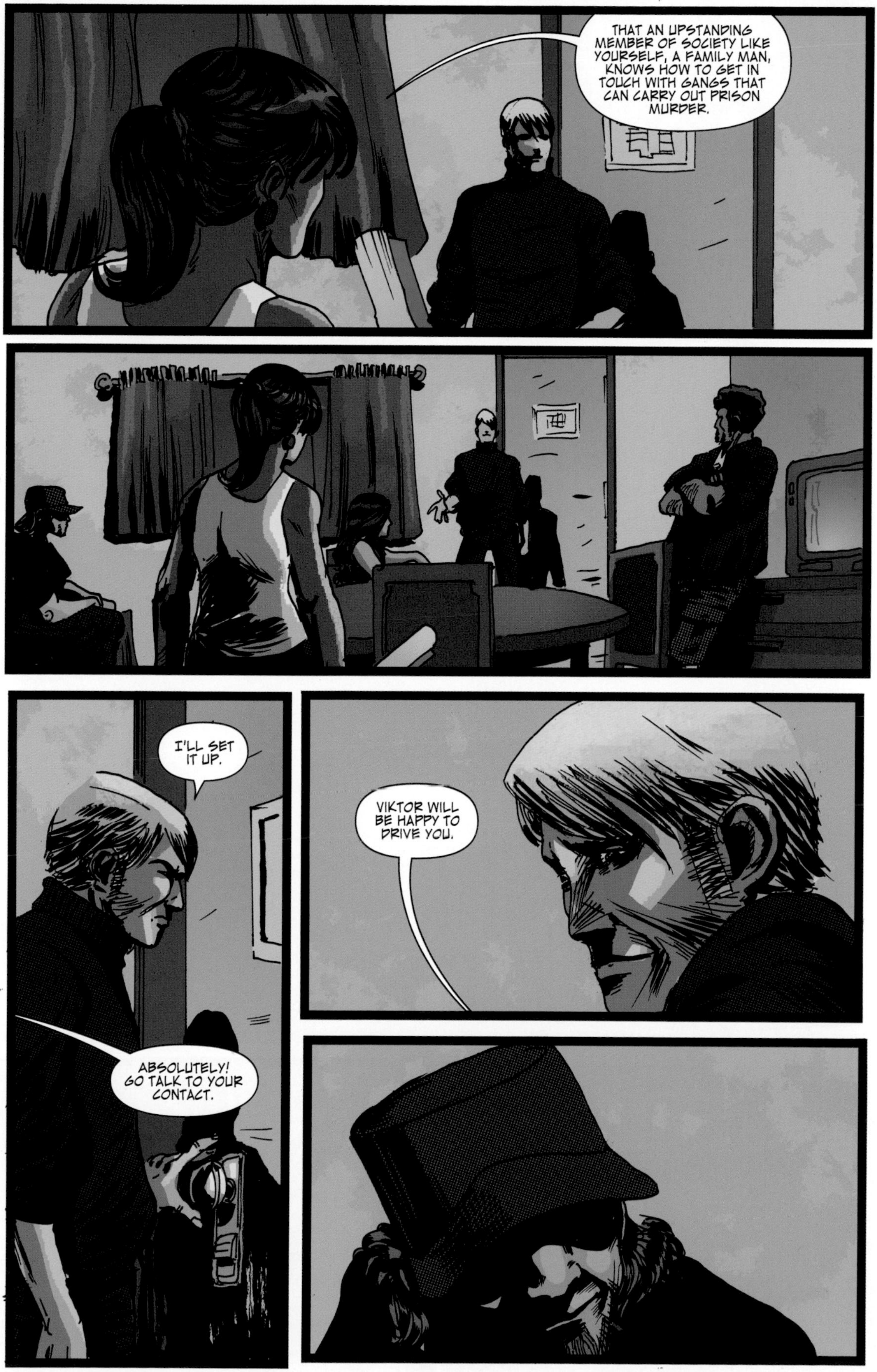
THAT AN UPSTANDING MEMBER OF SOCIETY LIKE YOURSELF, A FAMILY MAN, KNOWS HOW TO GET IN TOUCH WITH GANGS THAT CAN CARRY OUT PRISON MURDER.
I'LL SET IT UP.
VIKTOR WILL BE HAPPY TO DRIVE YOU.
ABSOLUTELY! GO TALK TO YOUR CONTACT.

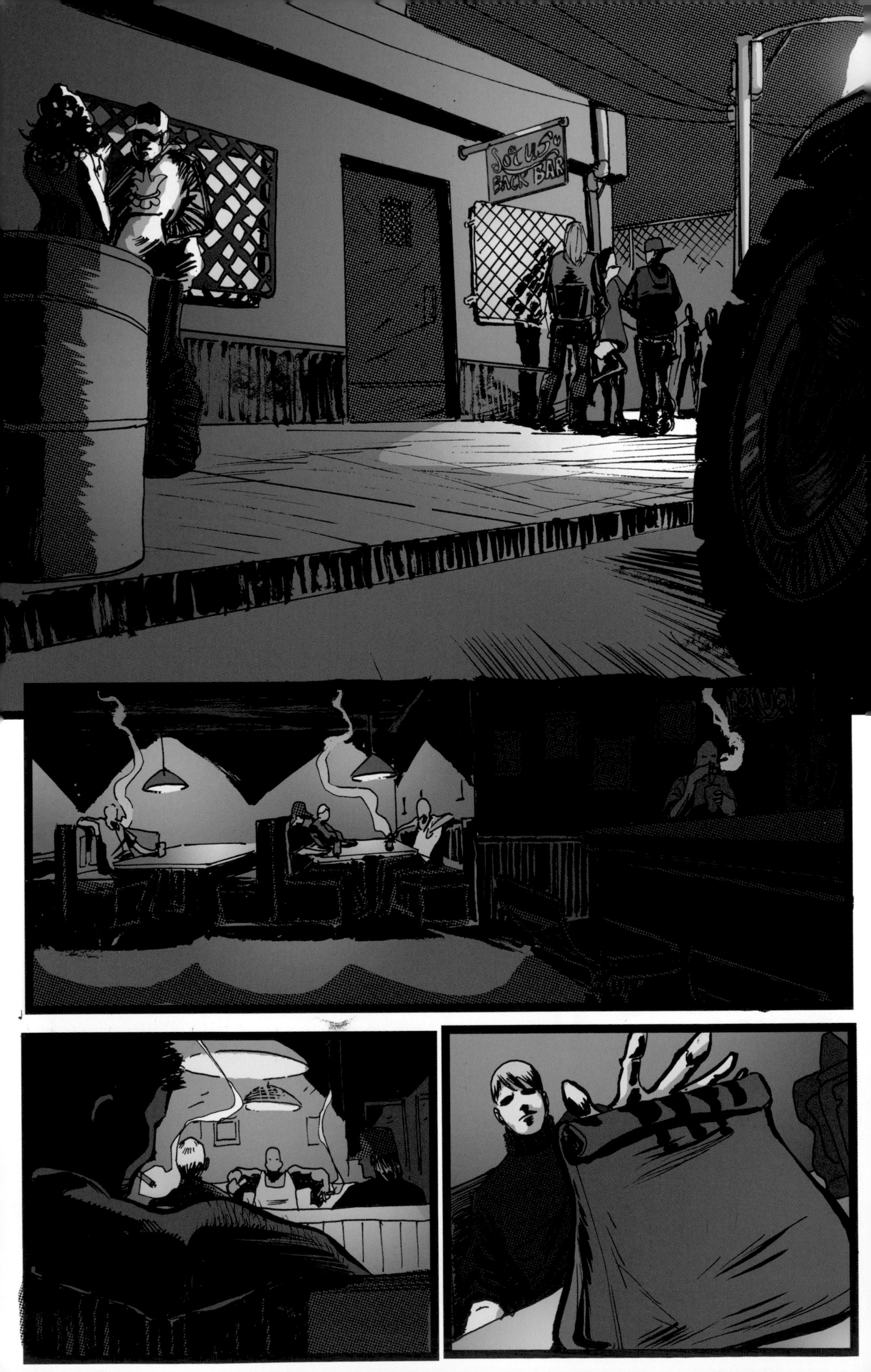
BACK BAR

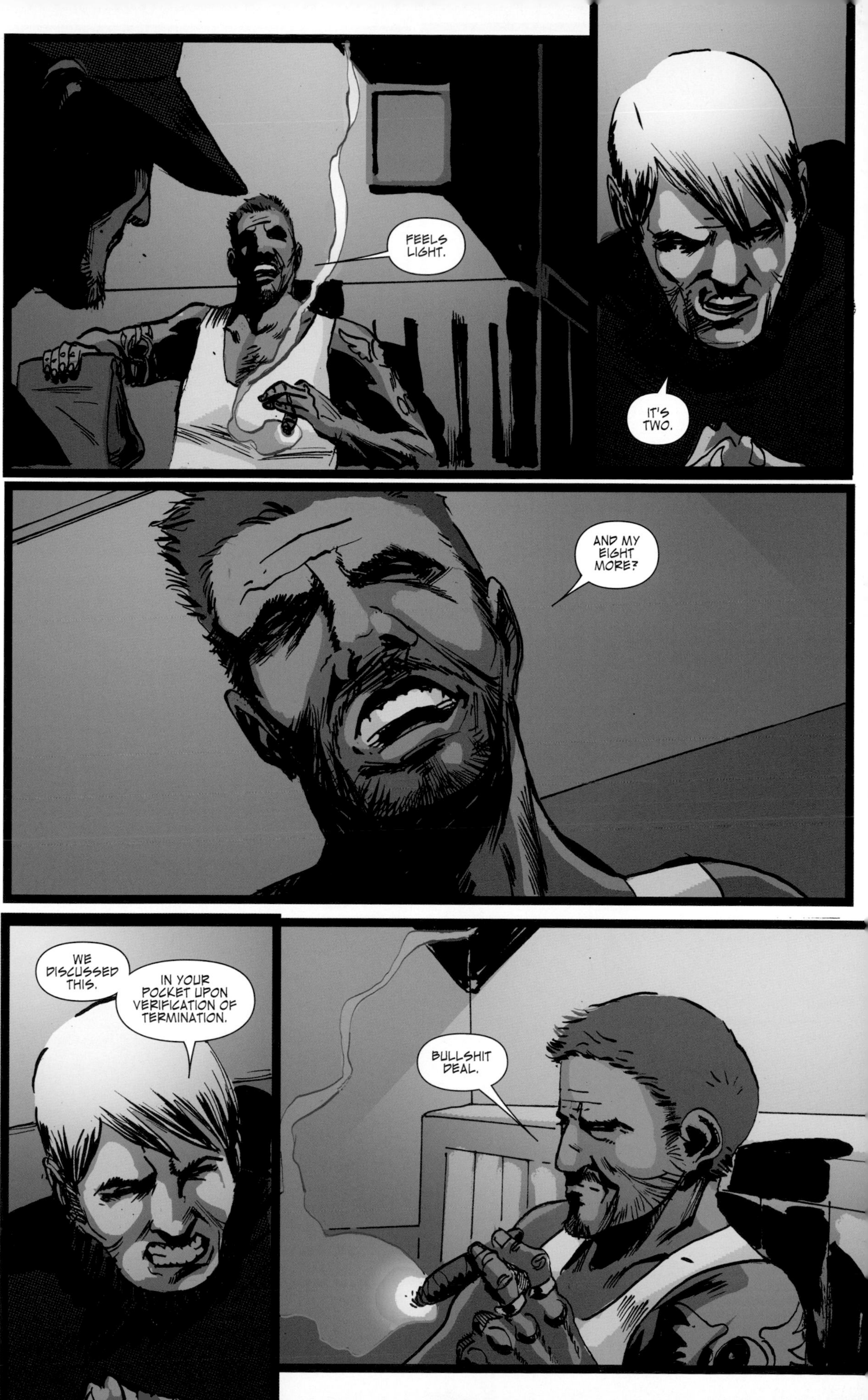
FEELS LIGHT.
IT'S TWO.
AND MY EIGHT MORE?
WE DISCUSSED THIS.
IN YOUR POCKET UPON VERIFICATION OF TERMINATION.
BULLSHIT DEAL.

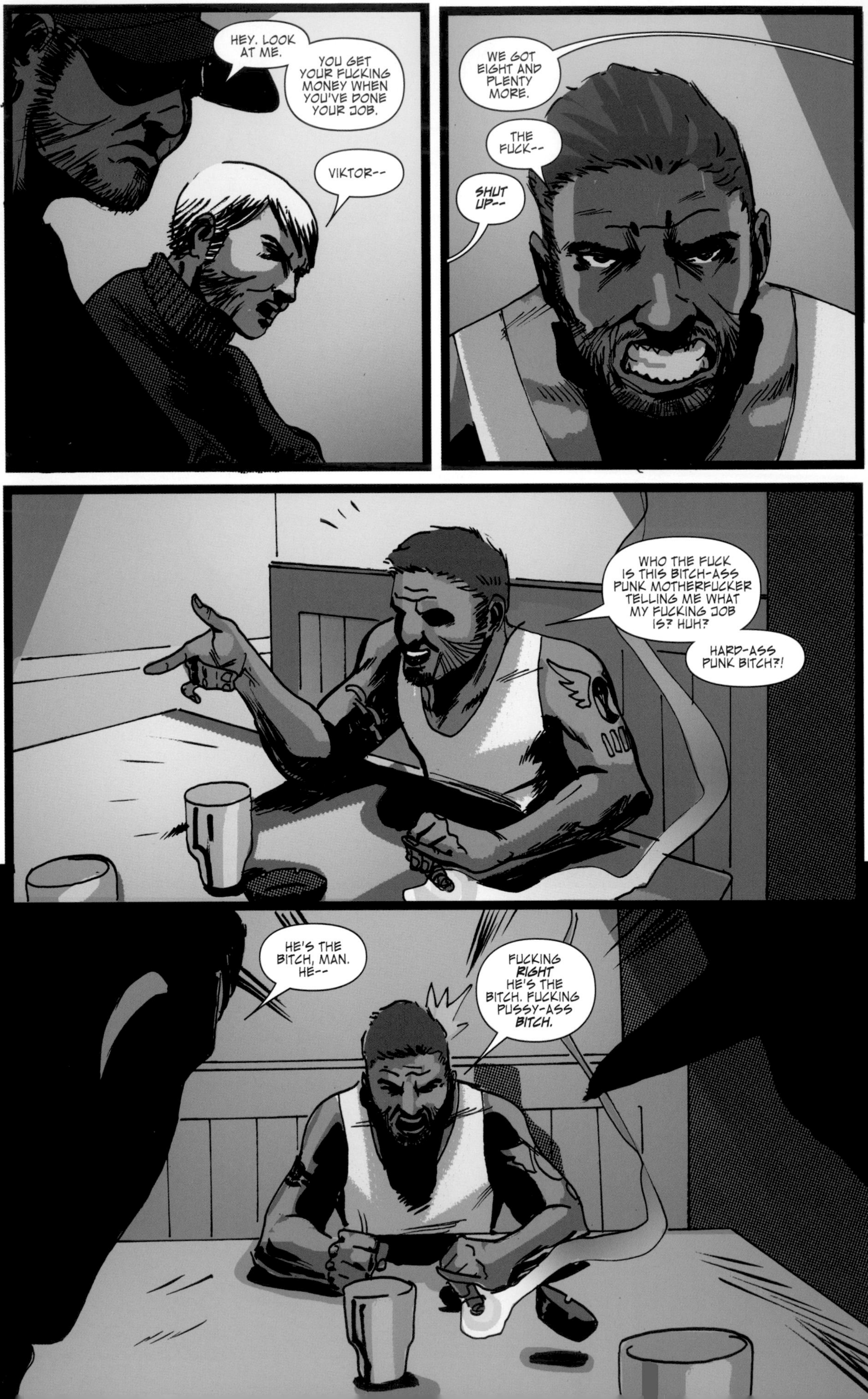
HEY. LOOK AT ME.
YOU GET YOUR FUCKING MONEY WHEN YOU'VE DONE YOUR JOB.
VIKTOR--
WE GOT EIGHT AND PLENTY MORE.
THE FUCK--
SHUT UP--
WHO THE FUCK IS THIS BITCH-ASS PUNK MOTHERFUCKER TELLING ME WHAT MY FUCKING JOB IS? HUH?
HARD-ASS PUNK BITCH?!
HE'S THE BITCH, MAN. HE--
FUCKING RIGHT HE'S THE BITCH. FUCKING PUSSY-ASS BITCH.

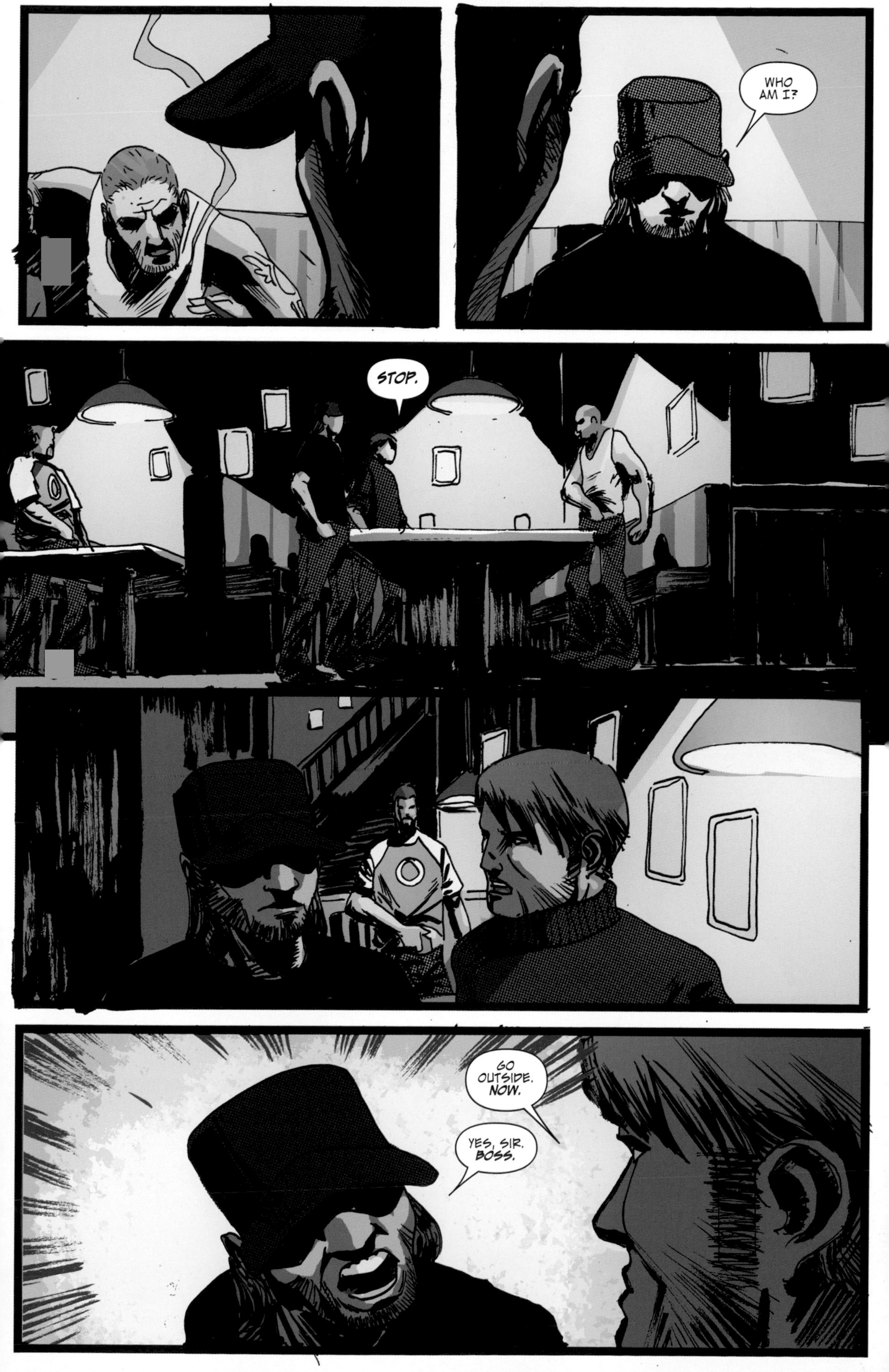
WHO AM I?
STOP.
GO OUTSIDE. NOW.
YES, SIR. BOSS.

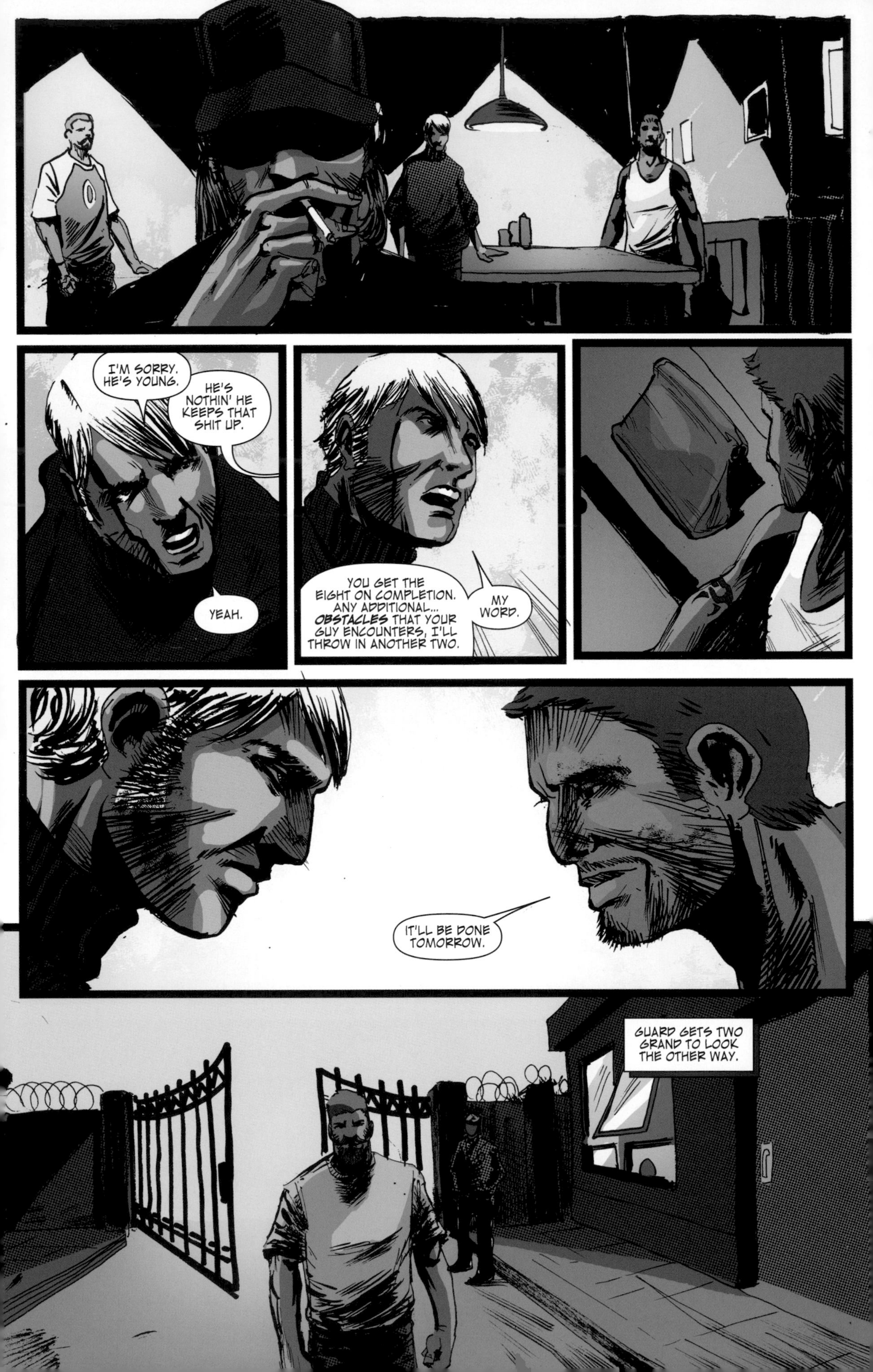

I'M SORRY. HE'S YOUNG.
HE'S NOTHIN' HE KEEPS THAT SHIT UP.
YEAH.
YOU GET THE EIGHT ON COMPLETION. ANY ADDITIONAL... OBSTACLES THAT YOUR GUY ENCOUNTERS, I'LL THROW IN ANOTHER TWO.
MY WORD.
IT'LL BE DONE TOMORROW.
GUARD GETS TWO GRAND TO LOOK THE OTHER WAY.

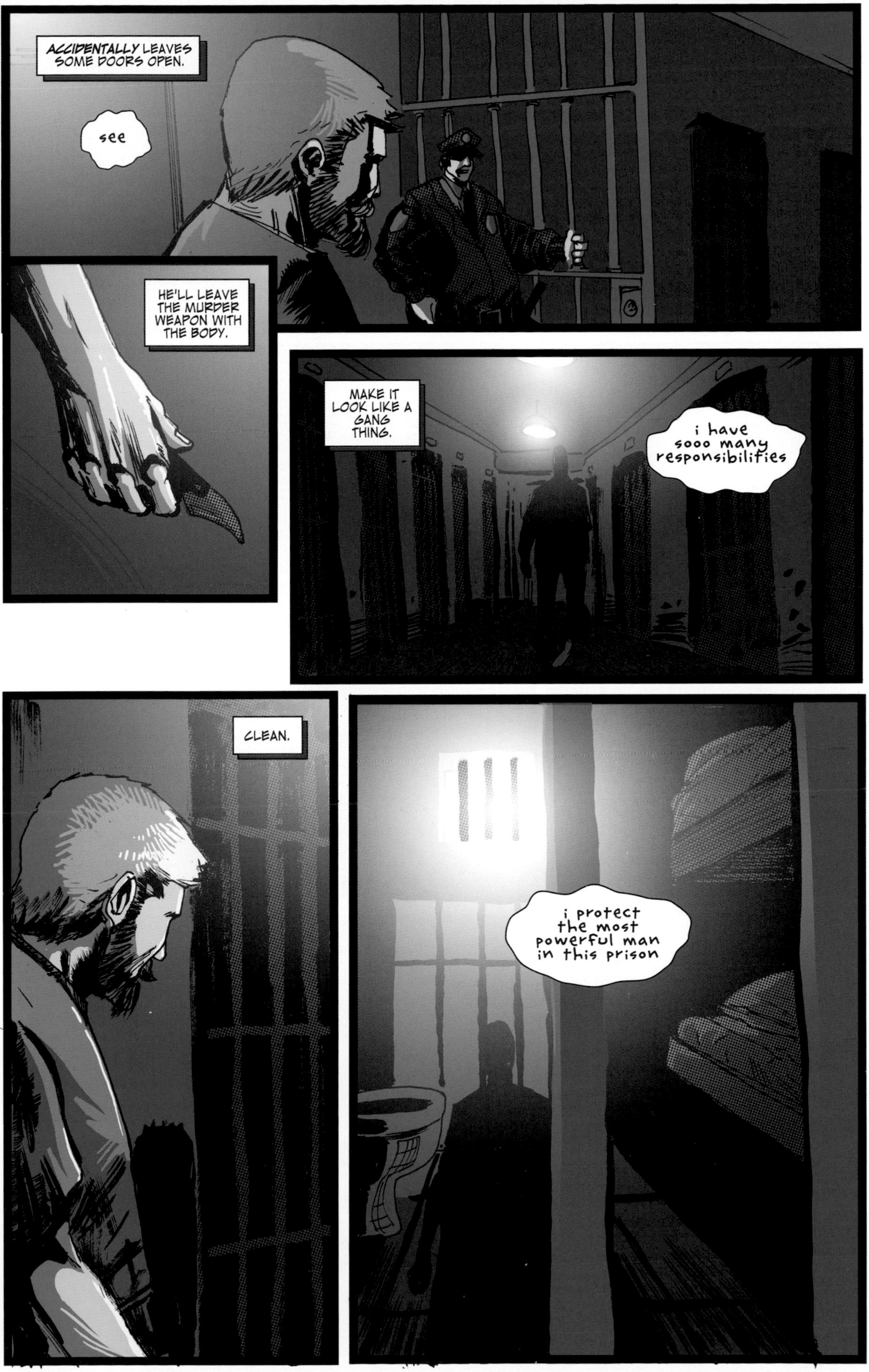
ACCIDENTALLY LEAVES SOME DOORS OPEN.
see
HE'LL LEAVE THE MURDER WEAPON WITH THE BODY.
MAKE IT LOOK LIKE A GANG THING.
i have sooo many responsibilities
CLEAN.
i protect the most powerful man in this prison

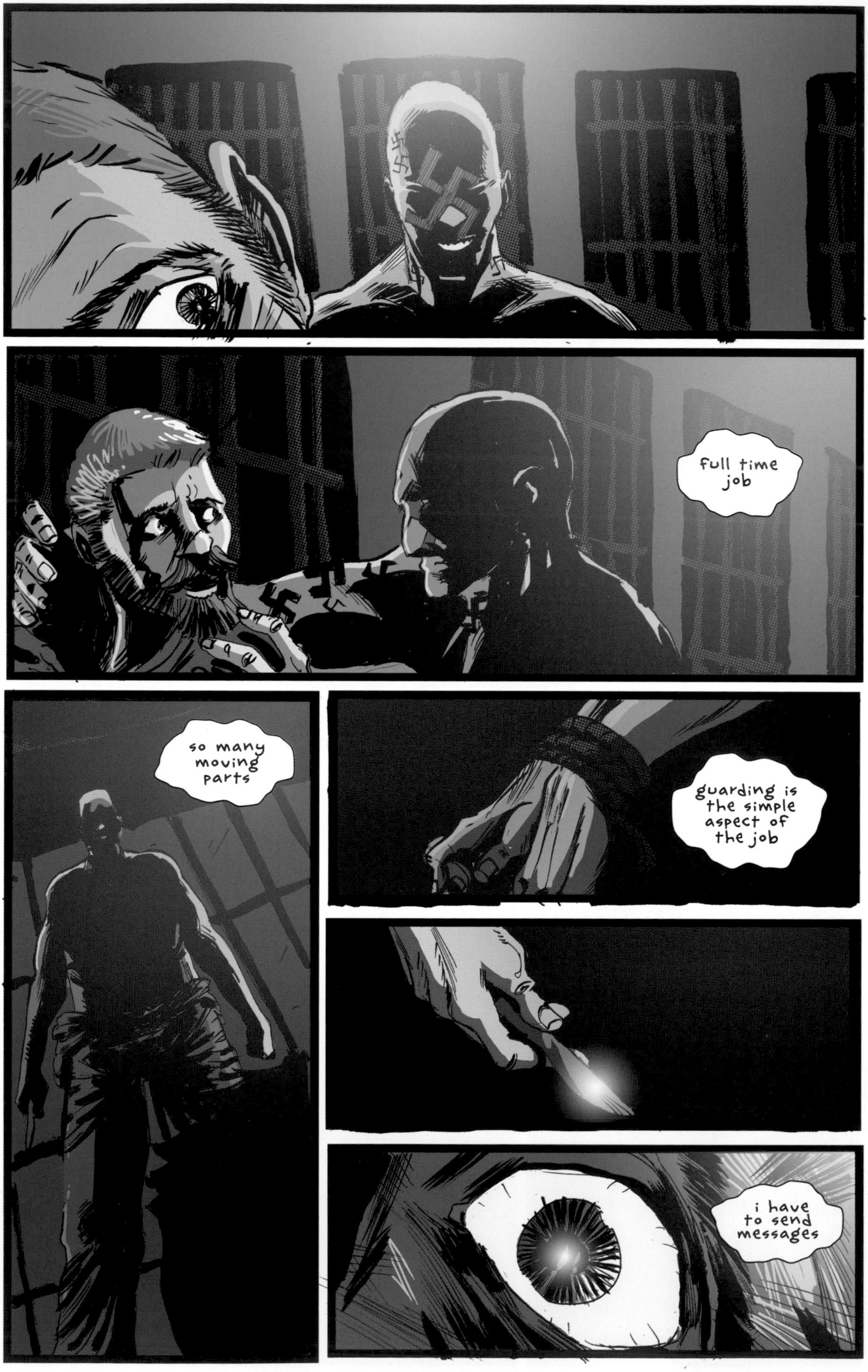
full time job
so many moving parts
guarding is the simple aspect of the job
i have to send messages

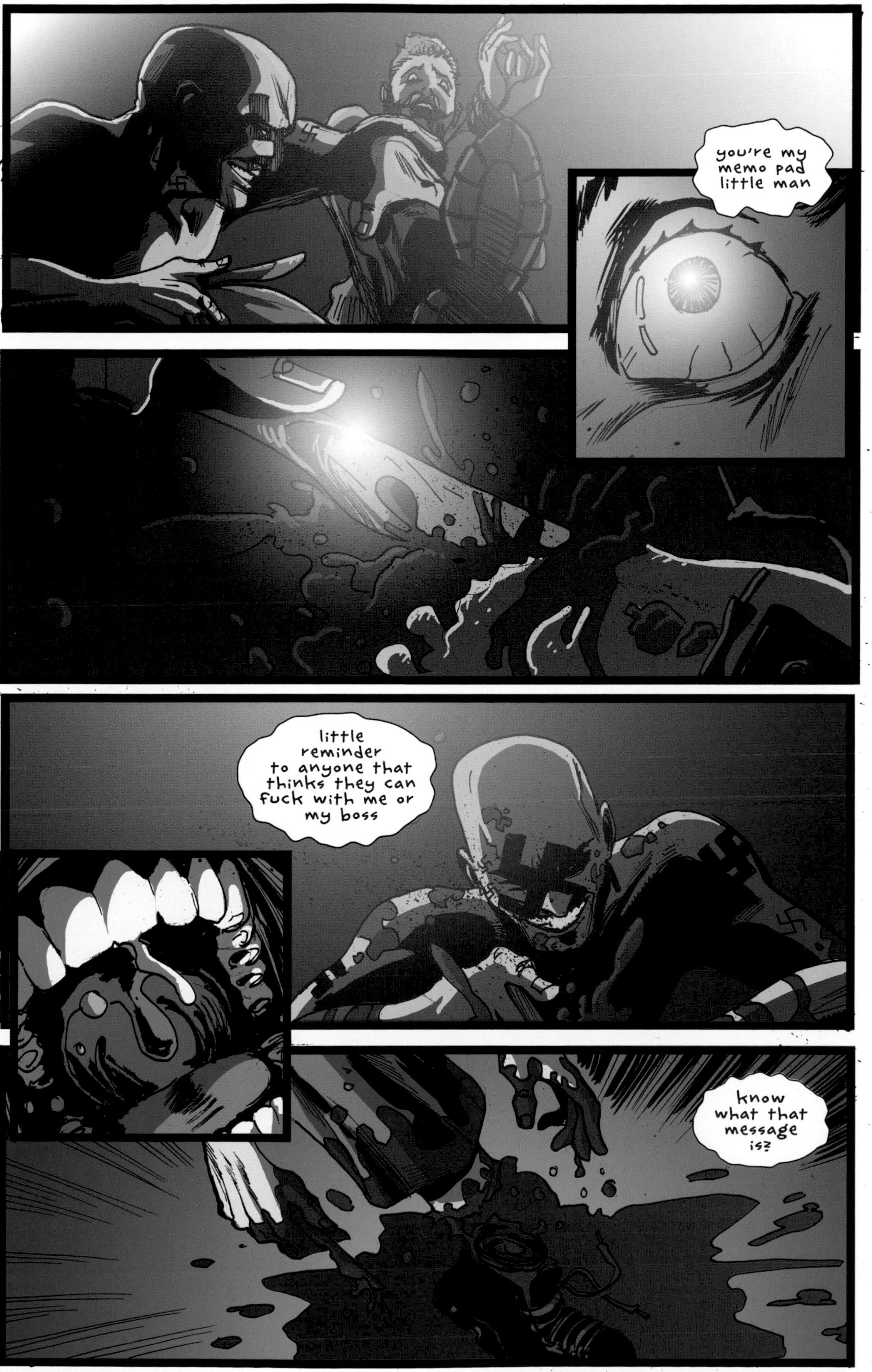
you're my memo pad little man
little reminder to anyone that thinks they can fuck with me or my boss
know what that message is?

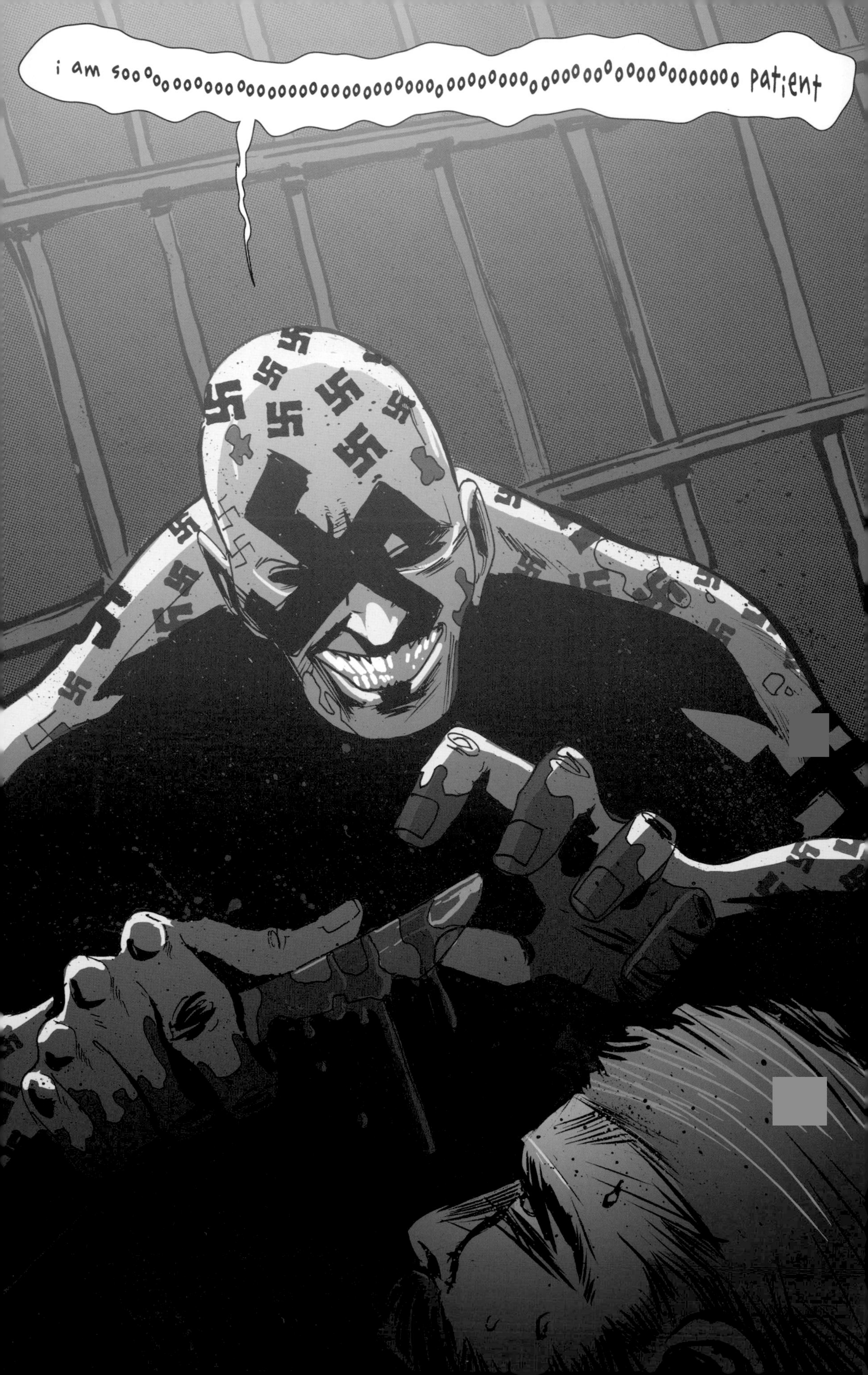
i am soooooooooooooooooooooooooooooooooooooooooooooooooooooooooooooooooooooo patient

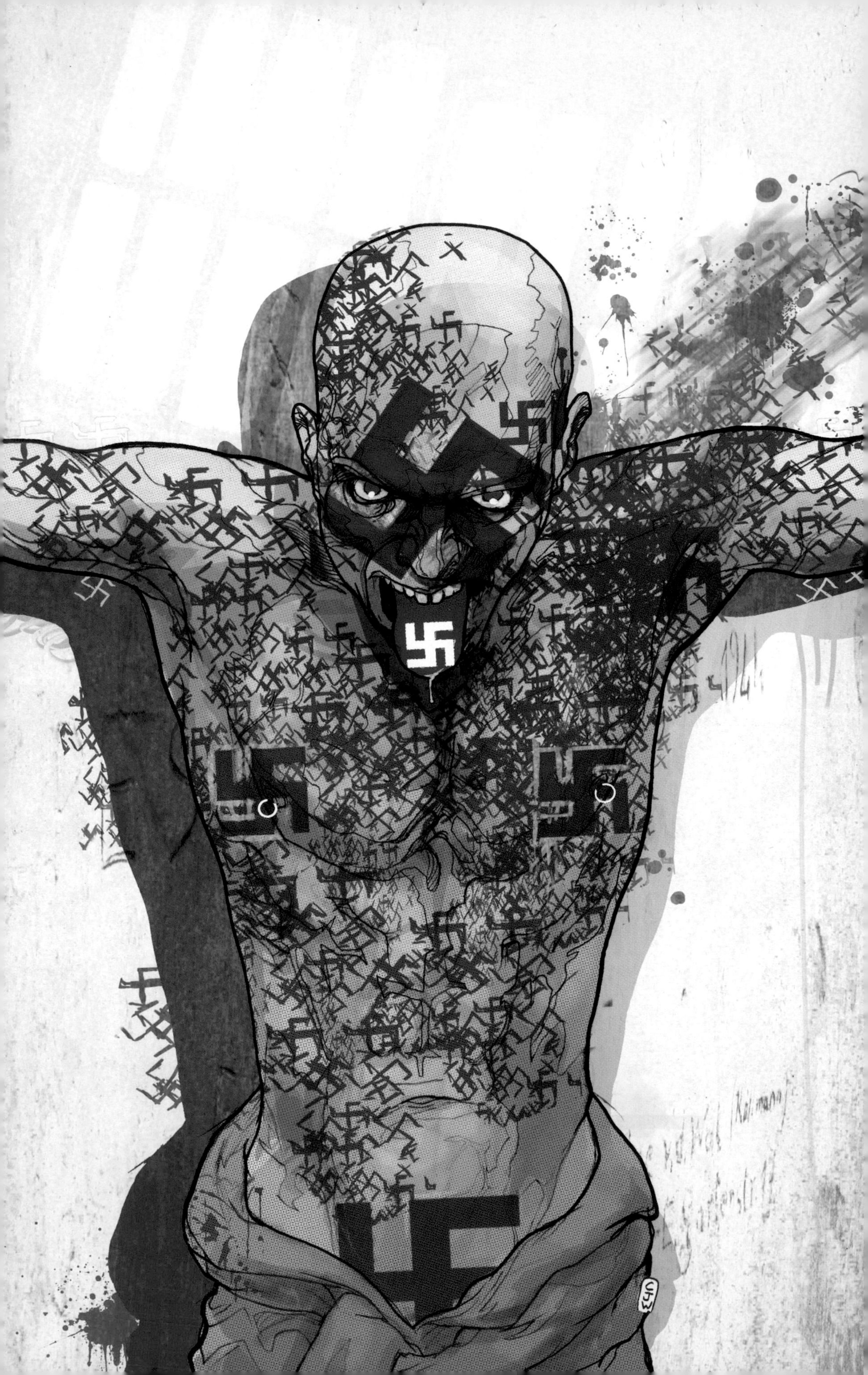

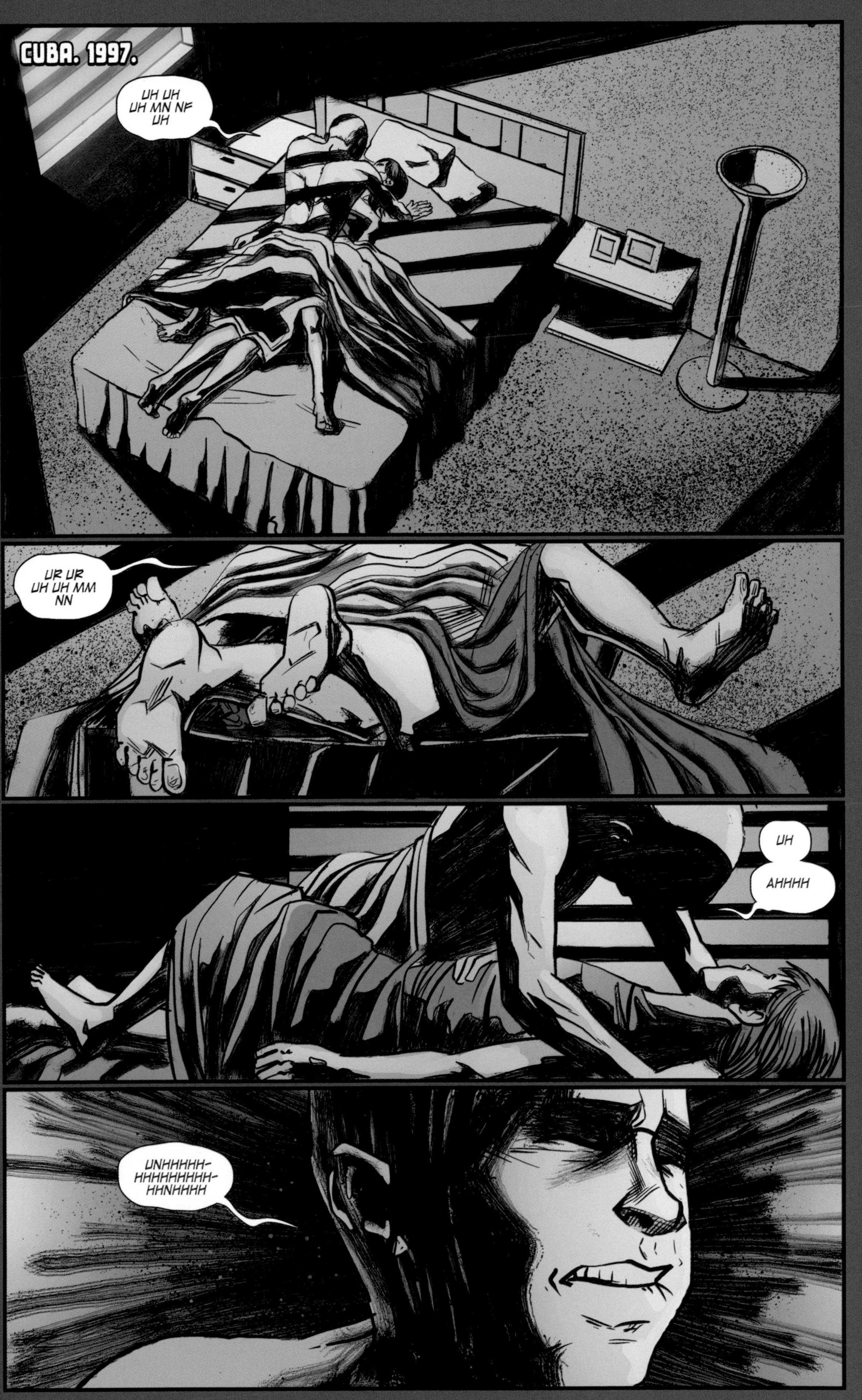
CUBA. 1997.
UH UH UH MN NF UH
UR UR UH UH MM NN
UH
AHHHH
UNHHHHH-HHHHHHHHH-HHNHHHH

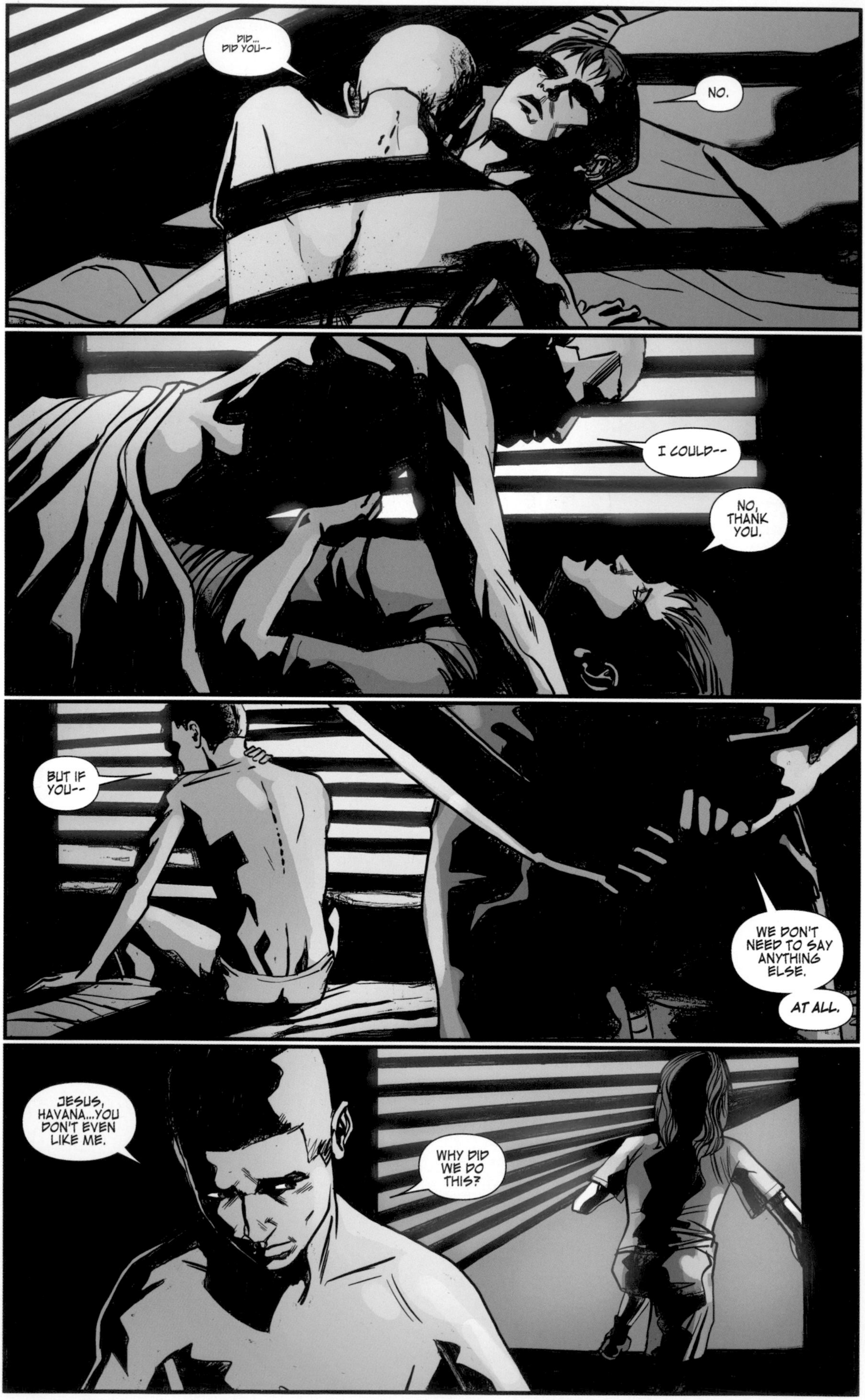
DID... DID YOU--
NO.
I COULD--
NO, THANK YOU.
BUT IF YOU--
WE DON'T NEED TO SAY ANYTHING ELSE.
AT ALL.
JESUS, HAVANA...YOU DON'T EVEN LIKE ME.
WHY DID WE DO THIS?

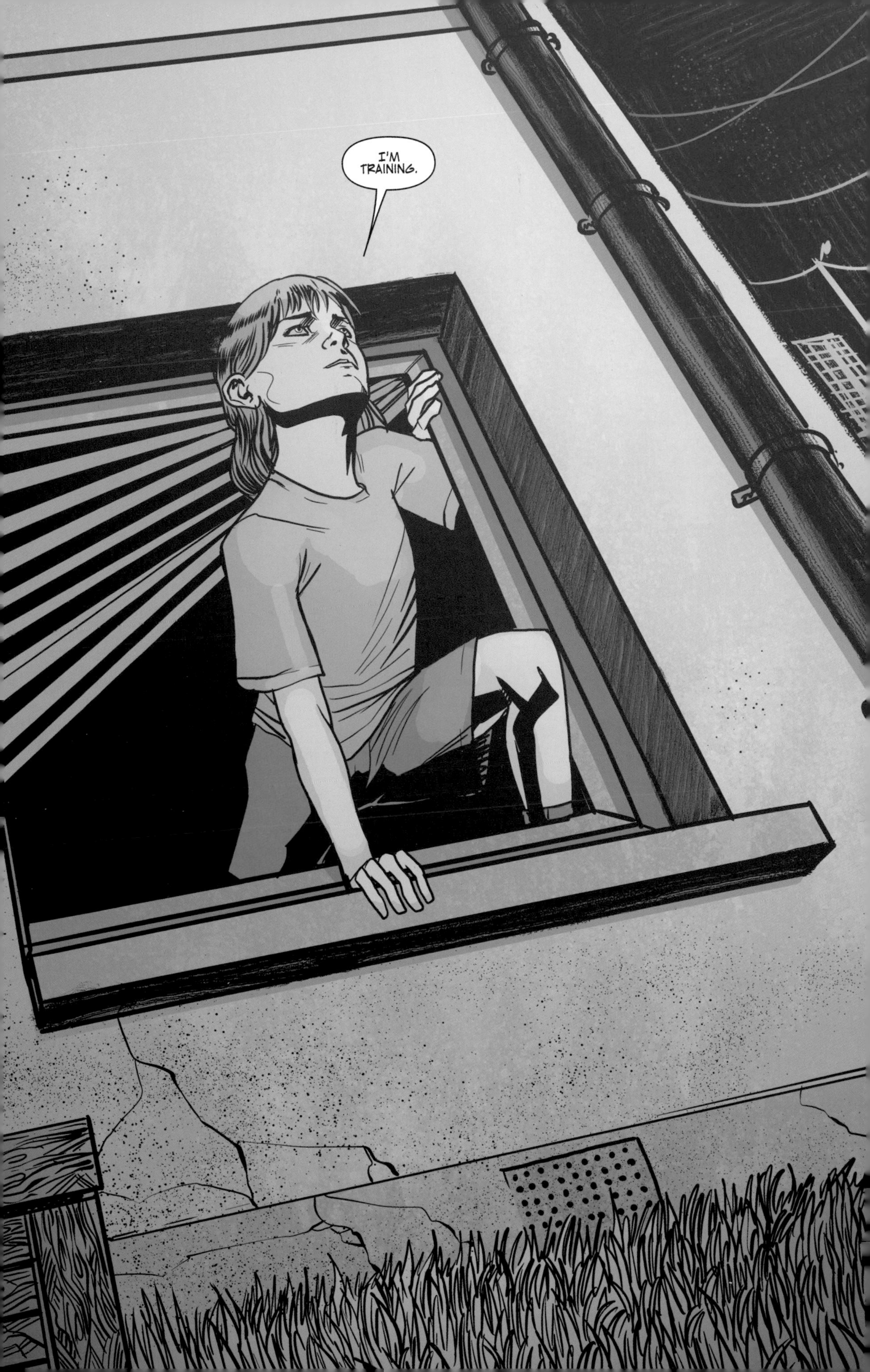
I'M TRAINING.

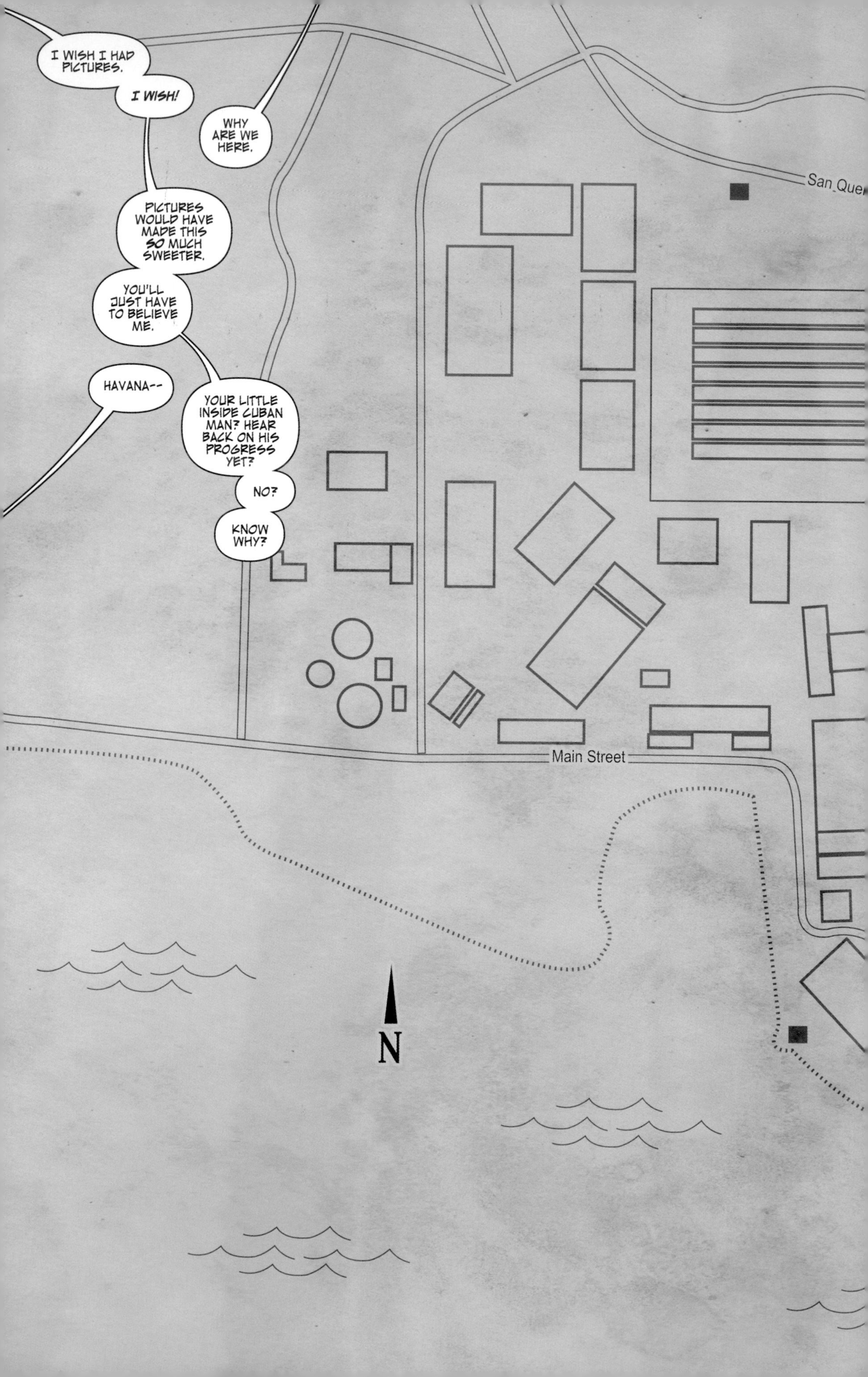
I WISH I HAD PICTURES.
I WISH!
WHY ARE WE HERE.
PICTURES WOULD HAVE MADE THIS SO MUCH SWEETER.
YOU'LL JUST HAVE TO BELIEVE ME.
HAVANA--
YOUR LITTLE INSIDE CUBAN MAN? HEAR BACK ON HIS PROGRESS YET?
NO?
KNOW WHY?
San Quen
Main Street
N

San Quentin Correctional Facility

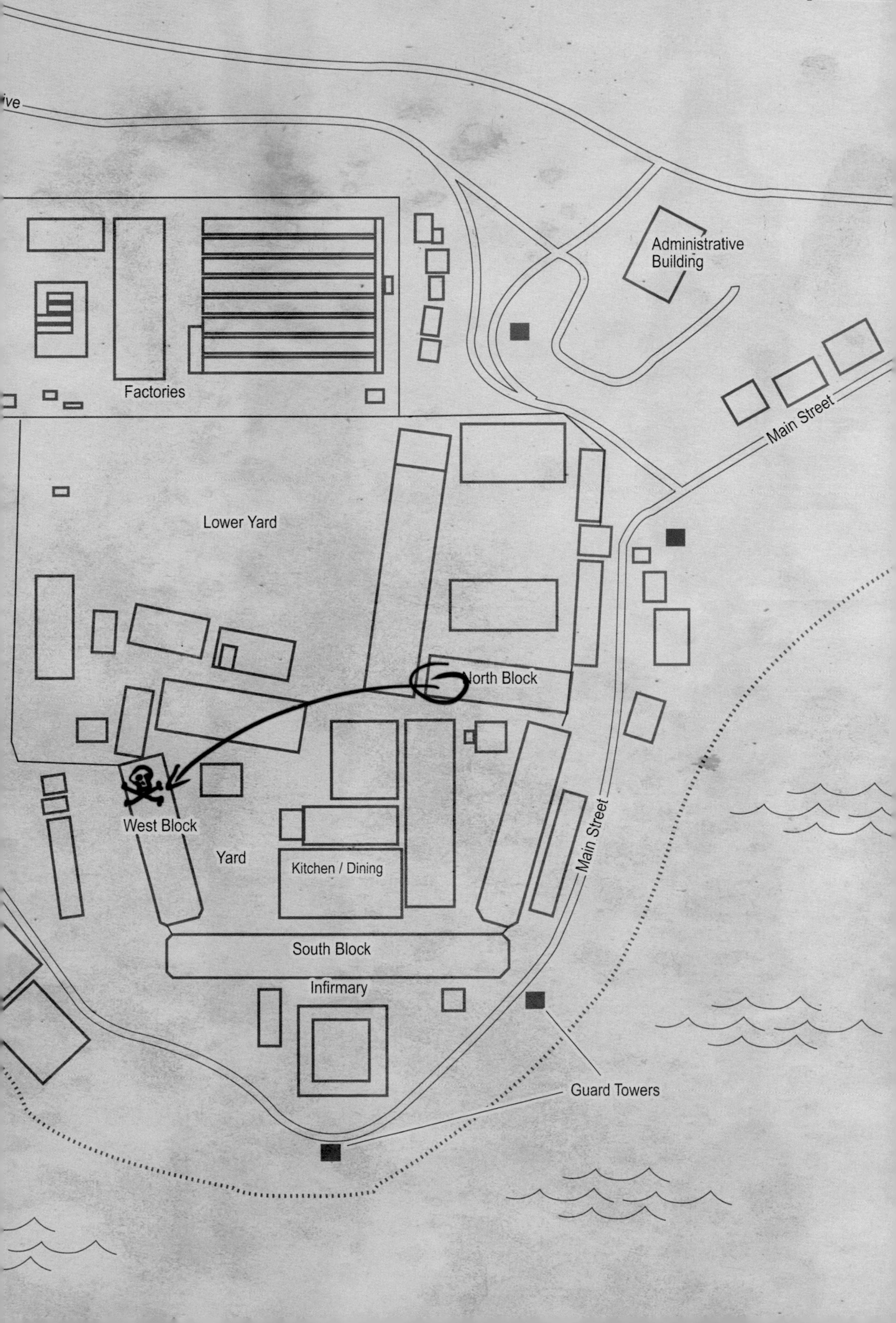
ive
Administrative Building
Factories
Main Street
Lower Yard
North Block
West Block
Yard
Kitchen / Dining
Main Street
South Block
Infirmary
Guard Towers

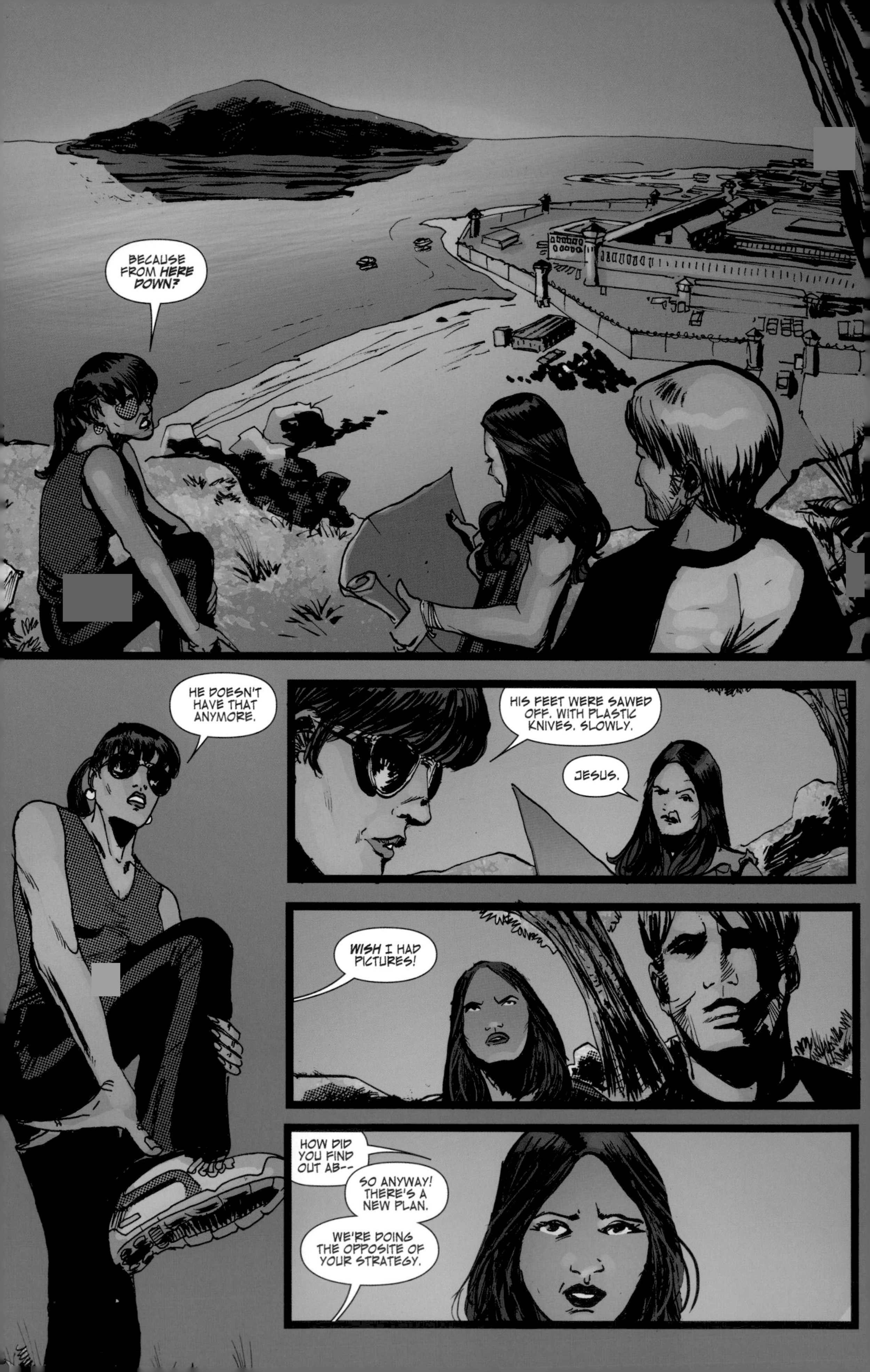
BECAUSE FROM HERE DOWN?
HE DOESN'T HAVE THAT ANYMORE.
HIS FEET WERE SAWED OFF. WITH PLASTIC KNIVES. SLOWLY.
JESUS.
WISH I HAD PICTURES!
HOW DID YOU FIND OUT AB--
SO ANYWAY! THERE'S A NEW PLAN.
WE'RE DOING THE OPPOSITE OF YOUR STRATEGY.

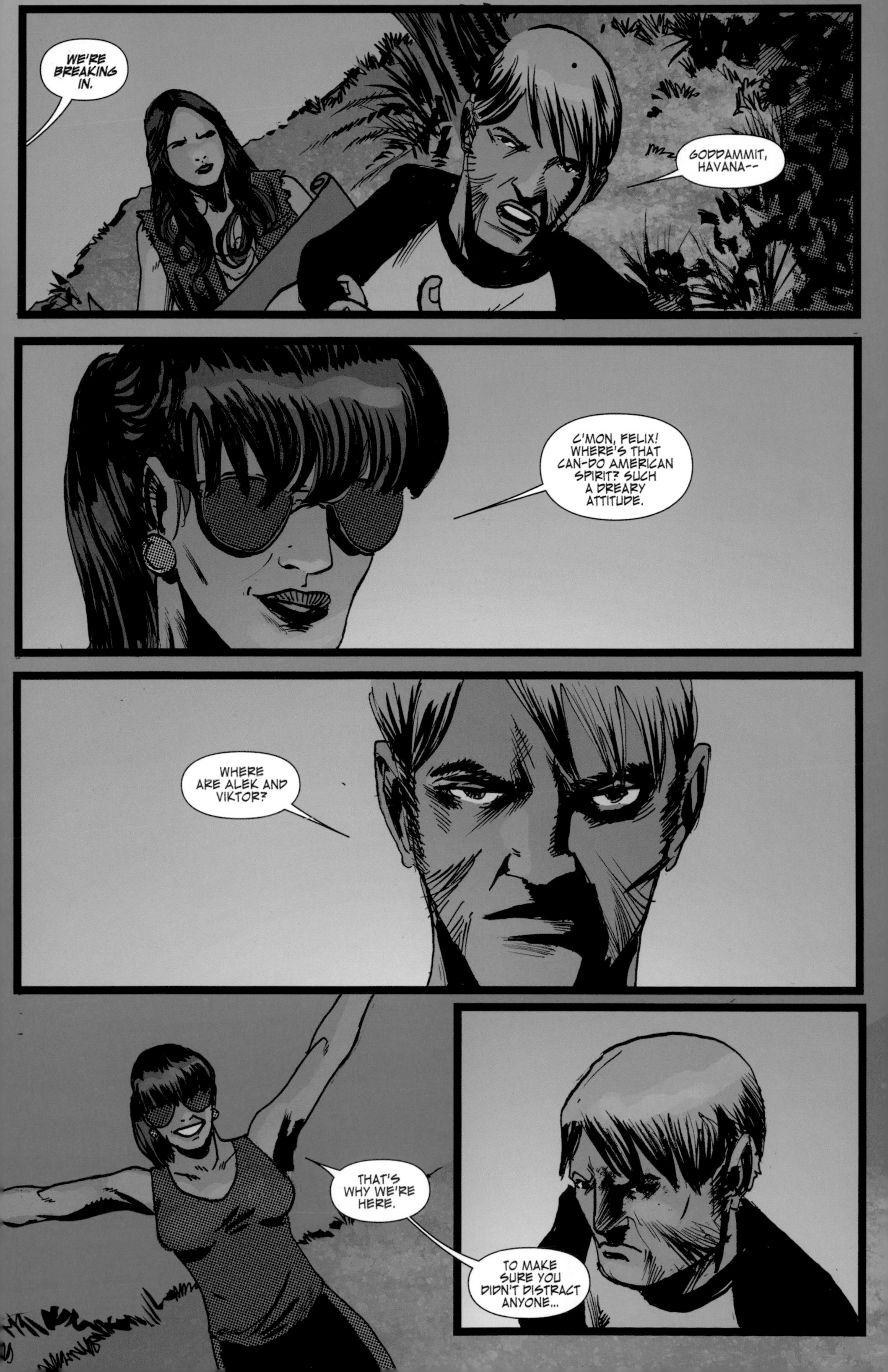
WE'RE BREAKING IN.
GODDAMMIT, HAVANA--
C'MON, FELIX! WHERE'S THAT CAN-DO AMERICAN SPIRIT? SUCH A DREARY ATTITUDE.
WHERE ARE ALEK AND VIKTOR?
THAT'S WHY WE'RE HERE.
TO MAKE SURE YOU DIDN'T DISTRACT ANYONE...

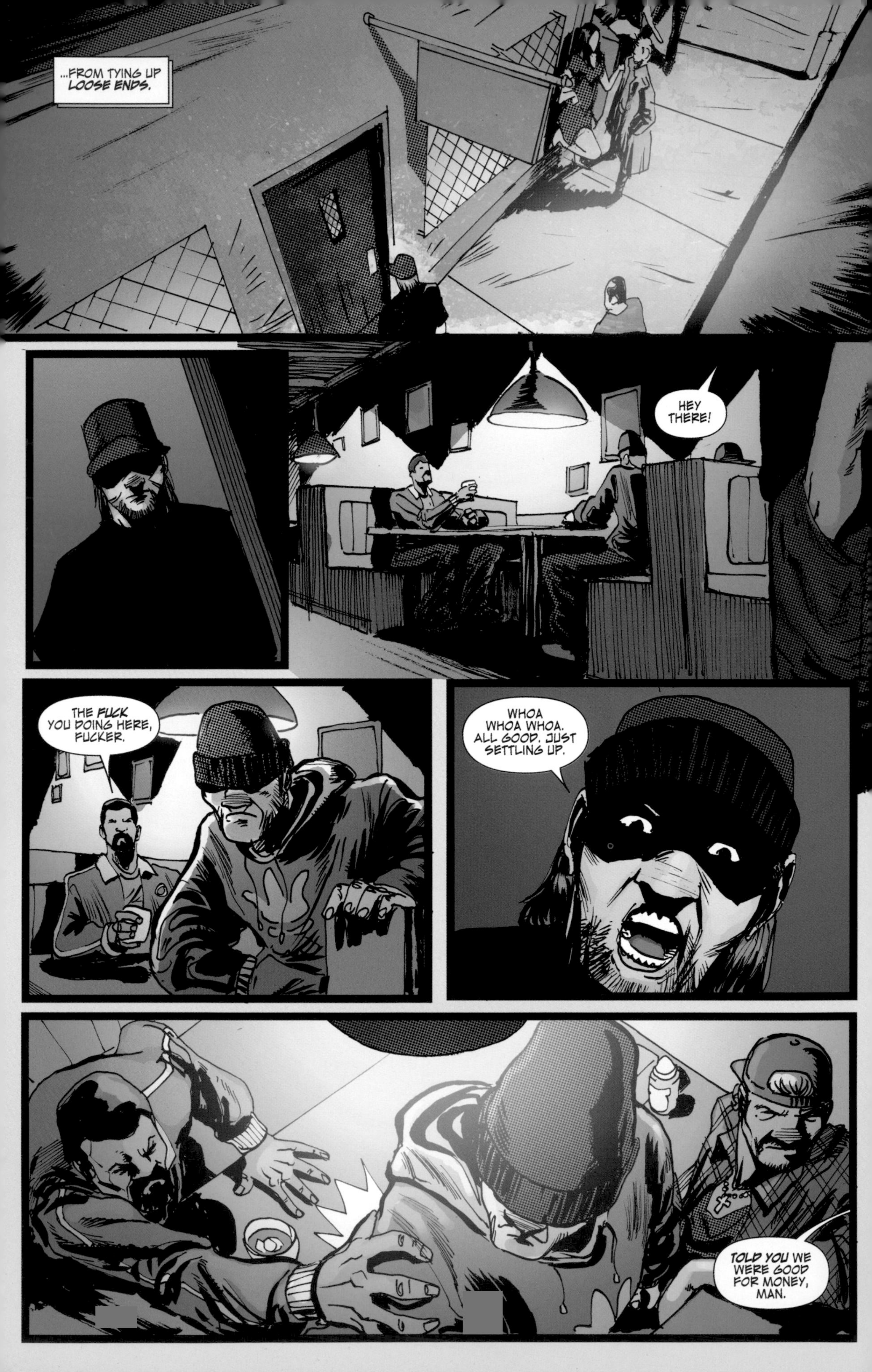
...FROM TYING UP LOOSE ENDS.
HEY THERE!
THE FUCK YOU DOING HERE, FUCKER.
WHOA WHOA WHOA. ALL GOOD. JUST SETTLING UP.
TOLD YOU WE WERE GOOD FOR MONEY, MAN.

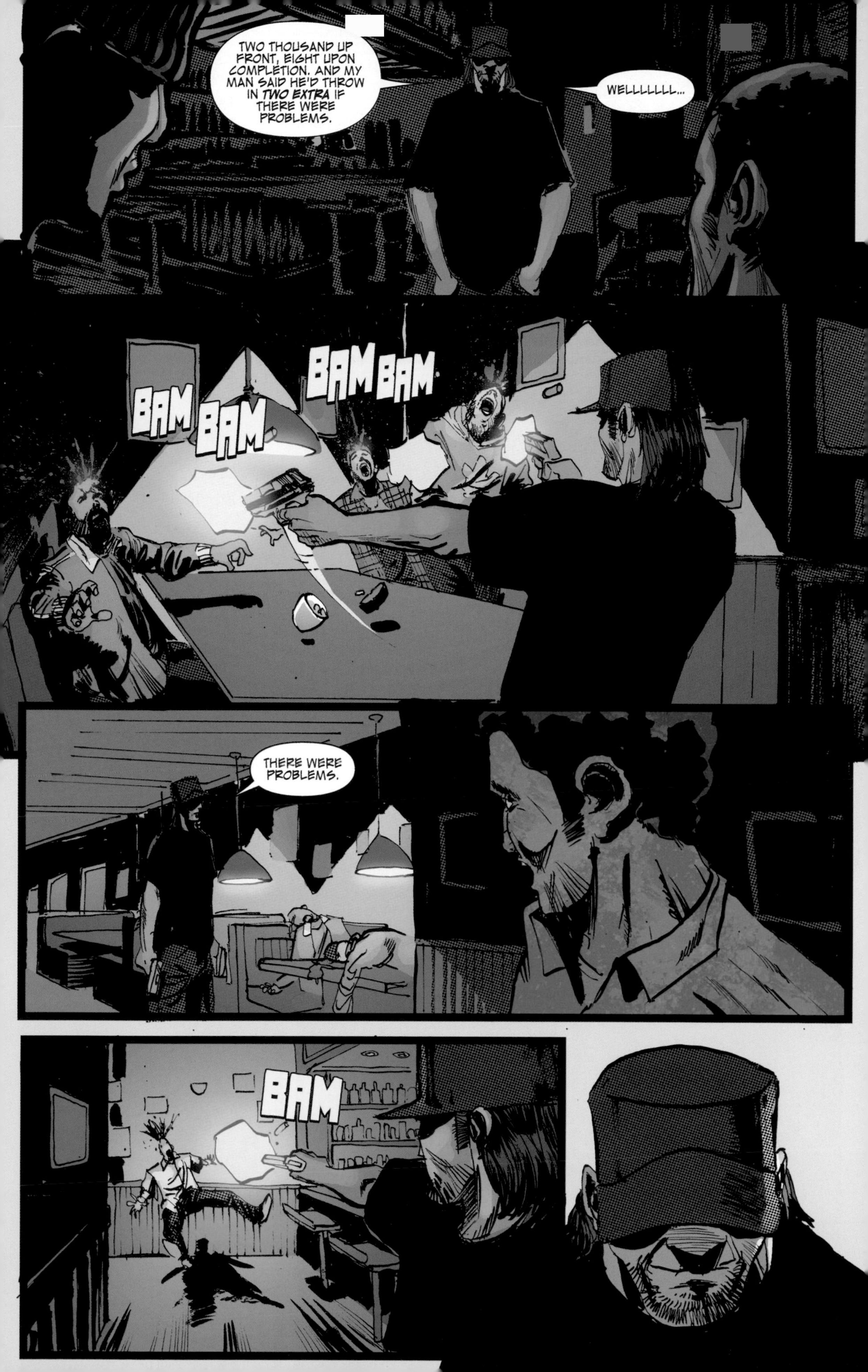
TWO THOUSAND UP FRONT, EIGHT UPON COMPLETION. AND MY MAN SAID HE'D THROW IN TWO EXTRA IF THERE WERE PROBLEMS.
WELLLLLLLL...
BAM
BAM
BAM BAM
THERE WERE PROBLEMS.
BAM

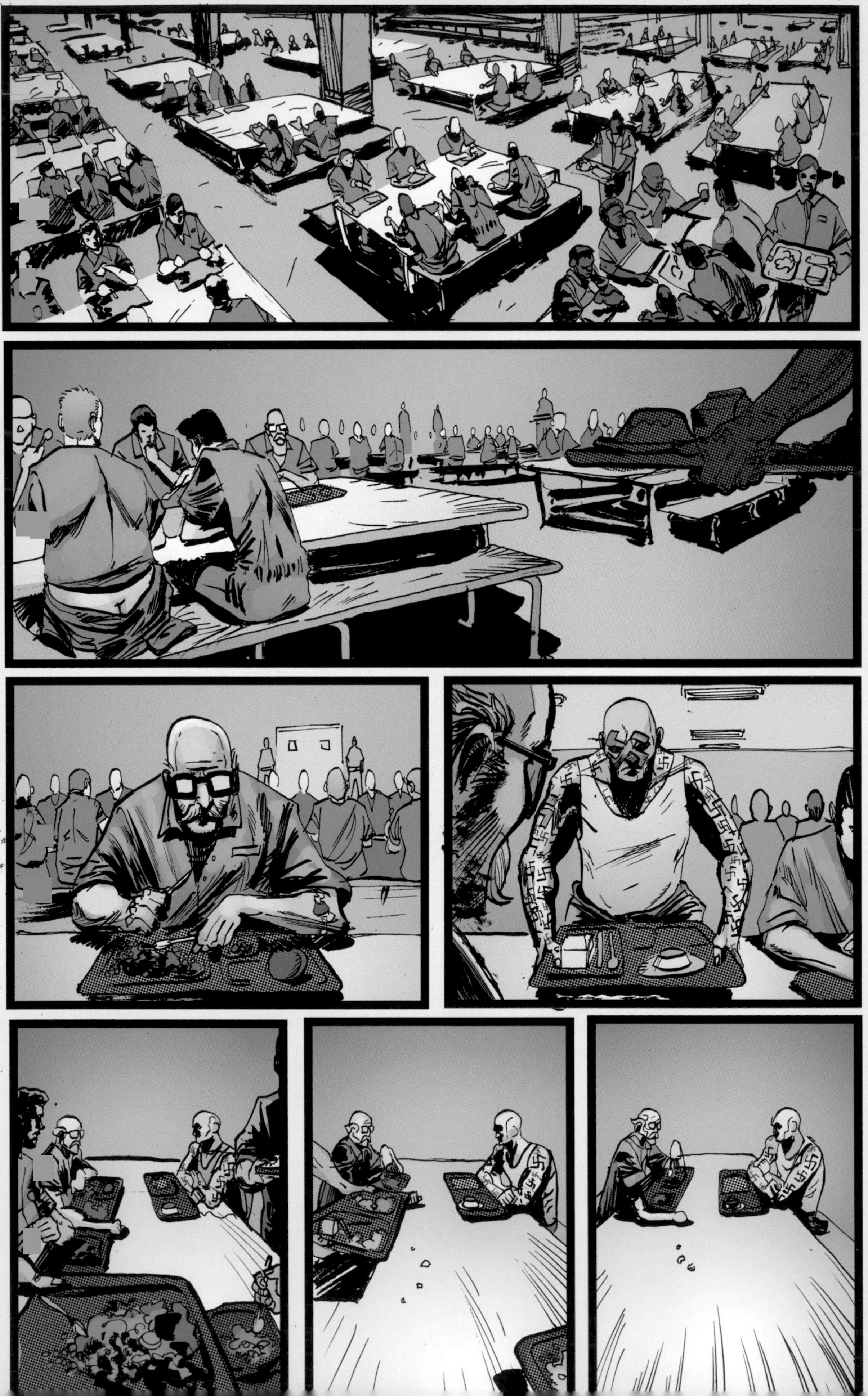

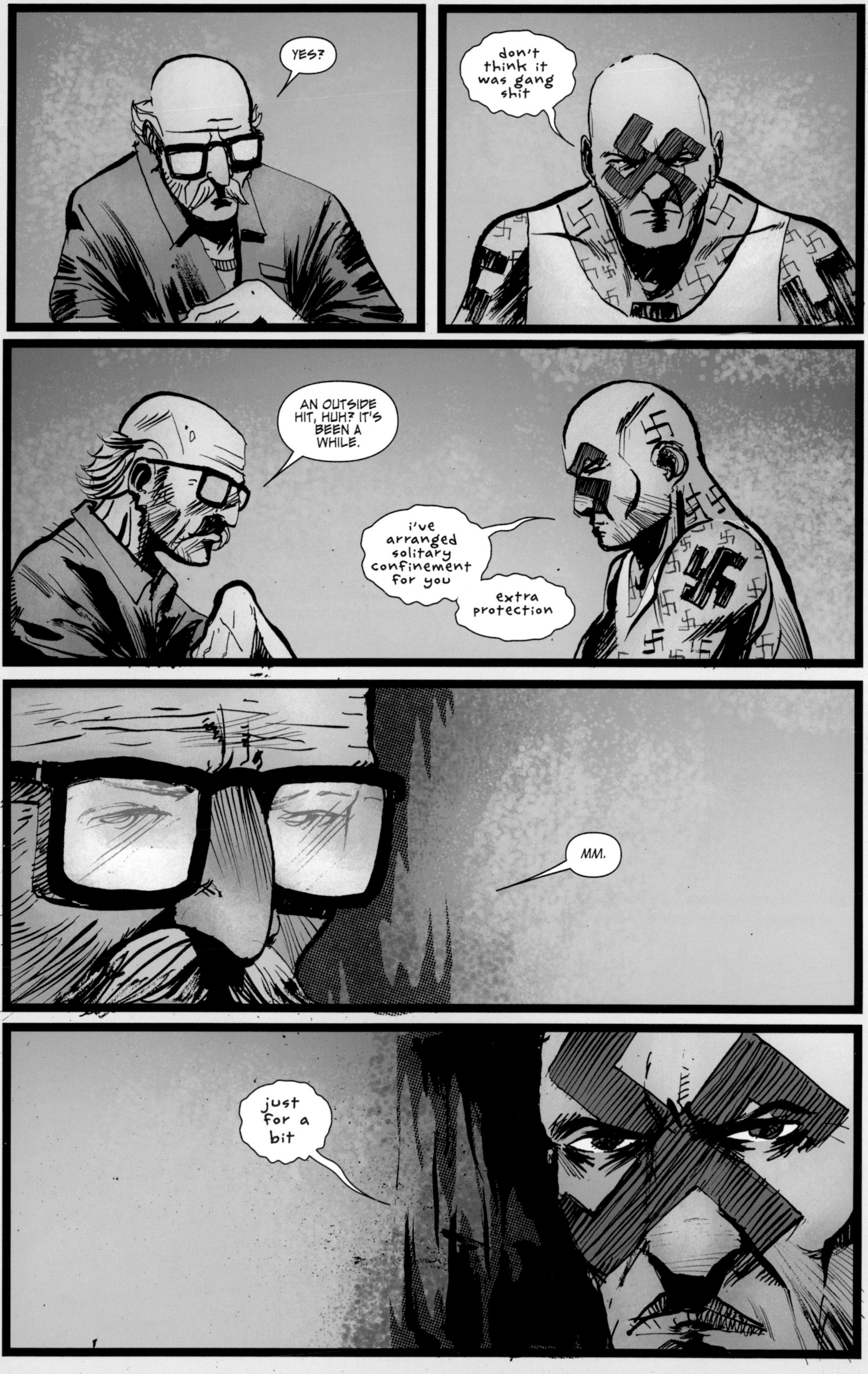
YES?
don't think it was gang shit
AN OUTSIDE HIT, HUH? IT'S BEEN A WHILE.
i've arranged solitary confinement for you
extra protection
MM.
just for a bit

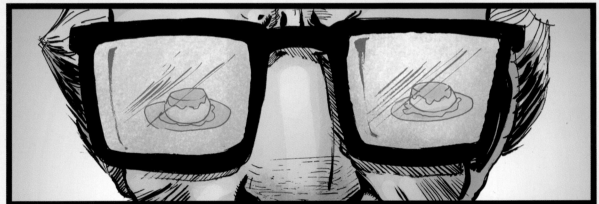

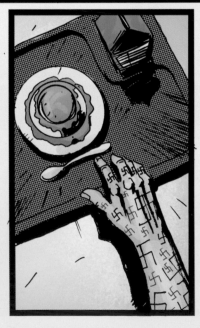

THANK YOU, FRED.

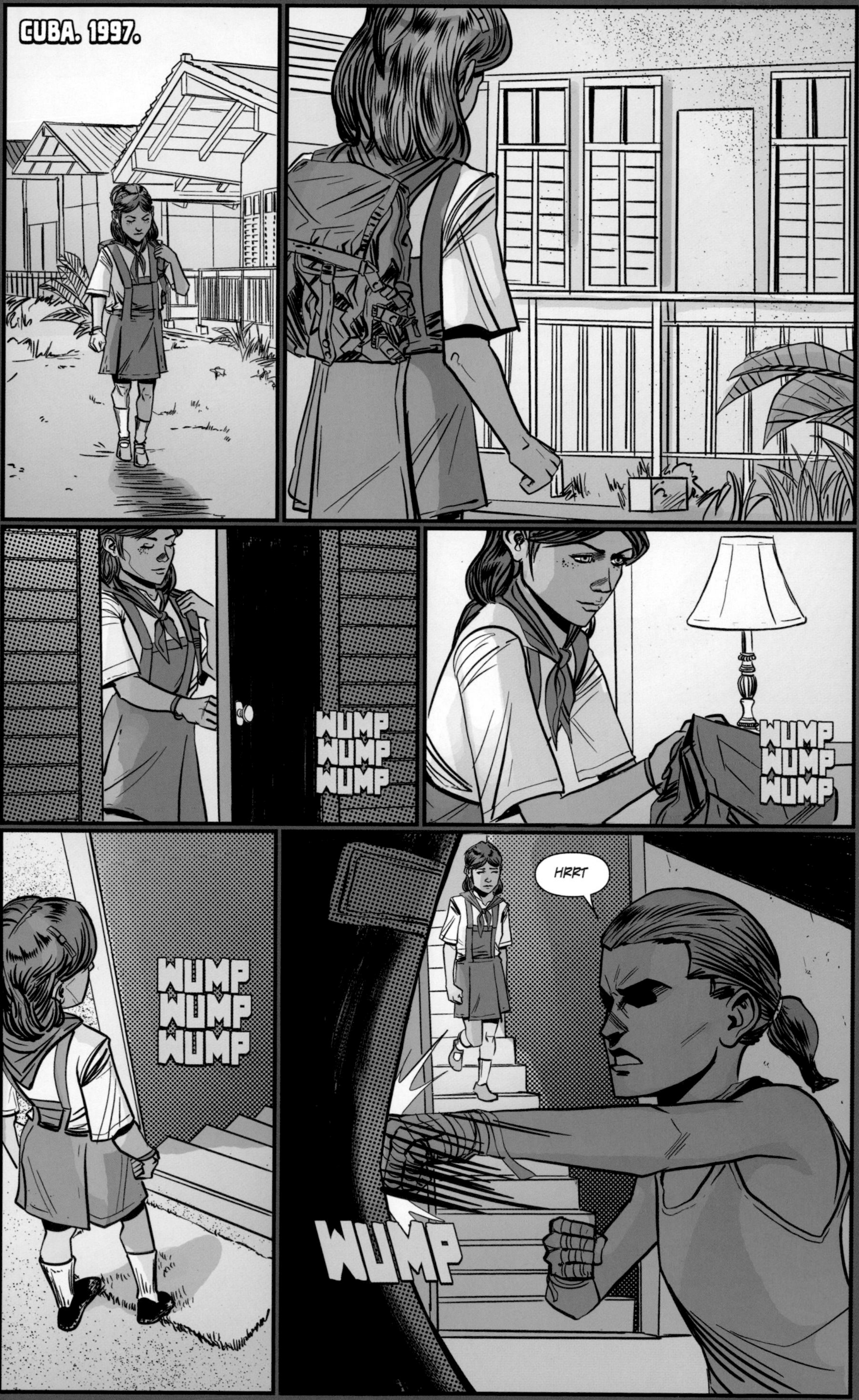
CUBA. 1997.
WUMP
WUMP
WUMP
WUMP
WUMP
WUMP
WUMP
WUMP
WUMP
HRRT
WUMP

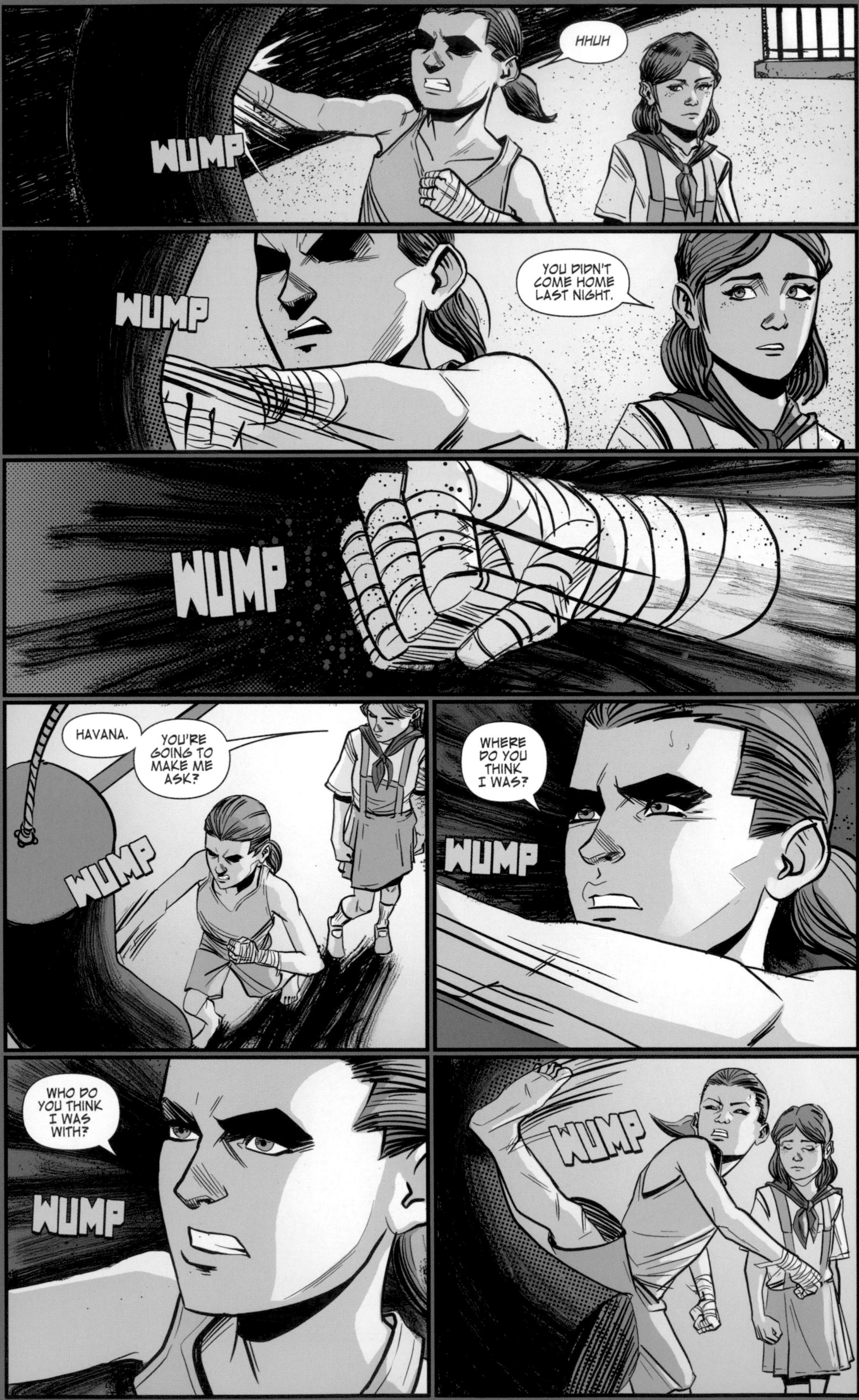
HHUH
WUMP
WUMP
YOU DIDN'T COME HOME LAST NIGHT.
WUMP
HAVANA.
YOU'RE GOING TO MAKE ME ASK?
WUMP
WHERE DO YOU THINK I WAS?
WUMP
WHO DO YOU THINK I WAS WITH?
WUMP
WUMP

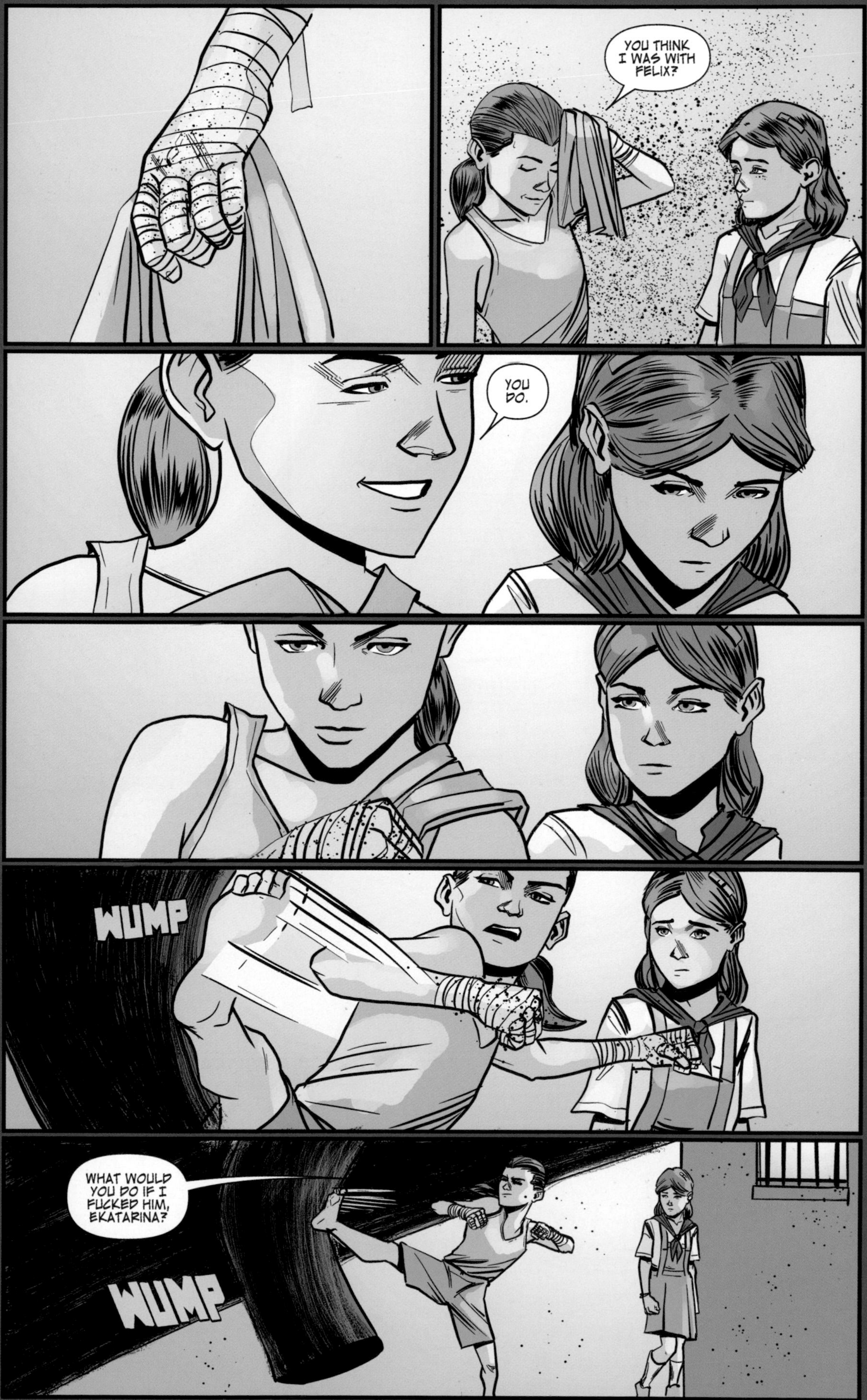
YOU THINK I WAS WITH FELIX?
YOU DO.
WUMP
WHAT WOULD YOU DO IF I FUCKED HIM, EKATARINA?
WUMP

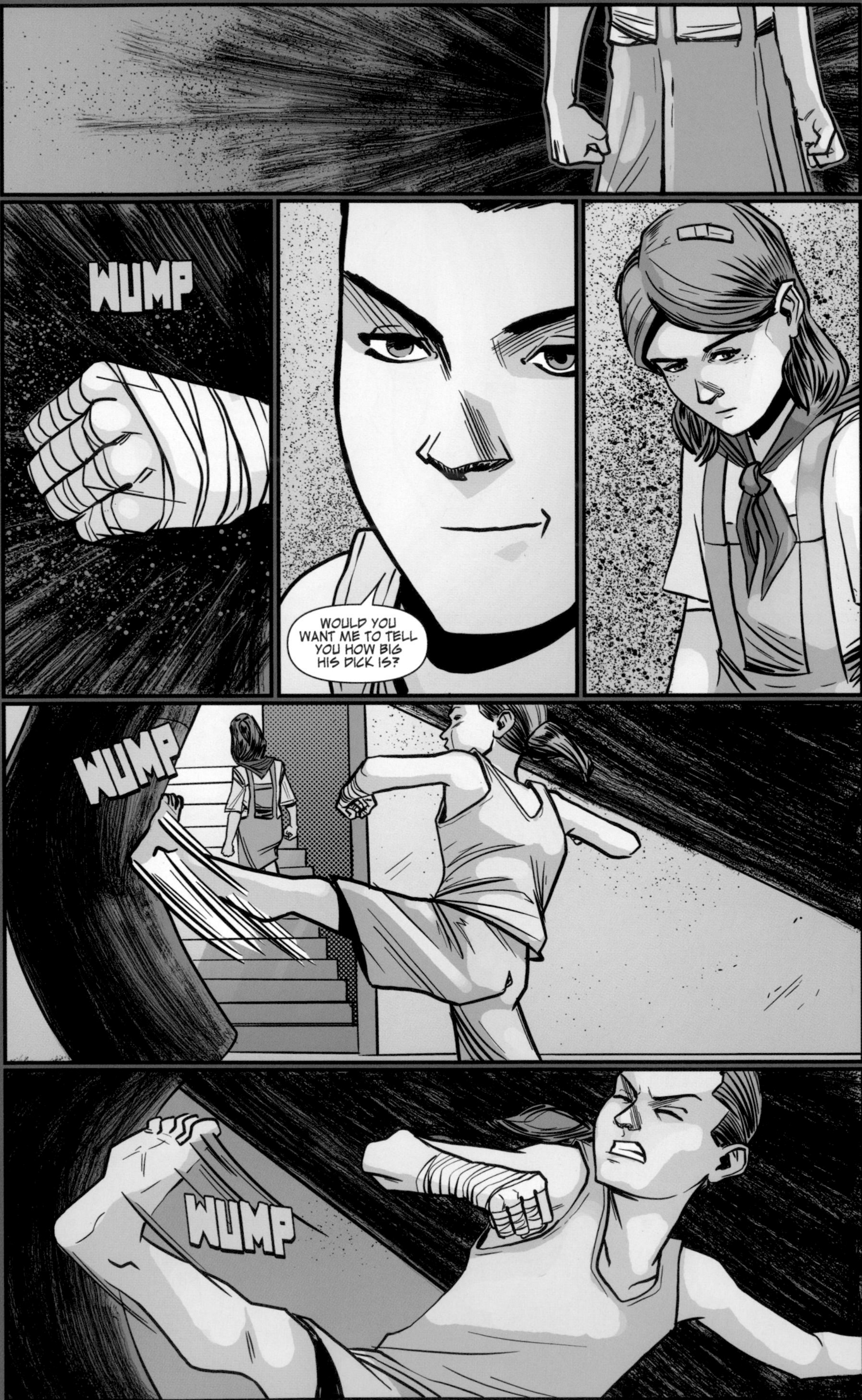
WUMP
WOULD YOU WANT ME TO TELL YOU HOW BIG HIS DICK IS?
WUMP
WUMP

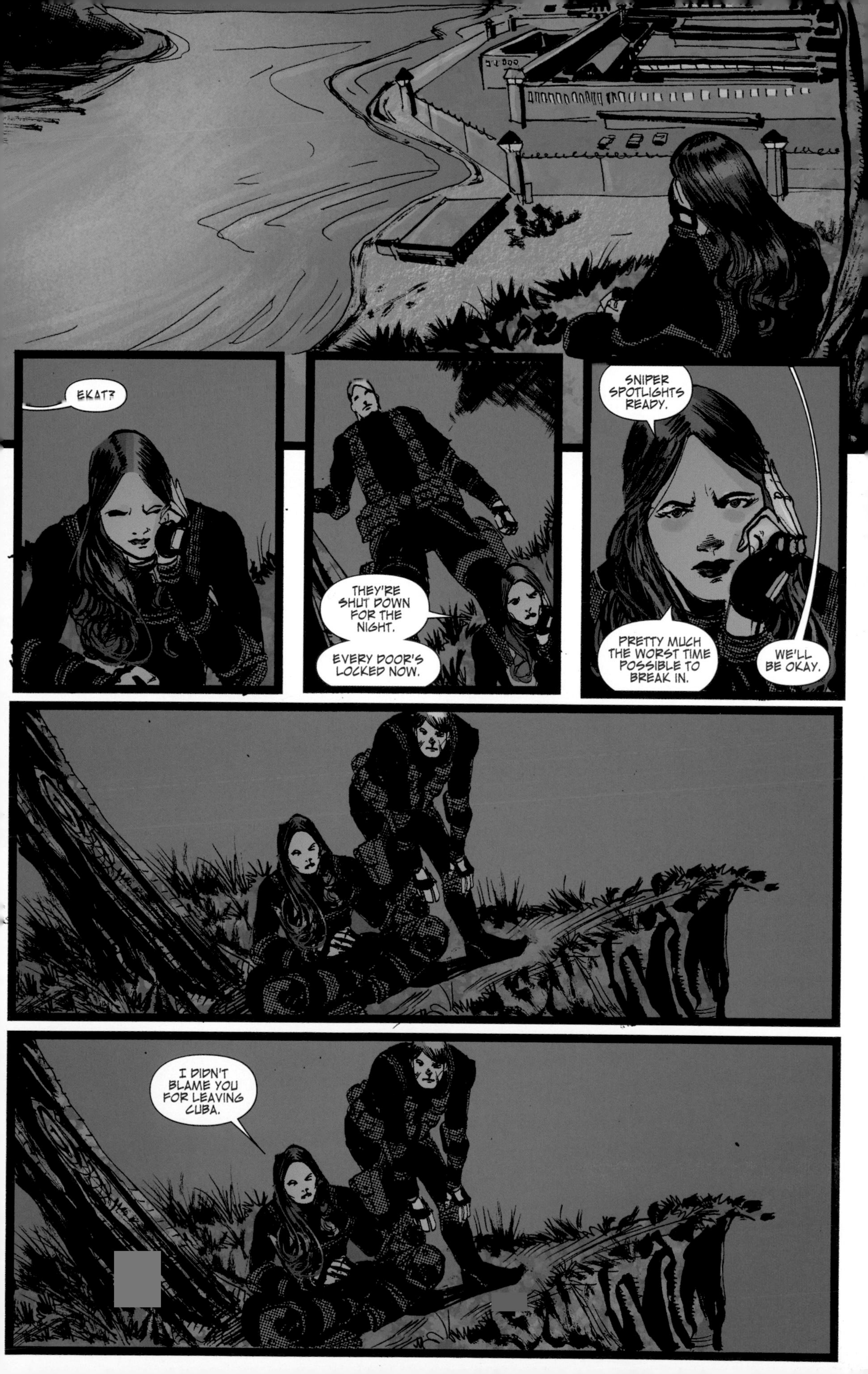
EKAT?
THEY'RE SHUT DOWN FOR THE NIGHT.
EVERY DOOR'S LOCKED NOW.
SNIPER SPOTLIGHTS READY.
PRETTY MUCH THE WORST TIME POSSIBLE TO BREAK IN.
WE'LL BE OKAY.
I DIDN'T BLAME YOU FOR LEAVING CUBA.

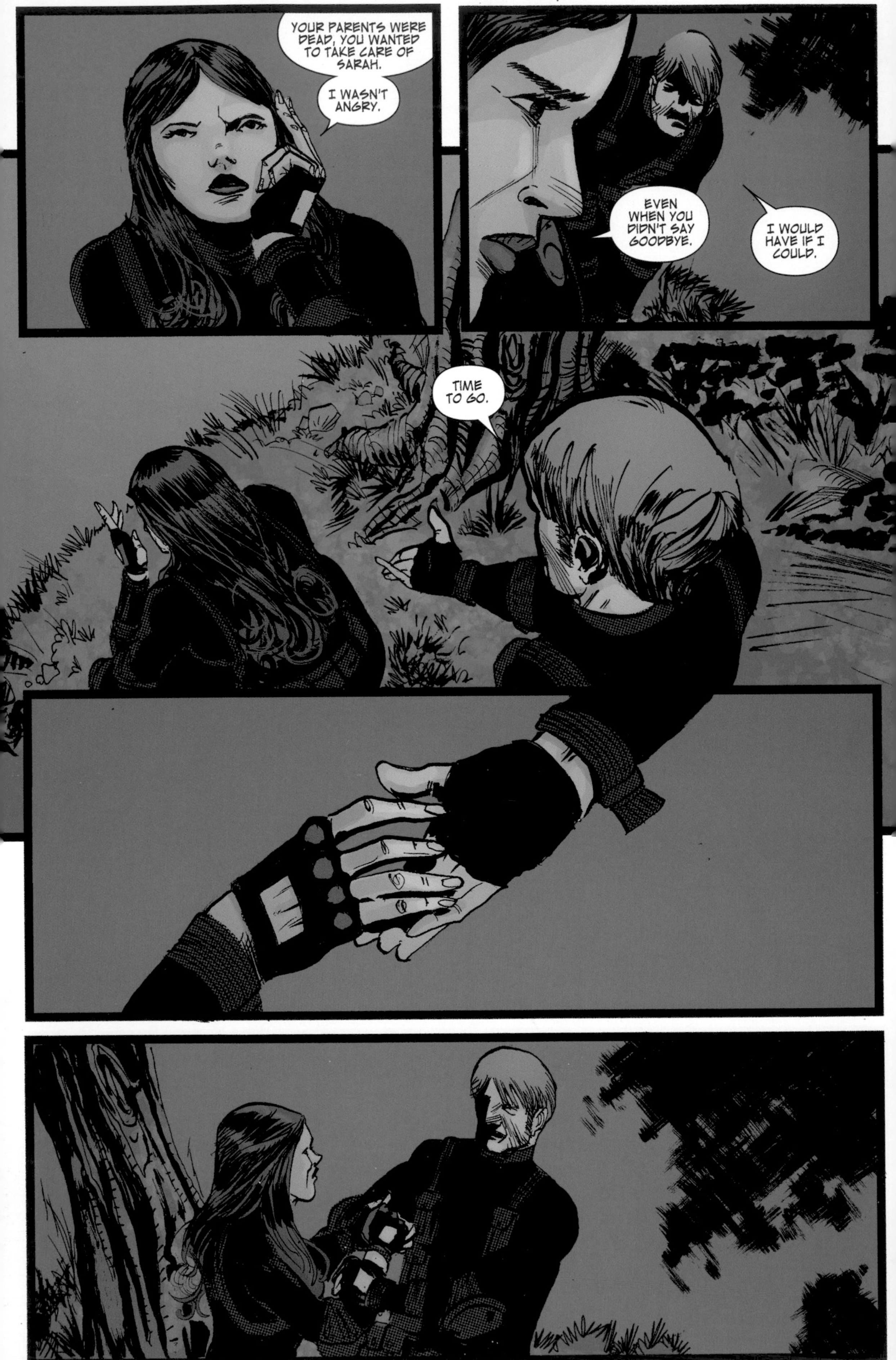

YOUR PARENTS WERE DEAD, YOU WANTED TO TAKE CARE OF SARAH.
I WASN'T ANGRY.
EVEN WHEN YOU DIDN'T SAY GOODBYE.
I WOULD HAVE IF I COULD.
TIME TO GO.

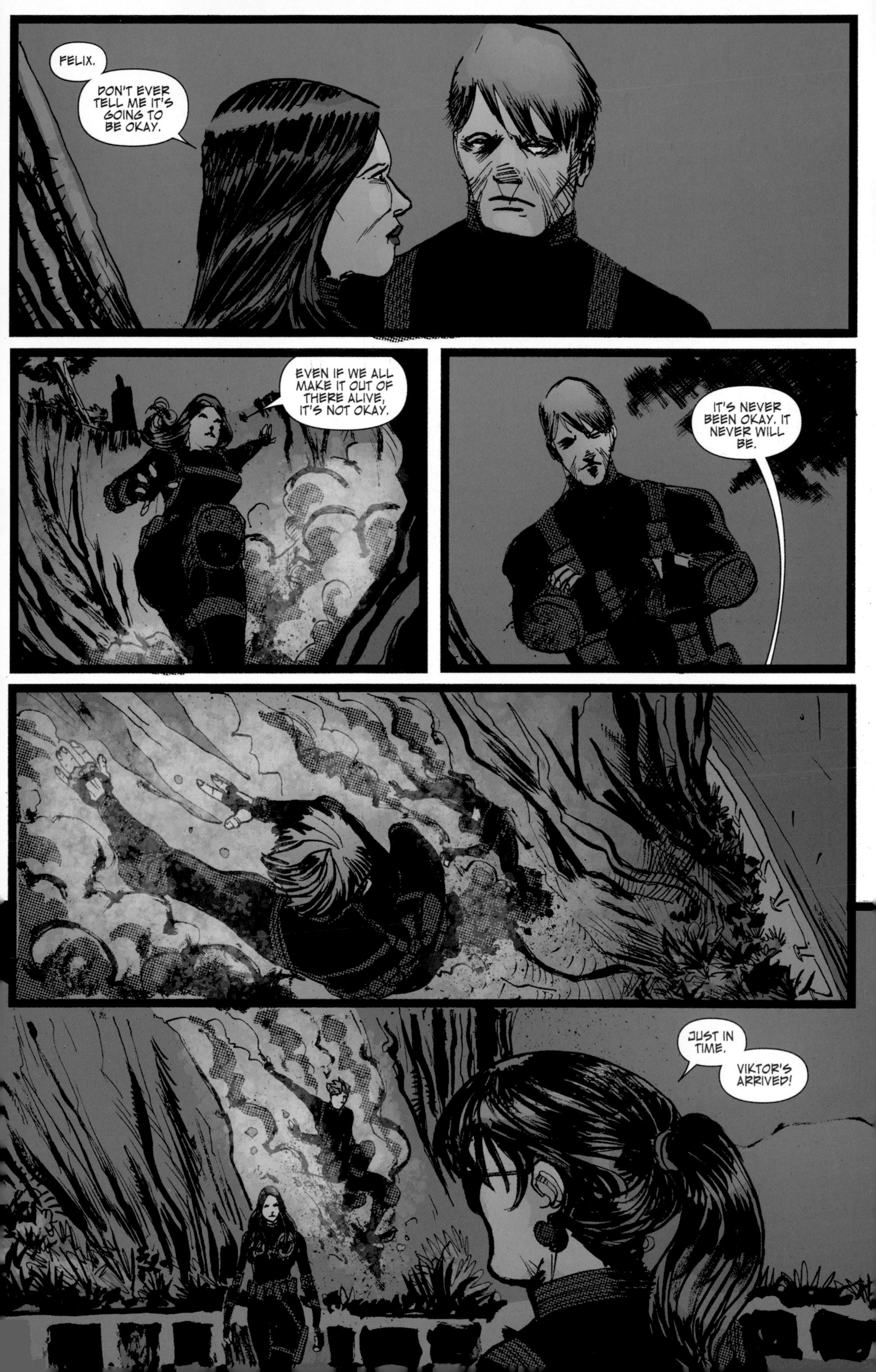
FELIX.
DON'T EVER TELL ME IT'S GOING TO BE OKAY.
EVEN IF WE ALL MAKE IT OUT OF THERE ALIVE, IT'S NOT OKAY.
IT'S NEVER BEEN OKAY. IT NEVER WILL BE.
JUST IN TIME.
VIKTOR'S ARRIVED!

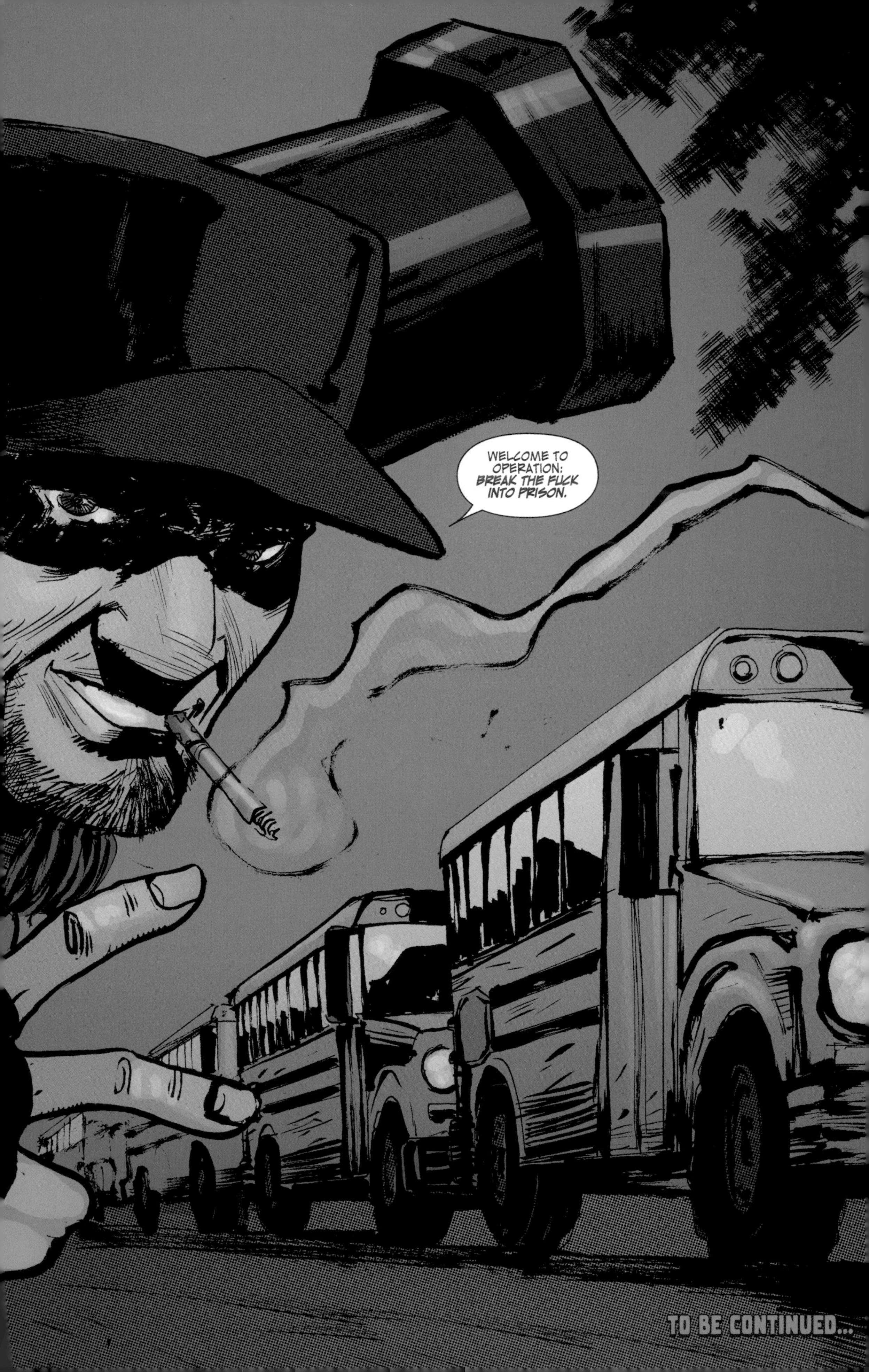
WELCOME TO OPERATION: BREAK THE FUCK INTO PRISON.
TO BE CONTINUED...

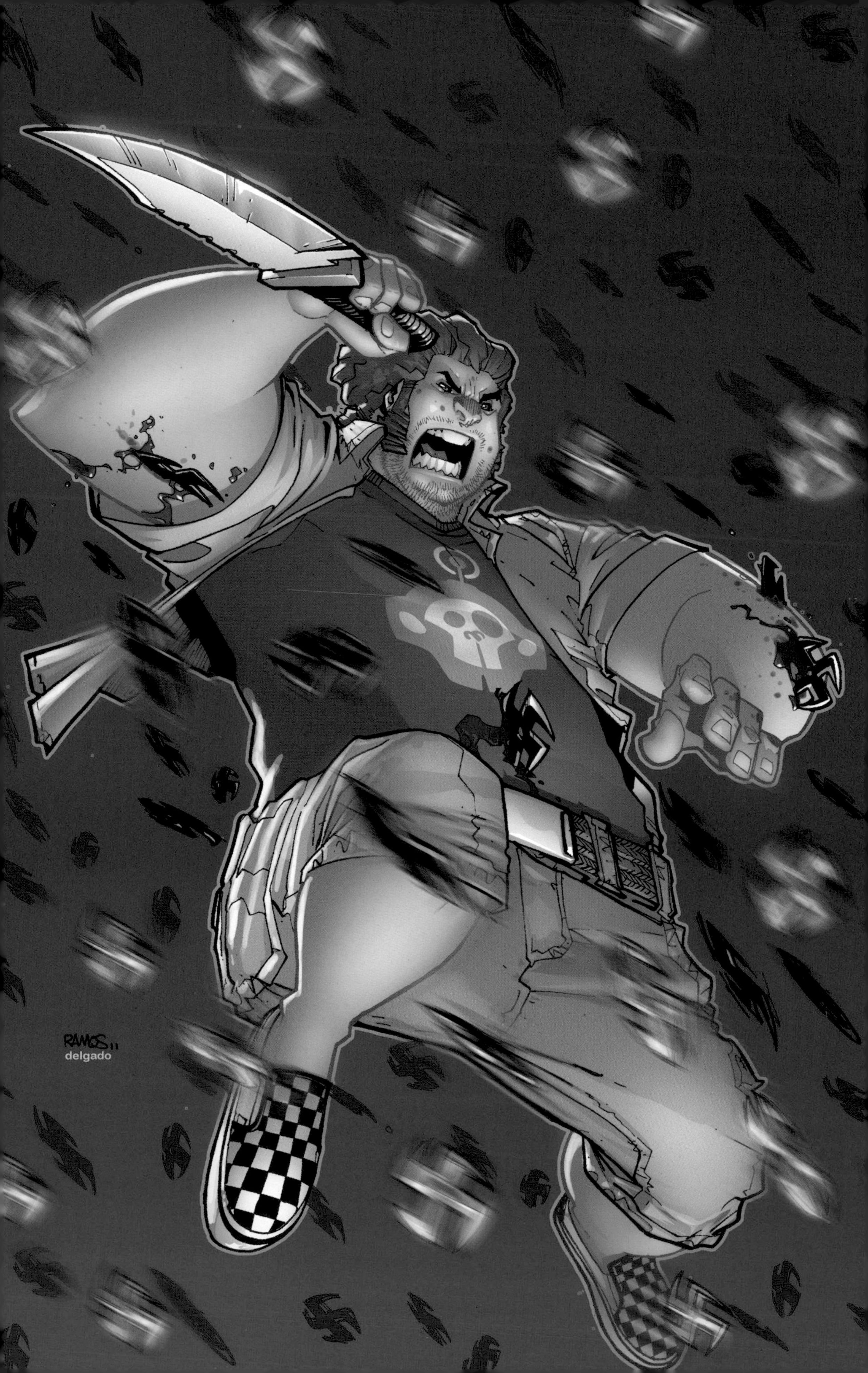
RAMOS 11
delgado

CASE FILE #421111056-Q
Radio Transcript, Acquired Via Satellite, 5-22-2012, 21

(radio feedback)

VOICE: Check in.
(female, believed to be Havana Machin)

VOICE: Check.
(male, believed to be Viktor Skipetrova)

VOICE: Check.
(female, believed to be Ekatarina Machin)

(seven second delay, scratching sound, radio feedback)

VOICE: Felix. Check the fuck in.
(female, believed to be Havana Machin)

VOICE: Check.
(male, believed to be Felix Botkina)

VOICE: Go.
(female, believed to be Havana Machin)

(sound, believed to be several large engines revving)

(revving sound increases)

(increases)

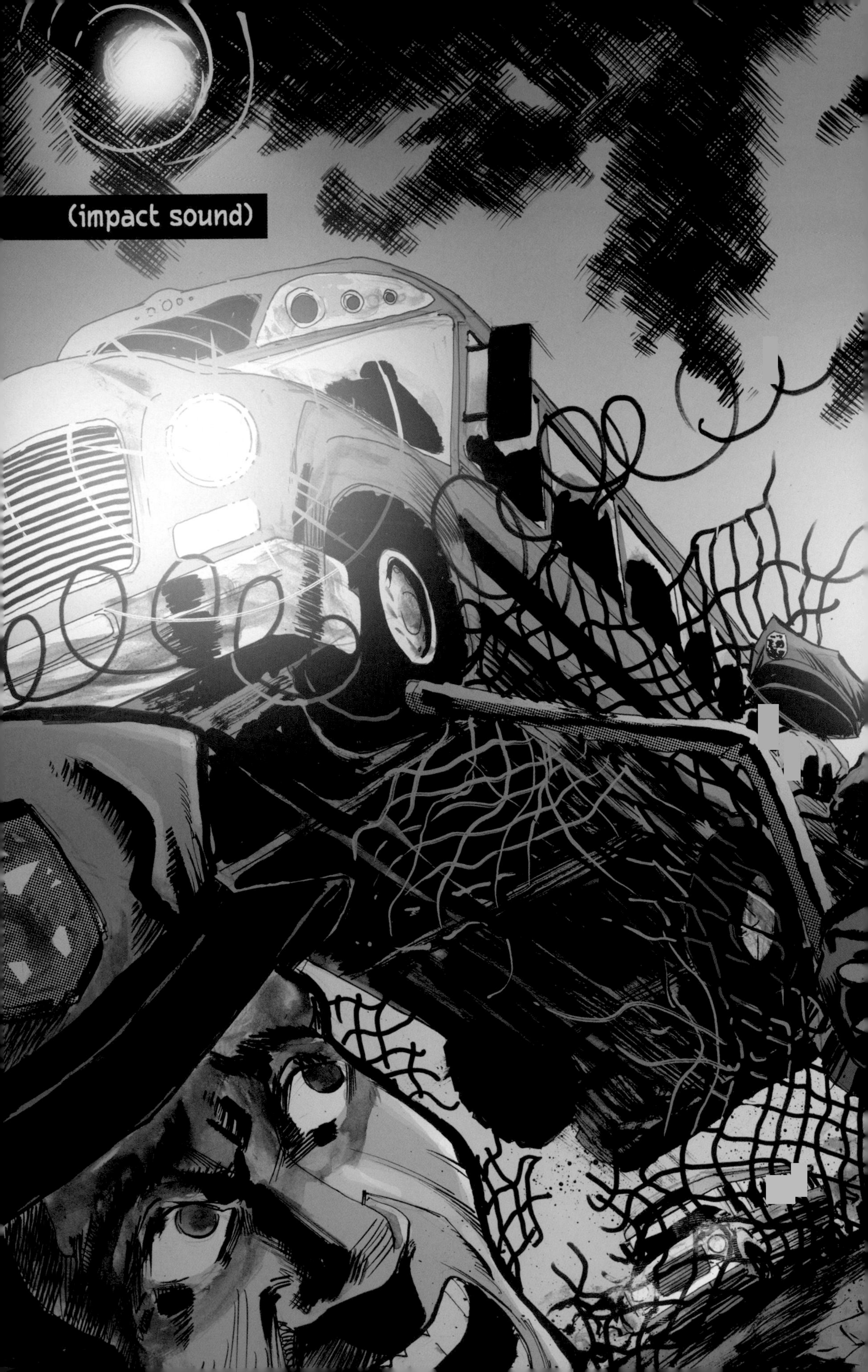
(impact sound)

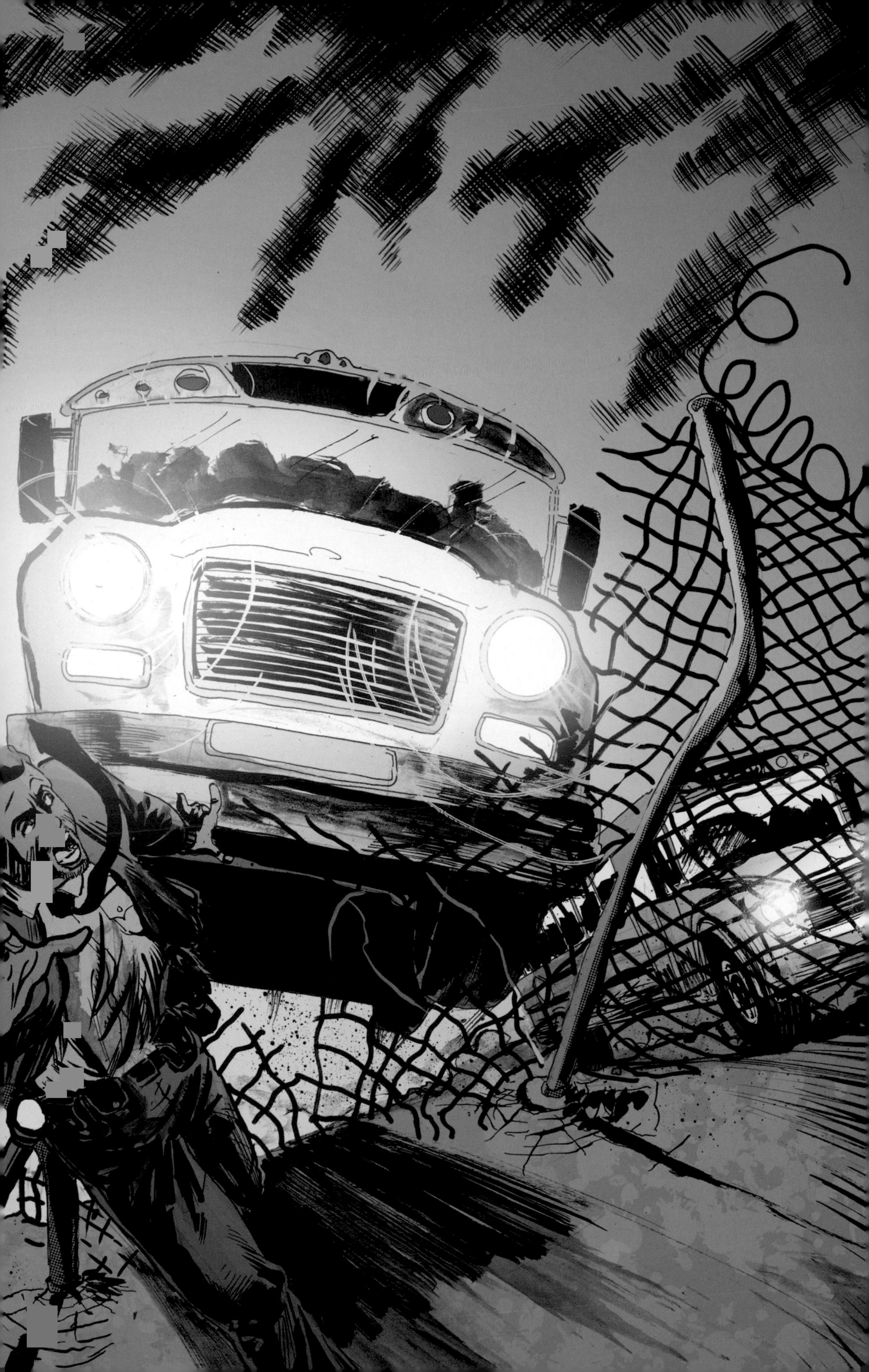

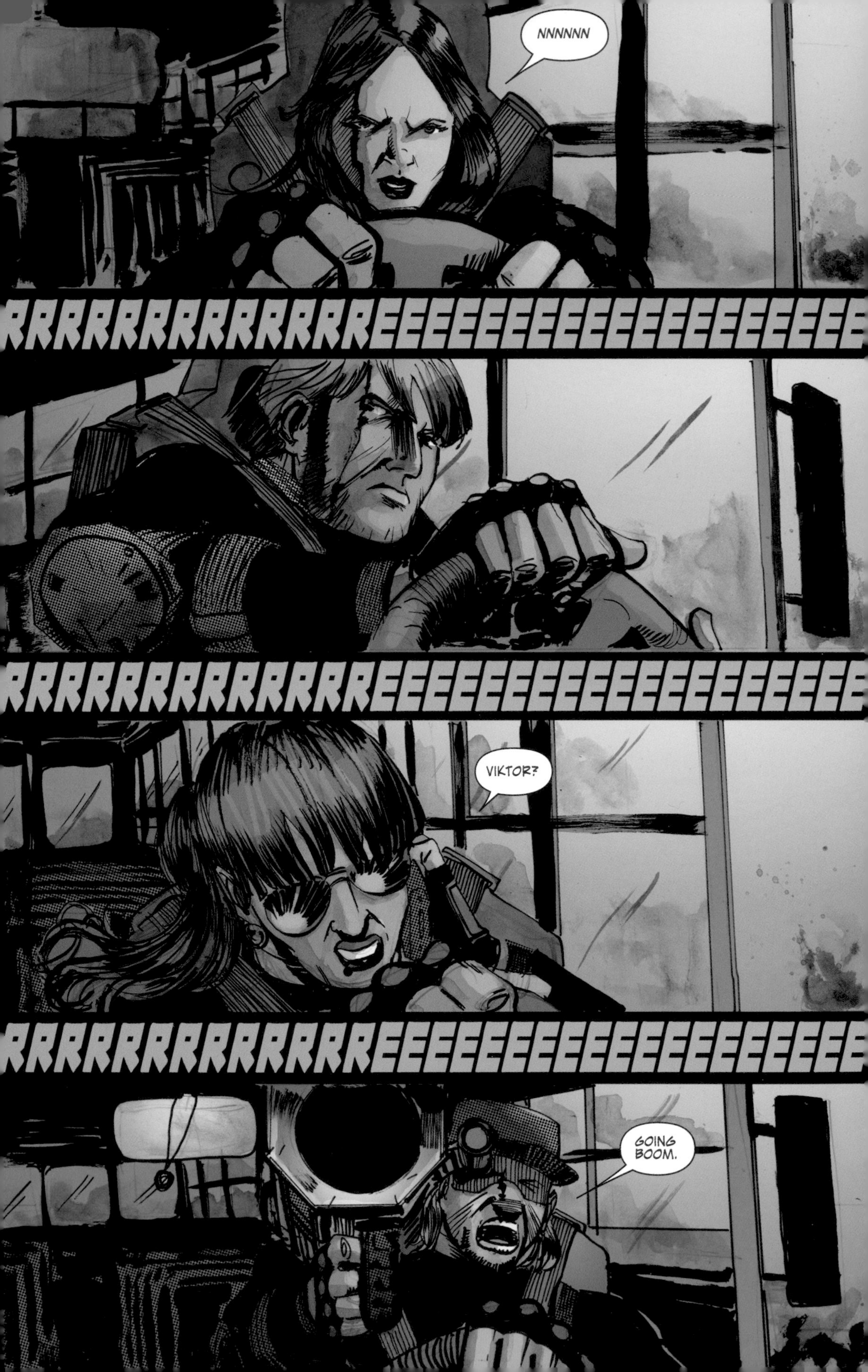
NNNNNN
RRRRRRRRRRRRREEEEEEEEEEEEEEEEEEE
RRRRRRRRRRRRREEEEEEEEEEEEEEEEEEE
VIKTOR?
RRRRRRRRRRRRREEEEEEEEEEEEEEEEEEE
GOING BOOM.

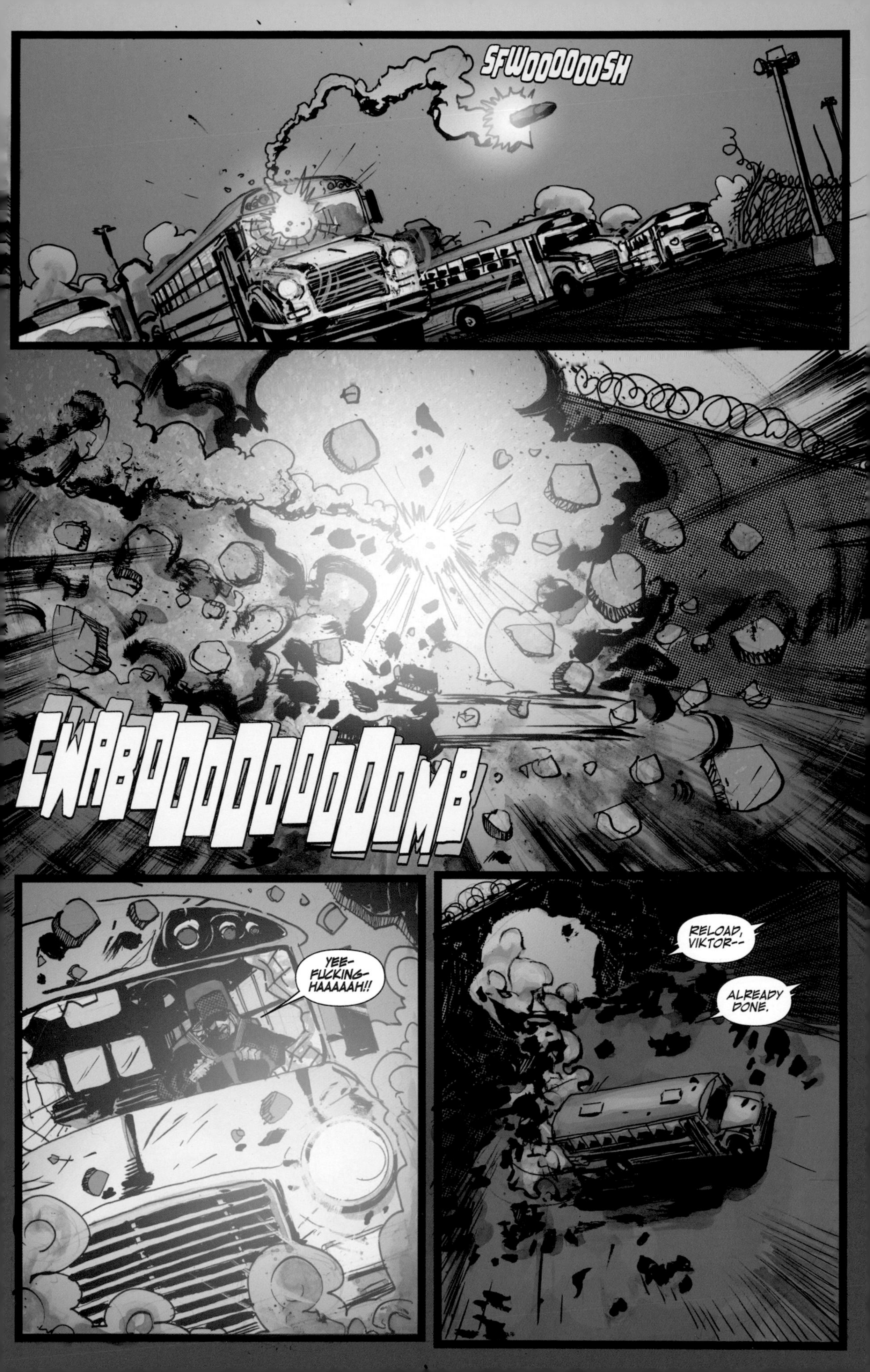
SFWOOOOOOSH
CWABOOOOOOOOOOMB
YEE-FUCKING-HAAAAAH!!
RELOAD, VIKTOR--
ALREADY DONE.

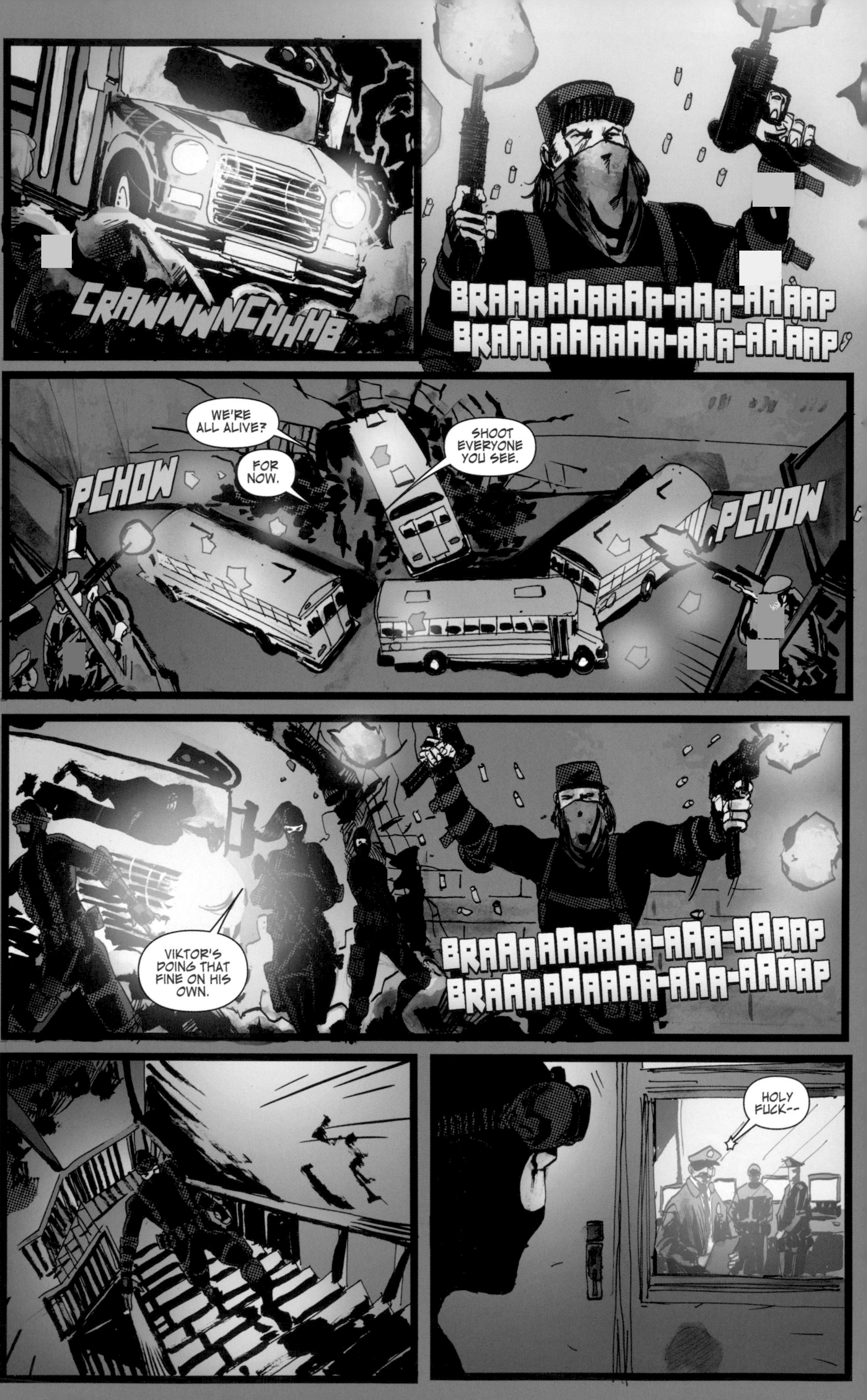
CRAWWWNCHHHB
BRAAAAAAAAA-AAA-AAAAP
BRAAAAAAAAA-AAA-AAAAP
WE'RE ALL ALIVE?
FOR NOW.
SHOOT EVERYONE YOU SEE.
PCHOW
PCHOW
VIKTOR'S DOING THAT FINE ON HIS OWN.
BRAAAAAAAAA-AAA-AAAAP
BRAAAAAAAAA-AAA-AAAAP
HOLY FUCK--

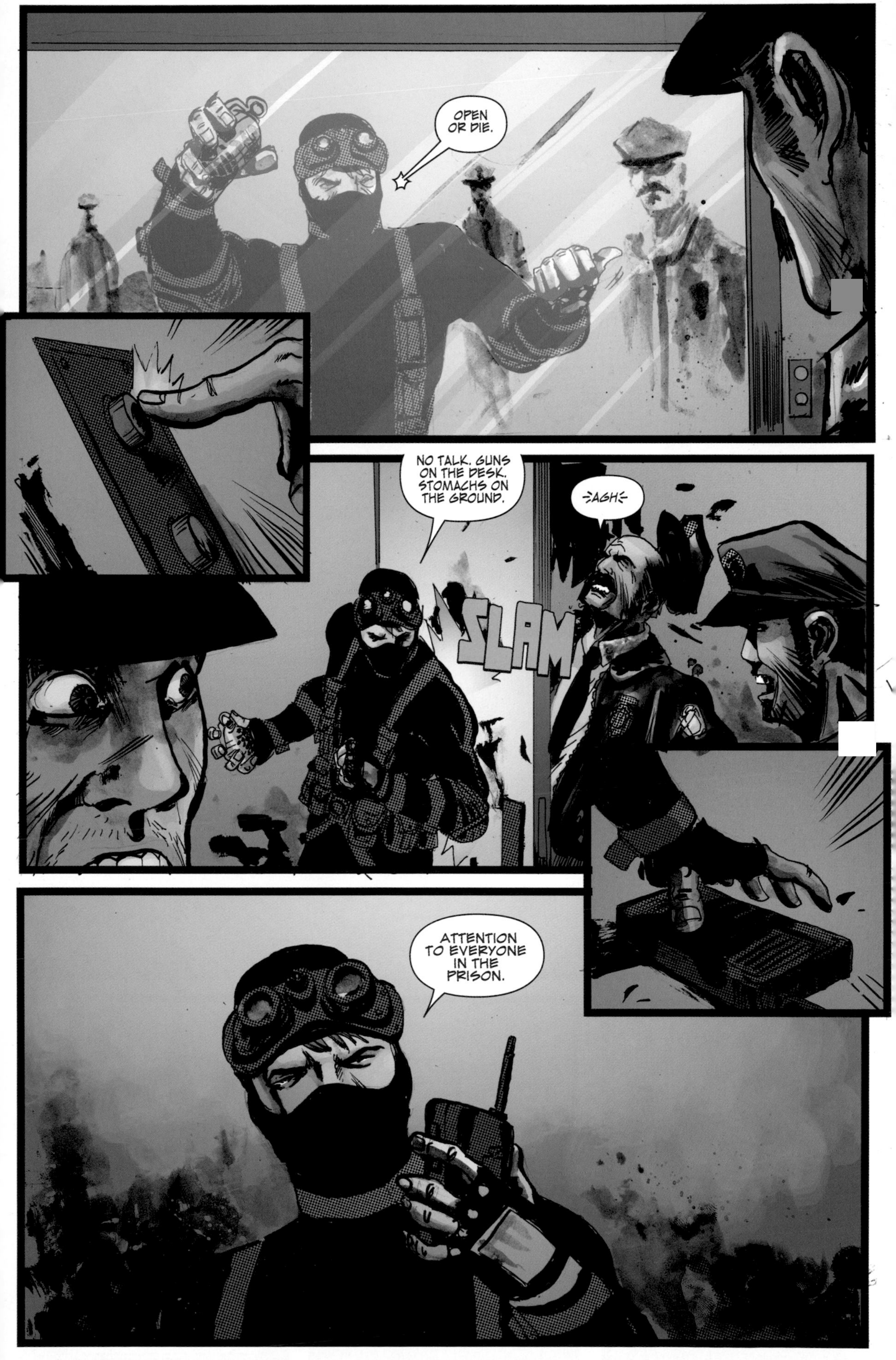
OPEN OR DIE.
NO TALK. GUNS ON THE DESK. STOMACHS ON THE GROUND.
SLAM
AGH
ATTENTION TO EVERYONE IN THE PRISON.

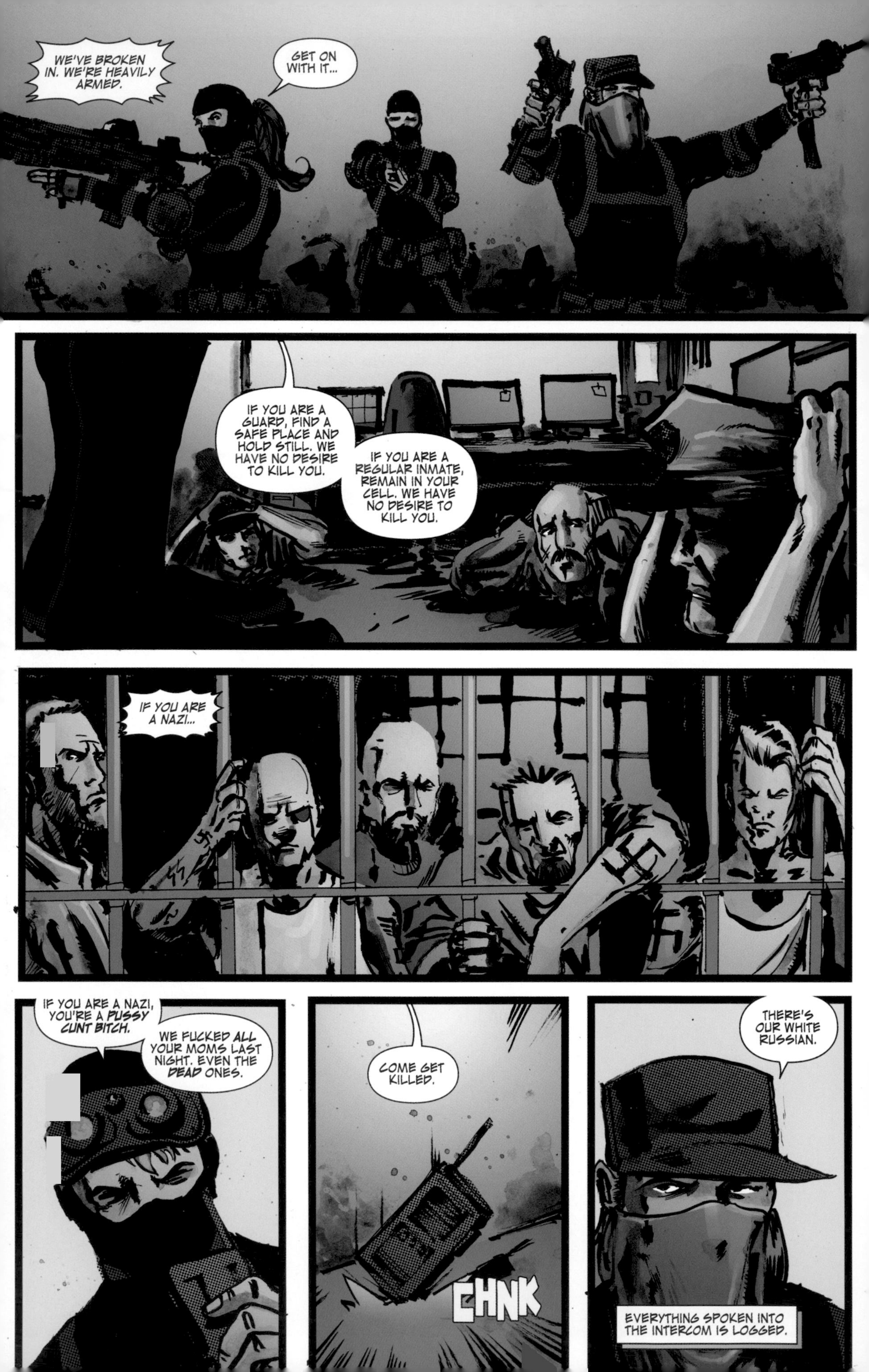
WE'VE BROKEN IN. WE'RE HEAVILY ARMED.
GET ON WITH IT...
IF YOU ARE A GUARD, FIND A SAFE PLACE AND HOLD STILL. WE HAVE NO DESIRE TO KILL YOU.
IF YOU ARE A REGULAR INMATE, REMAIN IN YOUR CELL. WE HAVE NO DESIRE TO KILL YOU.
IF YOU ARE A NAZI...
IF YOU ARE A NAZI, YOU'RE A PUSSY CUNT BITCH.
WE FUCKED ALL YOUR MOMS LAST NIGHT. EVEN THE DEAD ONES.
COME GET KILLED.
CHNK
THERE'S OUR WHITE RUSSIAN.
EVERYTHING SPOKEN INTO THE INTERCOM IS LOGGED.

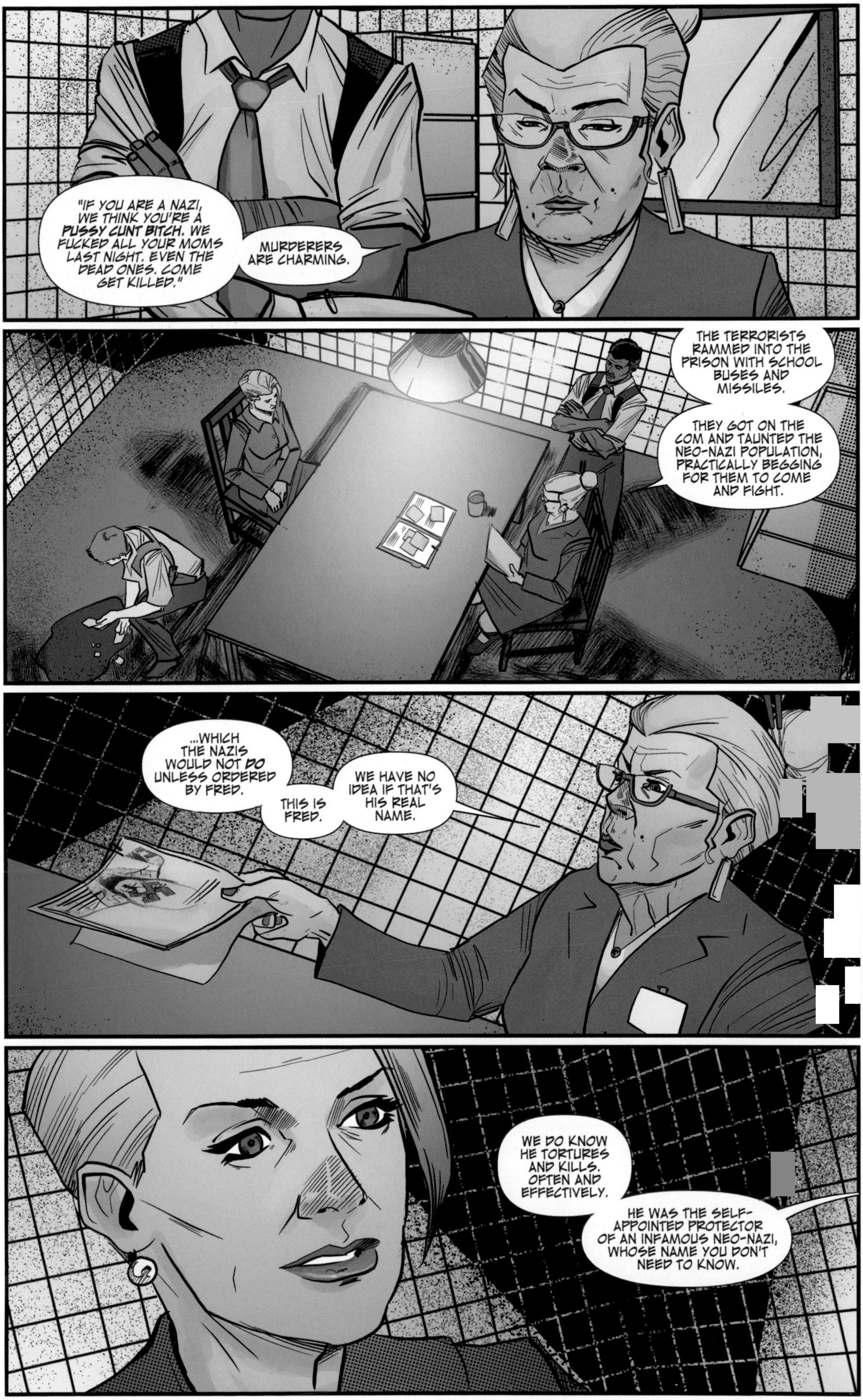
"IF YOU ARE A NAZI, WE THINK YOU'RE A PUSSY CUNT BITCH. WE FUCKED ALL YOUR MOMS LAST NIGHT. EVEN THE DEAD ONES. COME GET KILLED."
MURDERERS ARE CHARMING.
THE TERRORISTS RAMMED INTO THE PRISON WITH SCHOOL BUSES AND MISSILES.
THEY GOT ON THE COM AND TAUNTED THE NEO-NAZI POPULATION, PRACTICALLY BEGGING FOR THEM TO COME AND FIGHT.
...WHICH THE NAZIS WOULD NOT DO UNLESS ORDERED BY FRED.
THIS IS FRED.
WE HAVE NO IDEA IF THAT'S HIS REAL NAME.
WE DO KNOW HE TORTURES AND KILLS. OFTEN AND EFFECTIVELY.
HE WAS THE SELF-APPOINTED PROTECTOR OF AN INFAMOUS NEO-NAZI, WHOSE NAME YOU DON'T NEED TO KNOW.

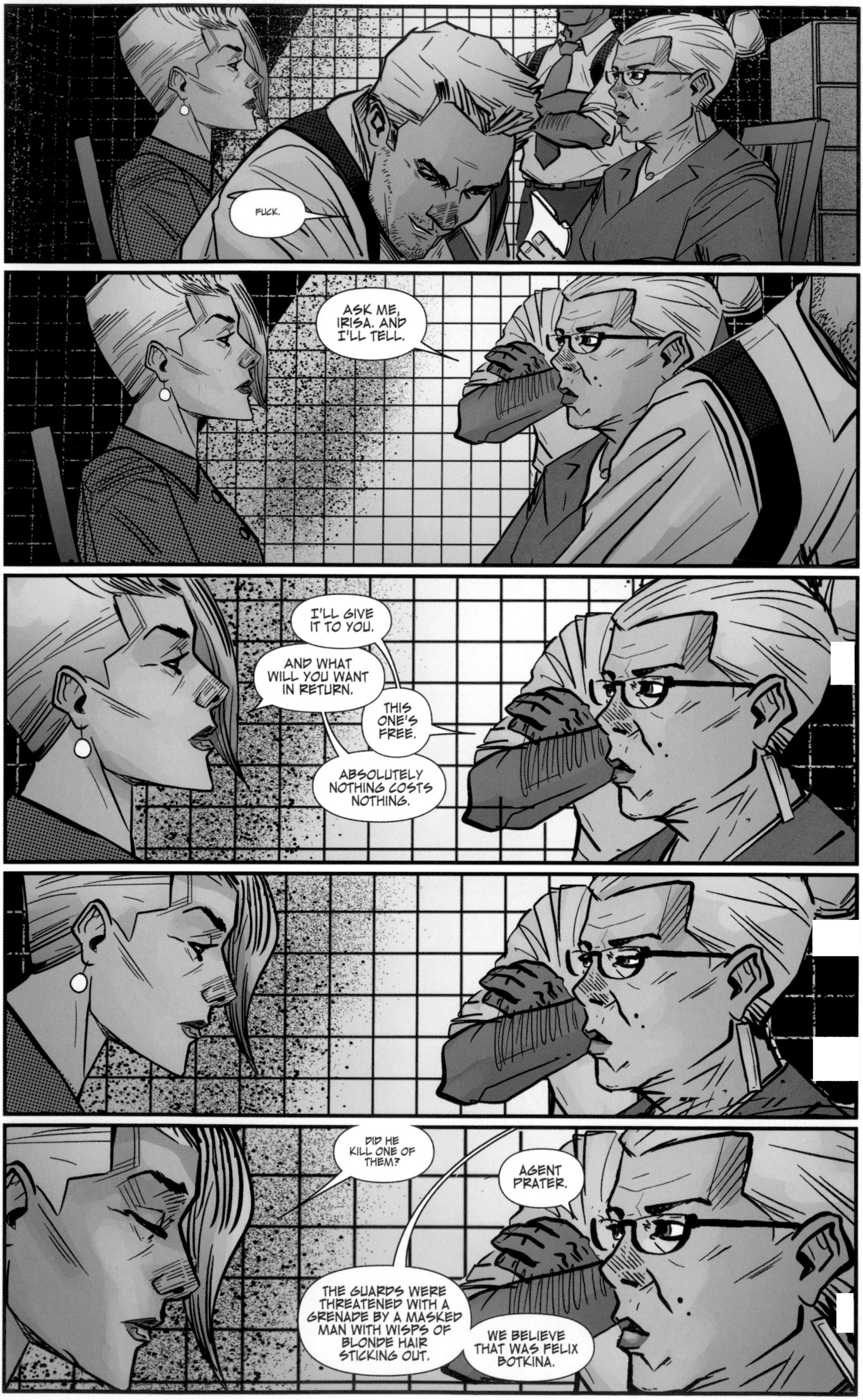
FUCK.
ASK ME, IRISA. AND I'LL TELL.
I'LL GIVE IT TO YOU.
AND WHAT WILL YOU WANT IN RETURN.
THIS ONE'S FREE.
ABSOLUTELY NOTHING COSTS NOTHING.
DID HE KILL ONE OF THEM?
AGENT PRATER.
THE GUARDS WERE THREATENED WITH A GRENADE BY A MASKED MAN WITH WISPS OF BLONDE HAIR STICKING OUT.
WE BELIEVE THAT WAS FELIX BOTKINA.

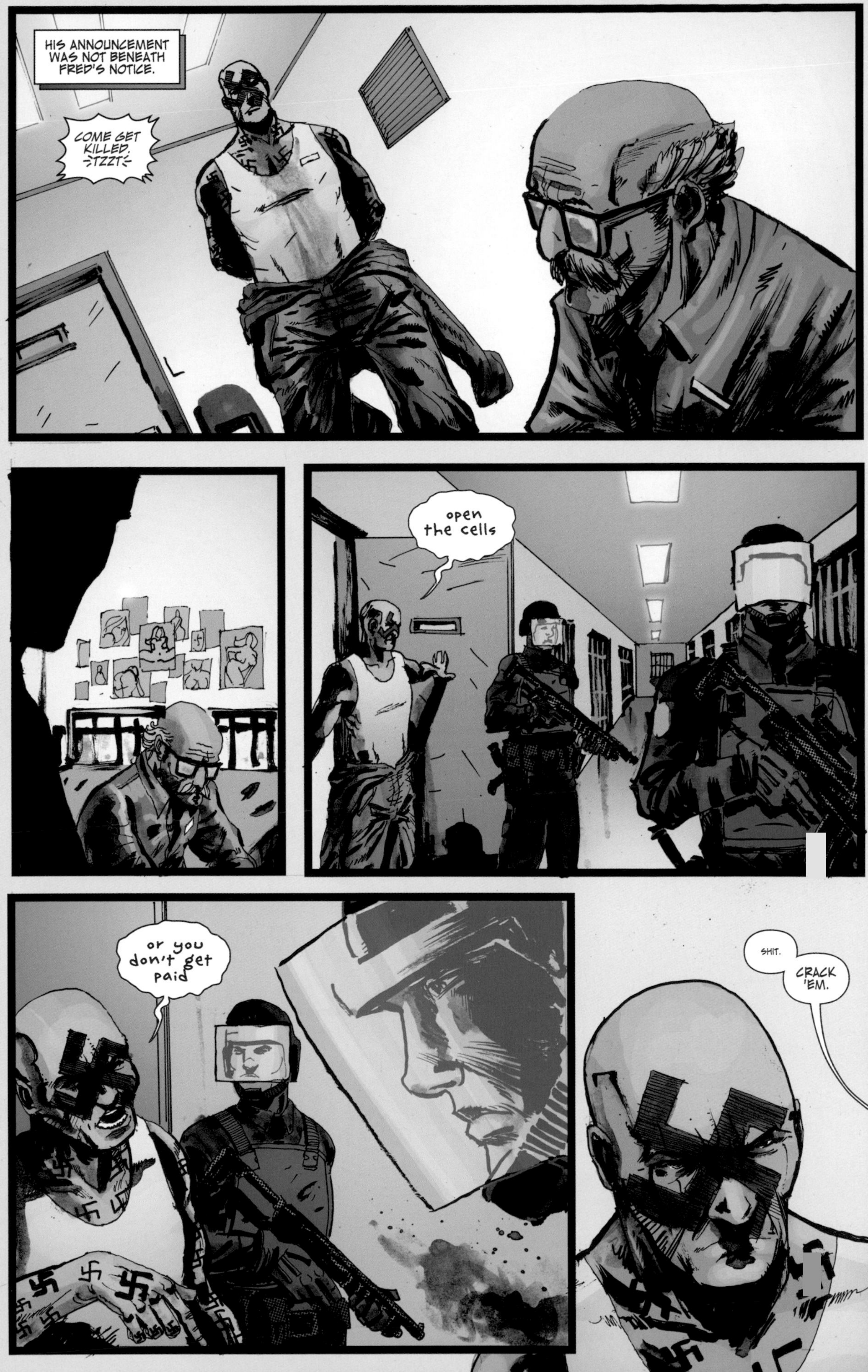

HIS ANNOUNCEMENT WAS NOT BENEATH FRED'S NOTICE.
COME GET KILLED. -TZZT-
open the cells
or you don't get paid
SHIT.
CRACK 'EM.

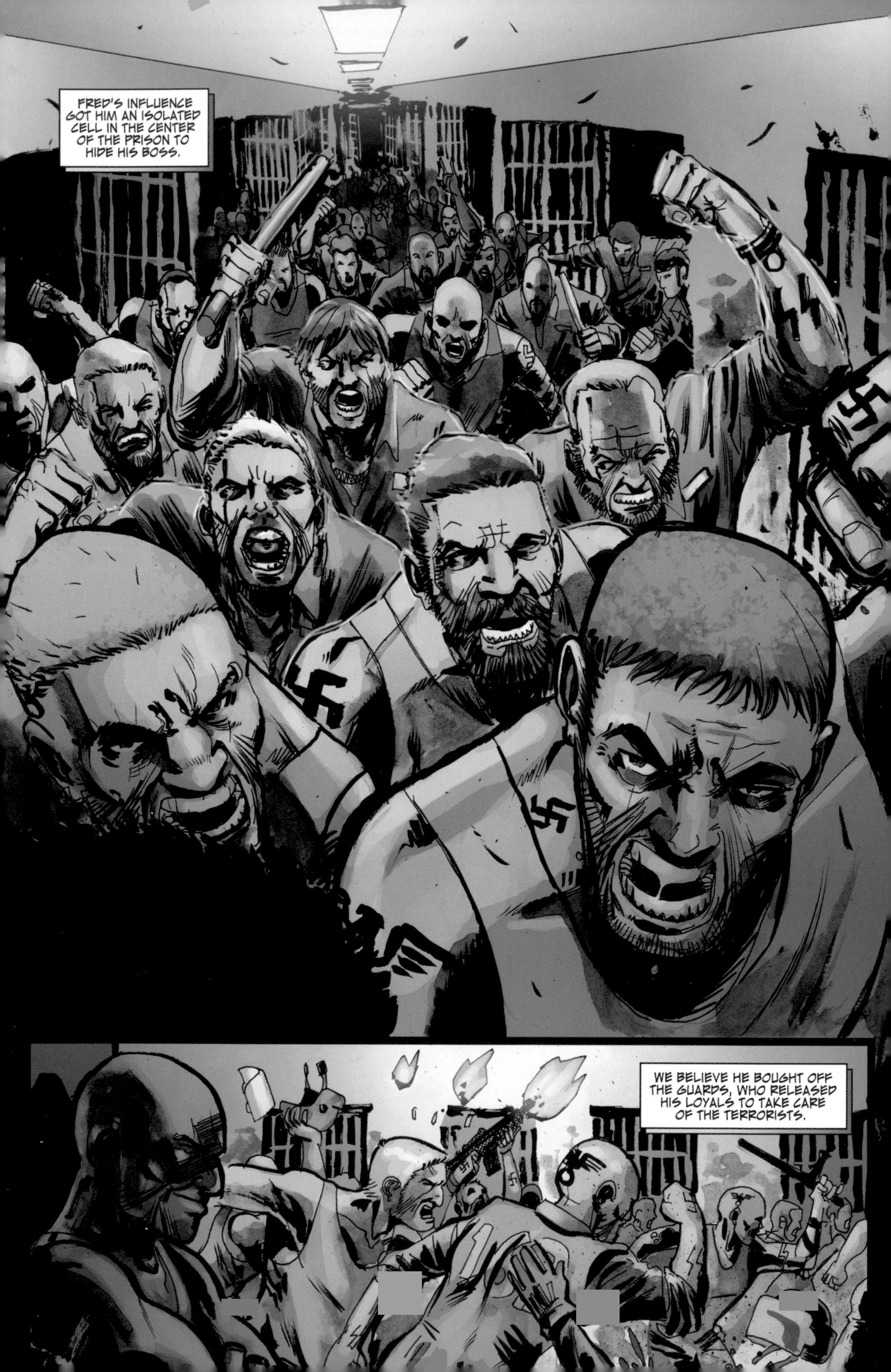

FRED'S INFLUENCE GOT HIM AN ISOLATED CELL IN THE CENTER OF THE PRISON TO HIDE HIS BOSS.
WE BELIEVE HE BOUGHT OFF THE GUARDS, WHO RELEASED HIS LOYALS TO TAKE CARE OF THE TERRORISTS.

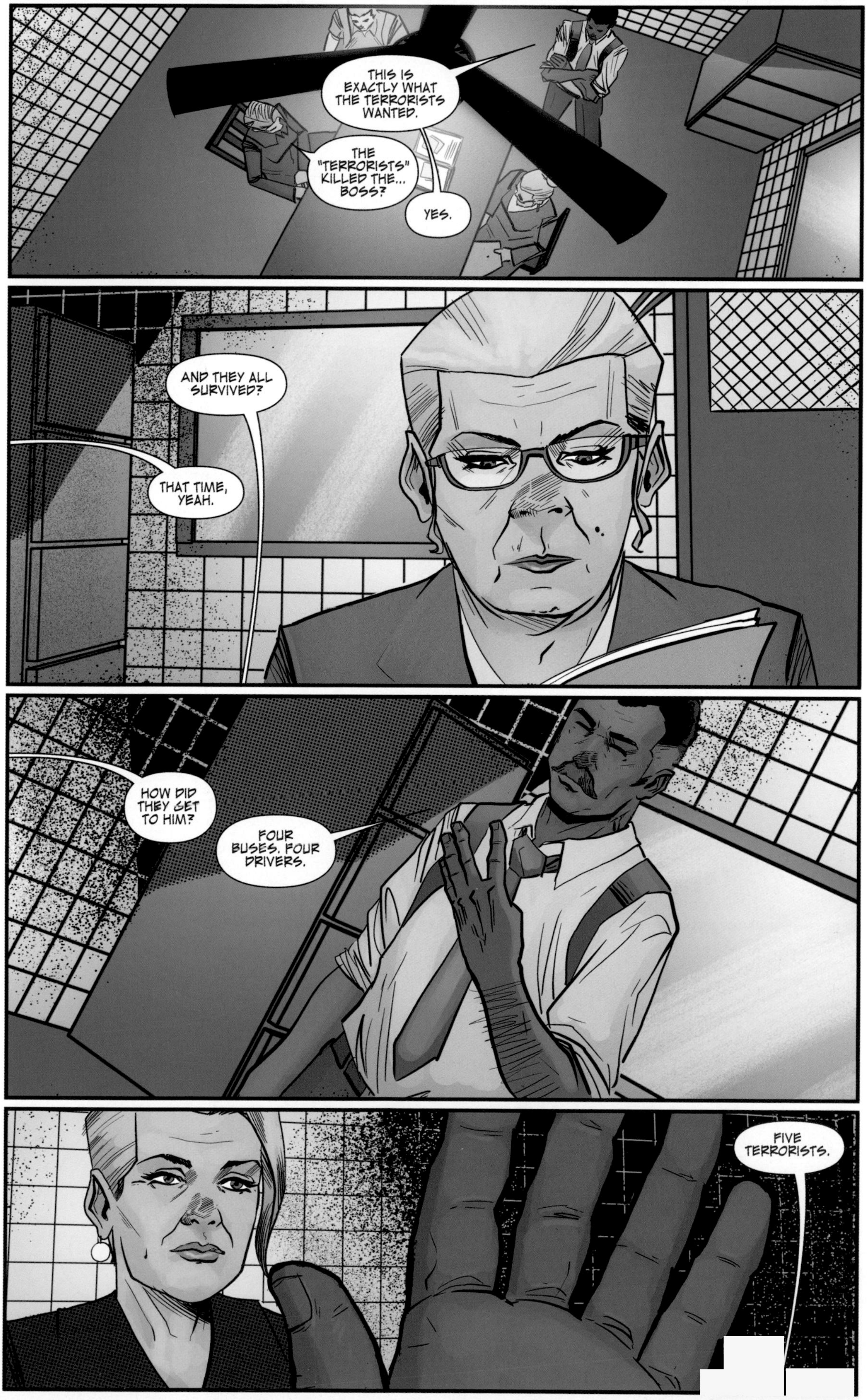
THIS IS EXACTLY WHAT THE TERRORISTS WANTED.
THE "TERRORISTS" KILLED THE... BOSS?
YES.
AND THEY ALL SURVIVED?
THAT TIME, YEAH.
HOW DID THEY GET TO HIM?
FOUR BUSES. FOUR DRIVERS.
FIVE TERRORISTS.

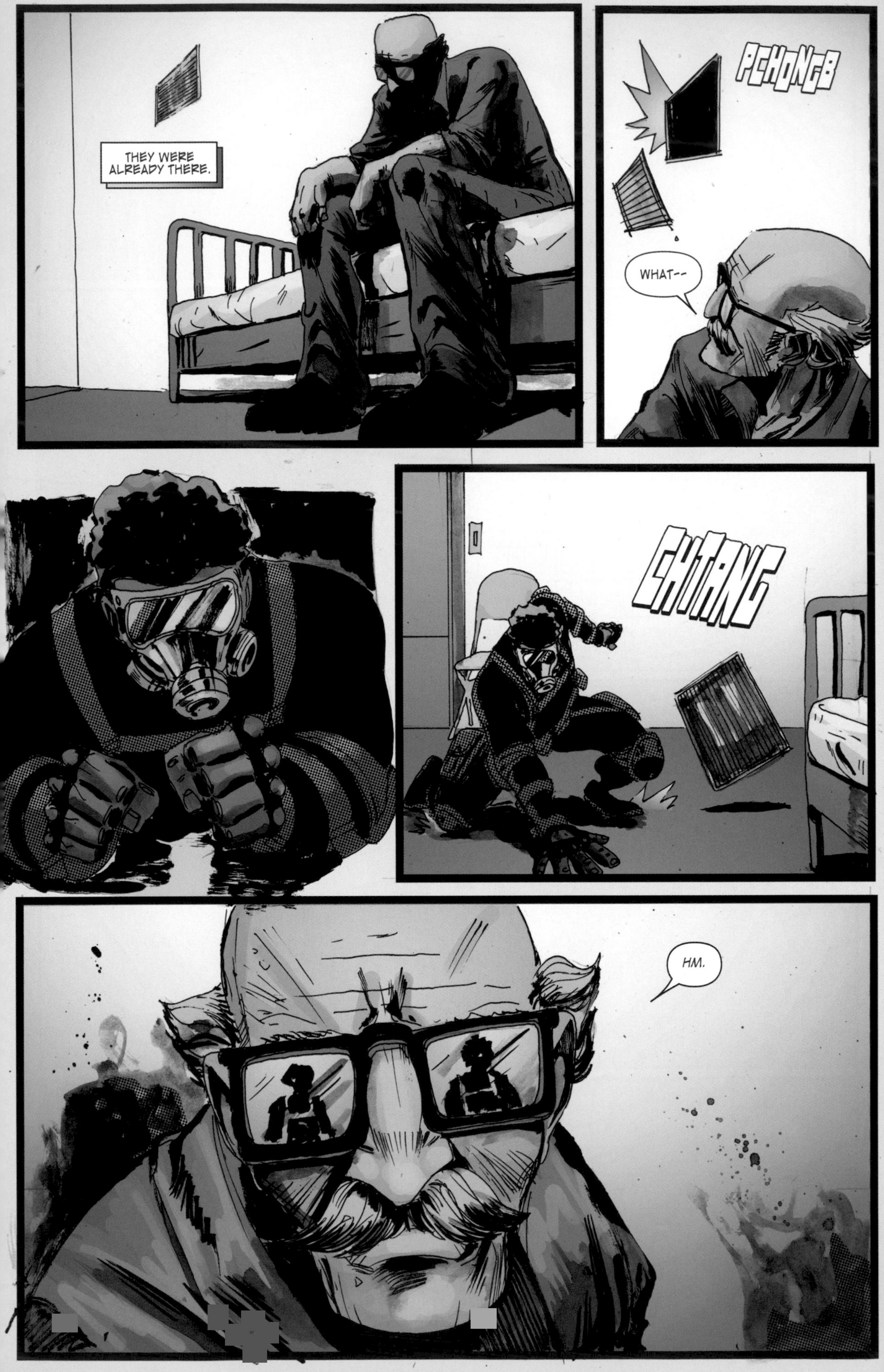
THEY WERE ALREADY THERE.
PCHONGB
WHAT--
CHTANG
HM.

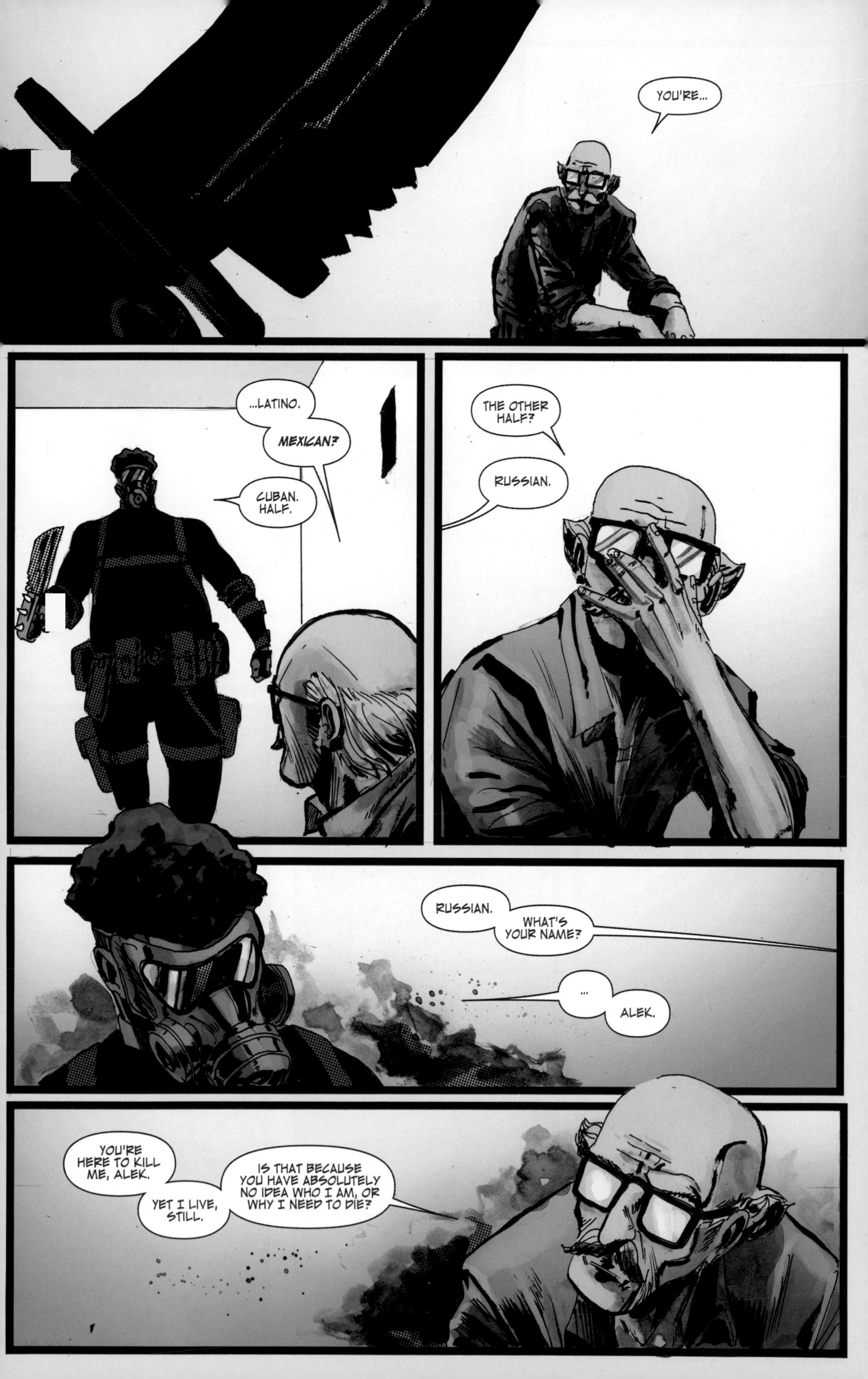
YOU'RE...
...LATINO.
MEXICAN?
CUBAN. HALF.
THE OTHER HALF?
RUSSIAN.
RUSSIAN.
WHAT'S YOUR NAME?
...
ALEK.
YOU'RE HERE TO KILL ME, ALEK.
YET I LIVE, STILL.
IS THAT BECAUSE YOU HAVE ABSOLUTELY NO IDEA WHO I AM, OR WHY I NEED TO DIE?

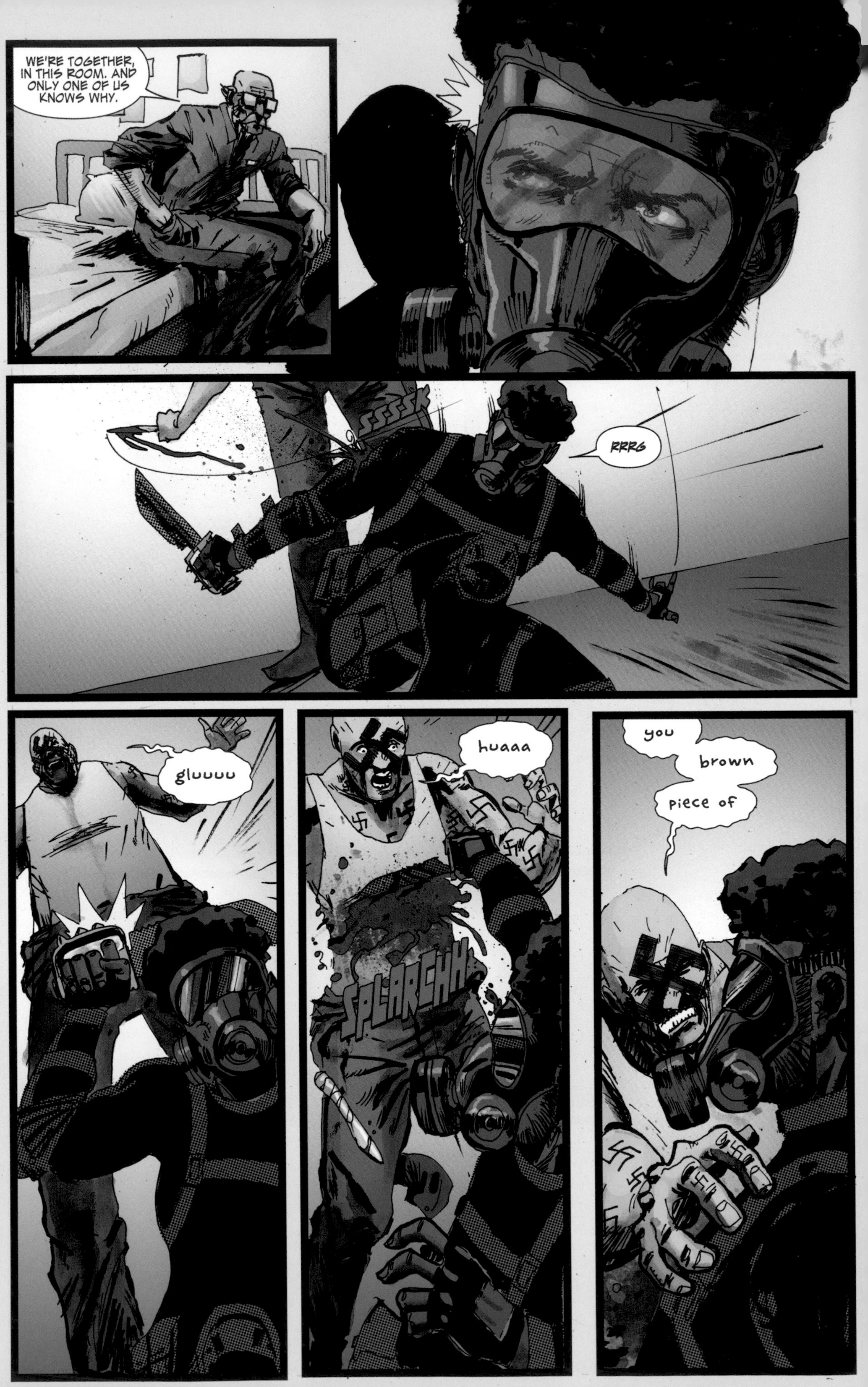
WE'RE TOGETHER, IN THIS ROOM. AND ONLY ONE OF US KNOWS WHY.
SSSSK
RRRG
gluuuu
huaaa
SPLARCHH
you
brown
piece of

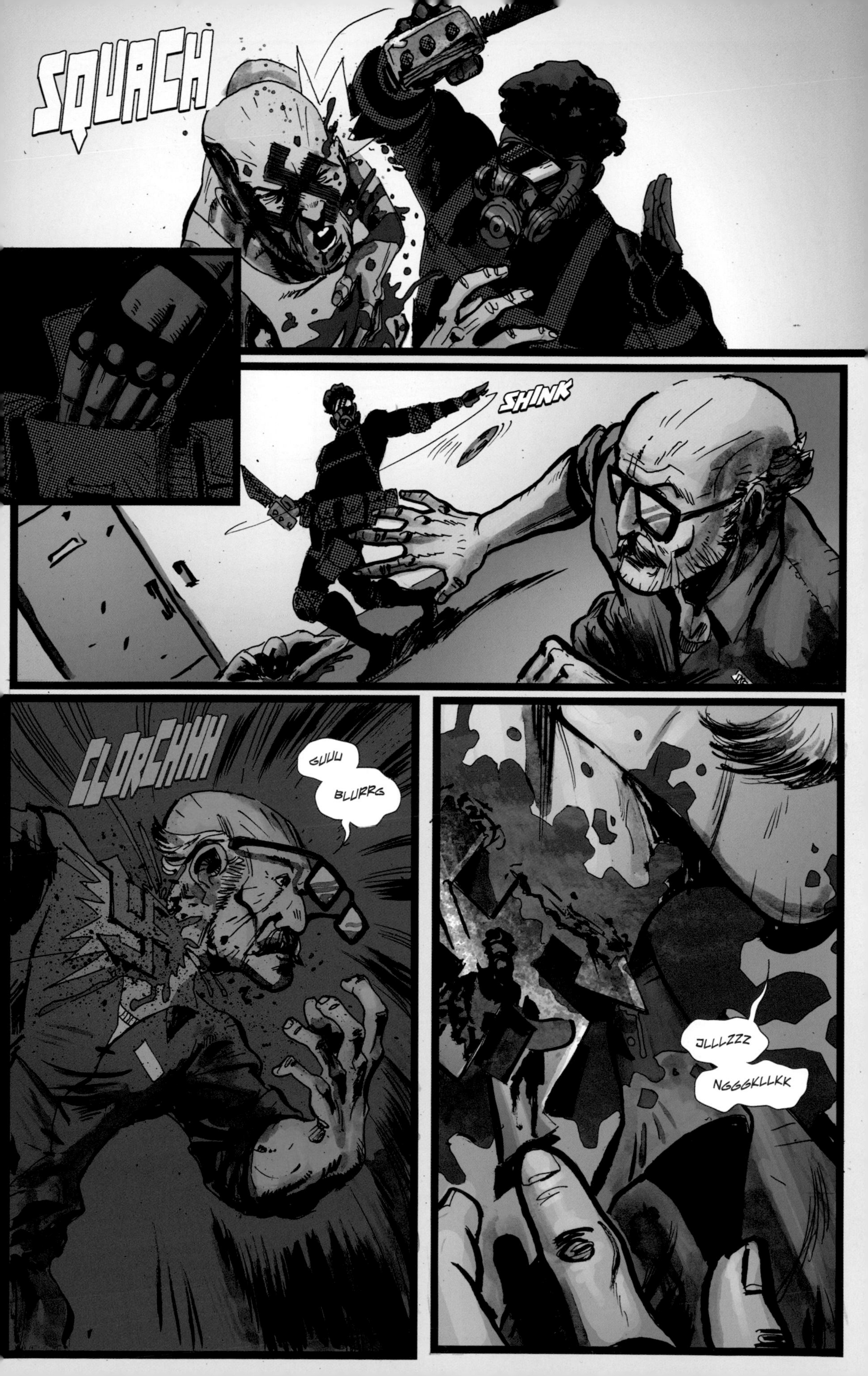
SQUACH
SHINK
CLORCHHH
GUUU
BLURRG
JLLLZZZ
NGGGKLLKK

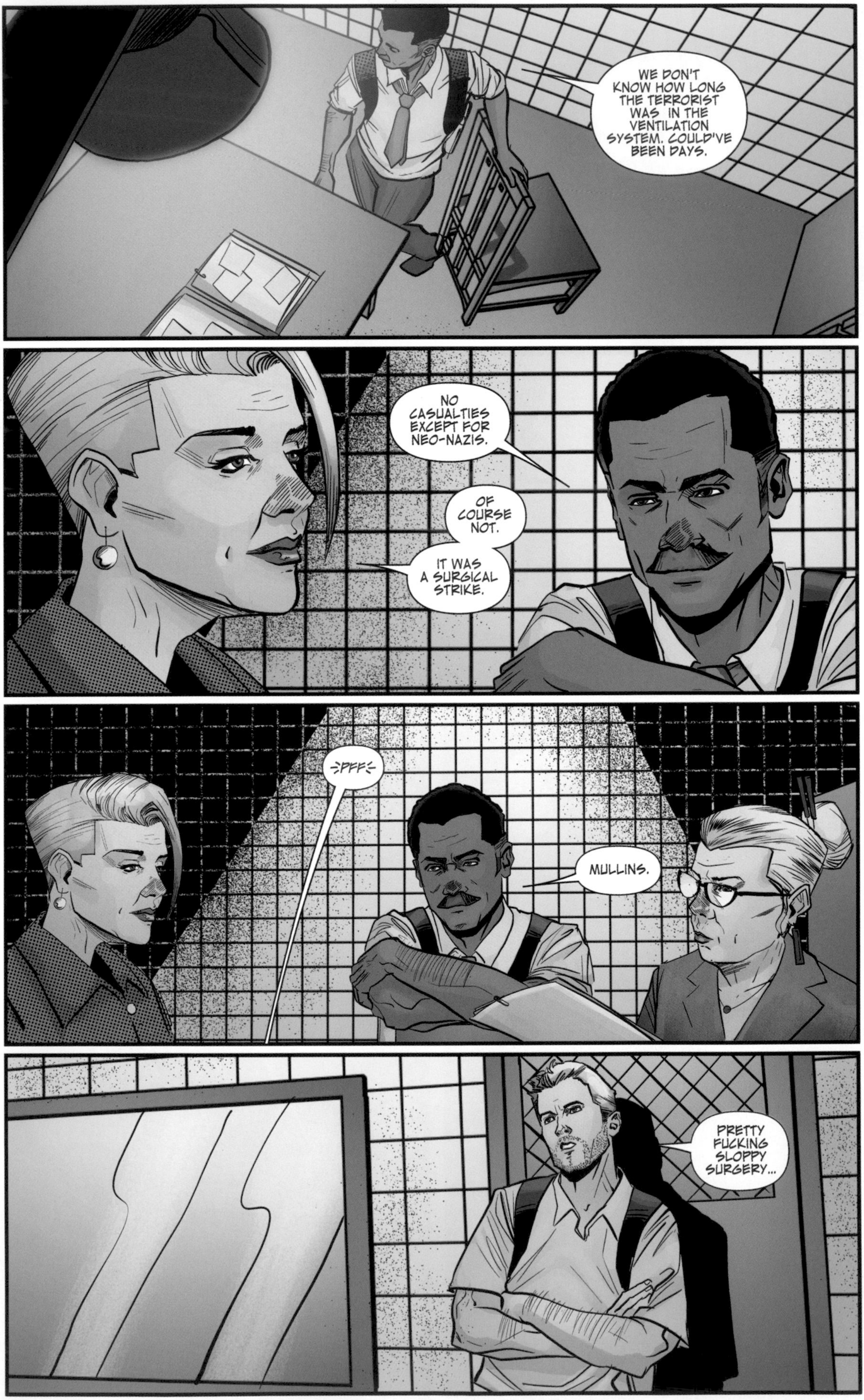
WE DON'T KNOW HOW LONG THE TERRORIST WAS IN THE VENTILATION SYSTEM. COULD'VE BEEN DAYS.
NO CASUALTIES EXCEPT FOR NEO-NAZIS.
OF COURSE NOT.
IT WAS A SURGICAL STRIKE.
PFF
MULLINS.
PRETTY FUCKING SLOPPY SURGERY...

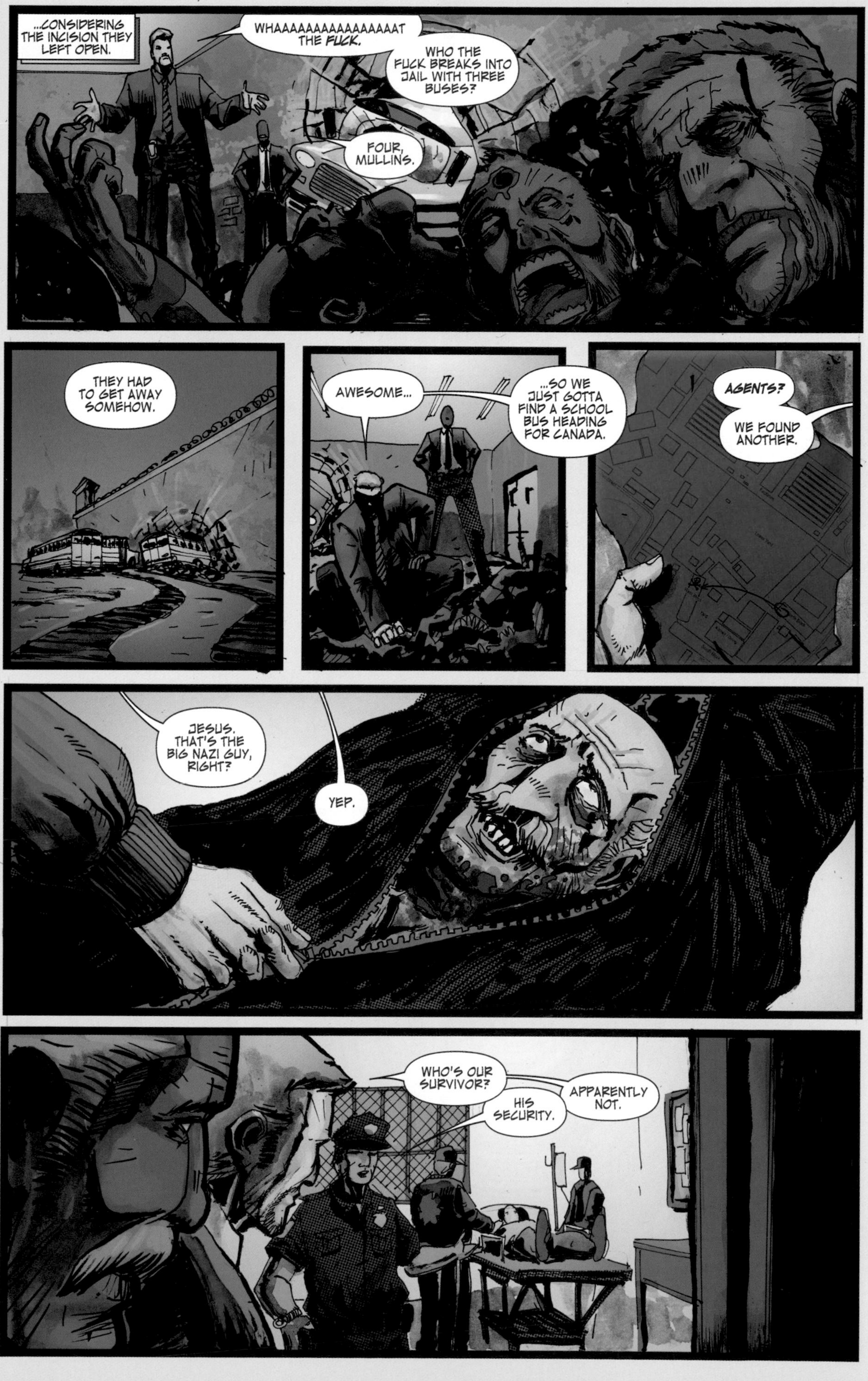
...CONSIDERING THE INCISION THEY LEFT OPEN.
WHAAAAAAAAAAAAAAAAT THE FUCK.
WHO THE FUCK BREAKS INTO JAIL WITH THREE BUSES?
FOUR, MULLINS.
THEY HAD TO GET AWAY SOMEHOW.
AWESOME...
...SO WE JUST GOTTA FIND A SCHOOL BUS HEADING FOR CANADA.
AGENTS?
WE FOUND ANOTHER.
JESUS. THAT'S THE BIG NAZI GUY, RIGHT?
YEP.
WHO'S OUR SURVIVOR?
HIS SECURITY.
APPARENTLY NOT.

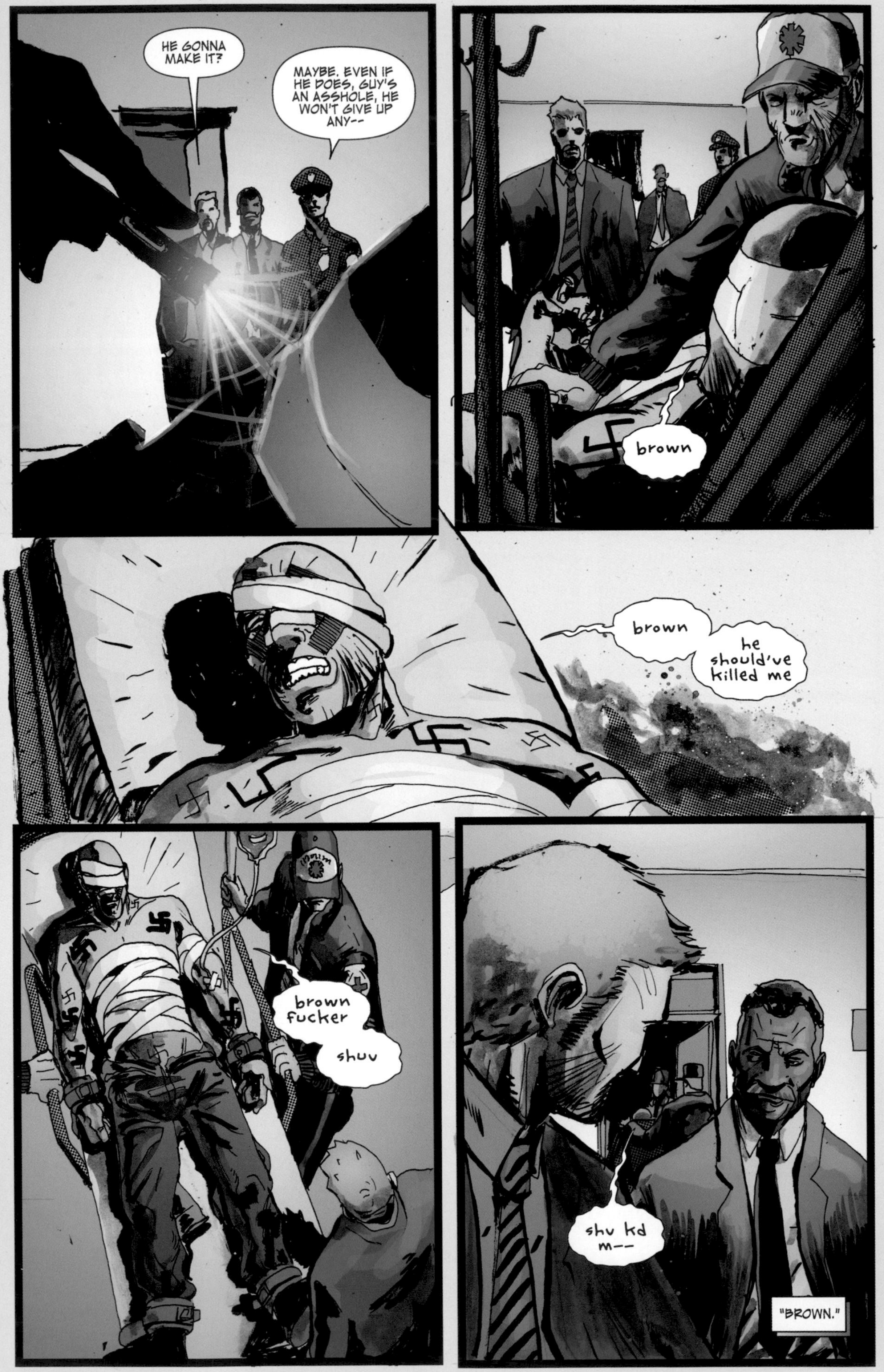
HE GONNA MAKE IT?
MAYBE. EVEN IF HE DOES, GUY'S AN ASSHOLE, HE WON'T GIVE UP ANY--
brown
brown
he should've killed me
brown fucker
shuv
shu kd m--
"BROWN."

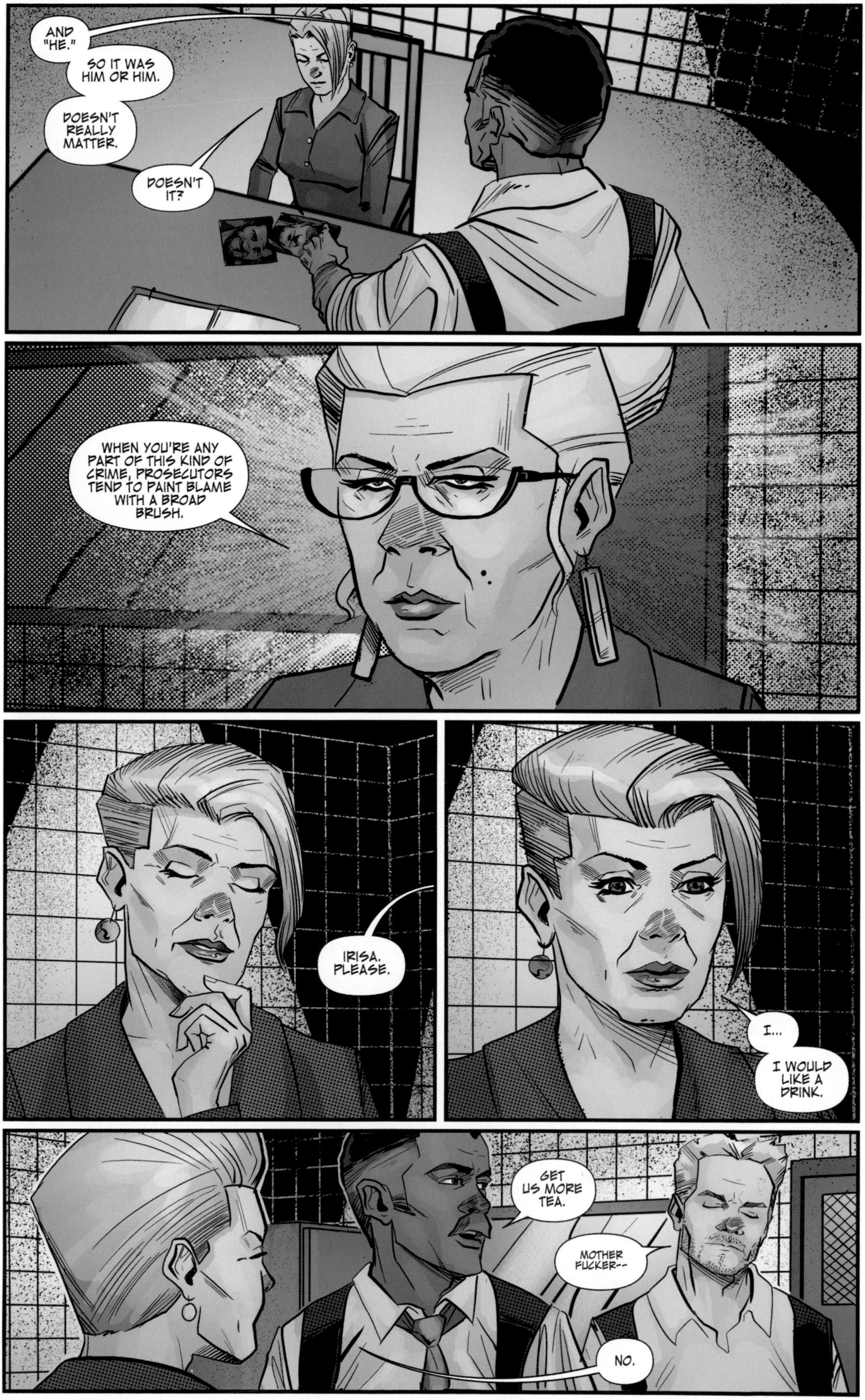
AND "HE."
SO IT WAS HIM OR HIM.
DOESN'T REALLY MATTER.
DOESN'T IT?
WHEN YOU'RE ANY PART OF THIS KIND OF CRIME, PROSECUTORS TEND TO PAINT BLAME WITH A BROAD BRUSH.
IRISA. PLEASE.
I...
I WOULD LIKE A DRINK.
GET US MORE TEA.
MOTHER FUCKER--
NO.

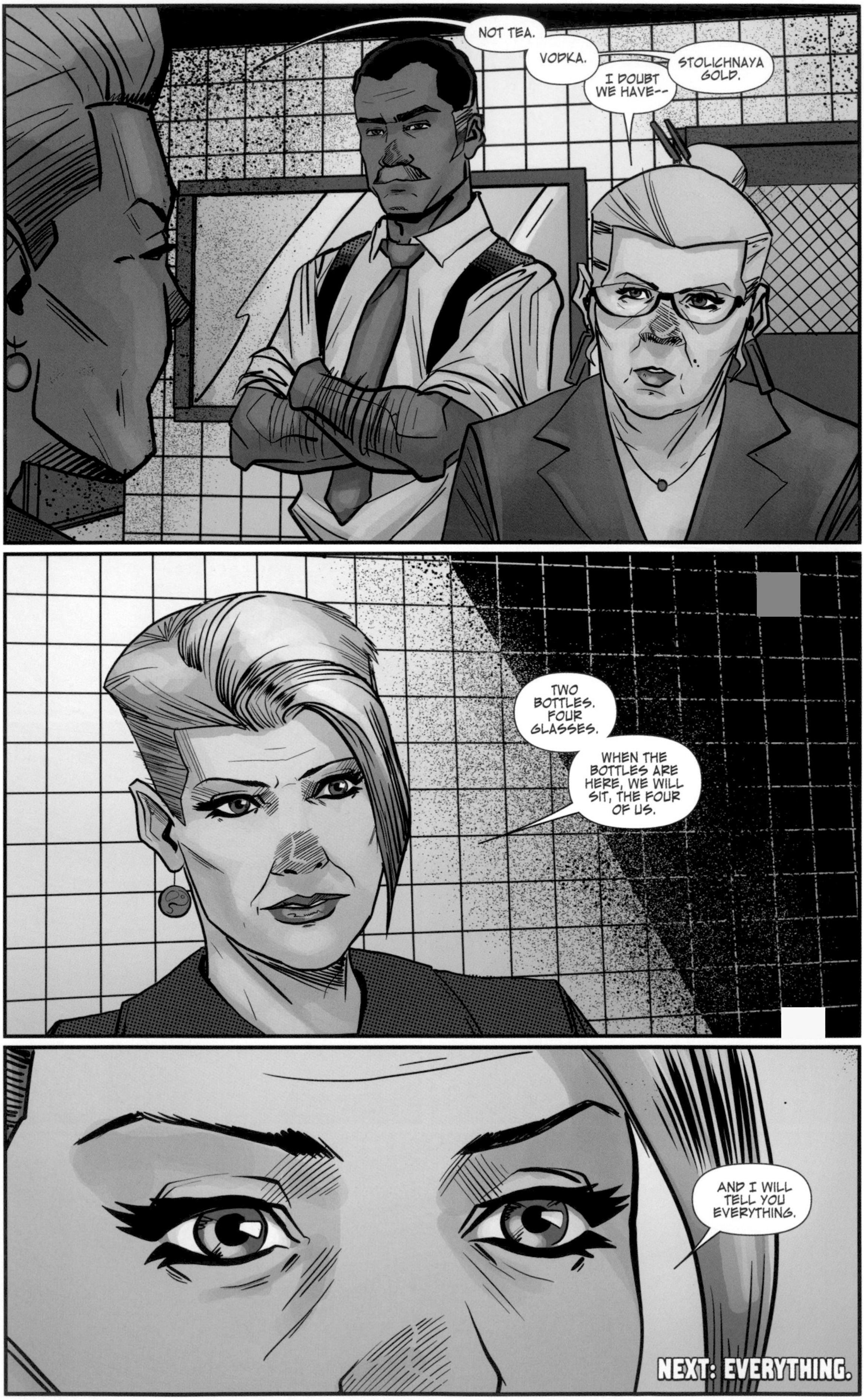
NOT TEA.
VODKA.
I DOUBT WE HAVE--
STOLICHNAYA GOLD.
TWO BOTTLES. FOUR GLASSES.
WHEN THE BOTTLES ARE HERE, WE WILL SIT, THE FOUR OF US.
AND I WILL TELL YOU EVERYTHING.
NEXT: EVERYTHING.

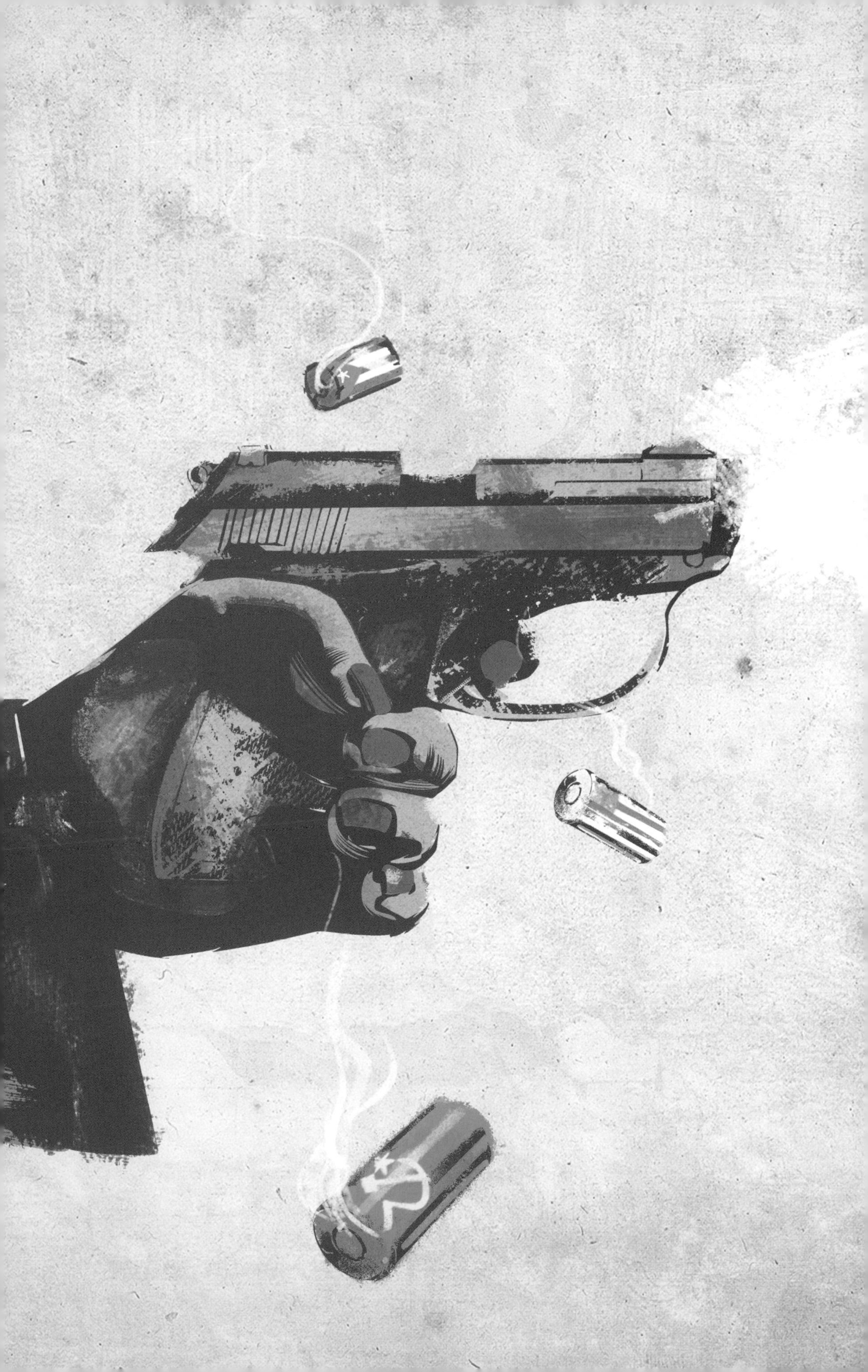

HAVANA VIKTOR FELIX ALEKSANDR EKATARINA

THE PRESIDENT IS KIDNAPPED.
HIS HAND IS CHOPPED OFF.

THE FBI BELIEVES A KGB CUBAN
SLEEPER CELL IS INVOLVED.

THE FBI HAVE BROUGHT IN AN
ELDERLY RUSSIAN WOMAN
NAMED IRISA FOR QUESTIONING.

IRISA DRINKS VODKA.

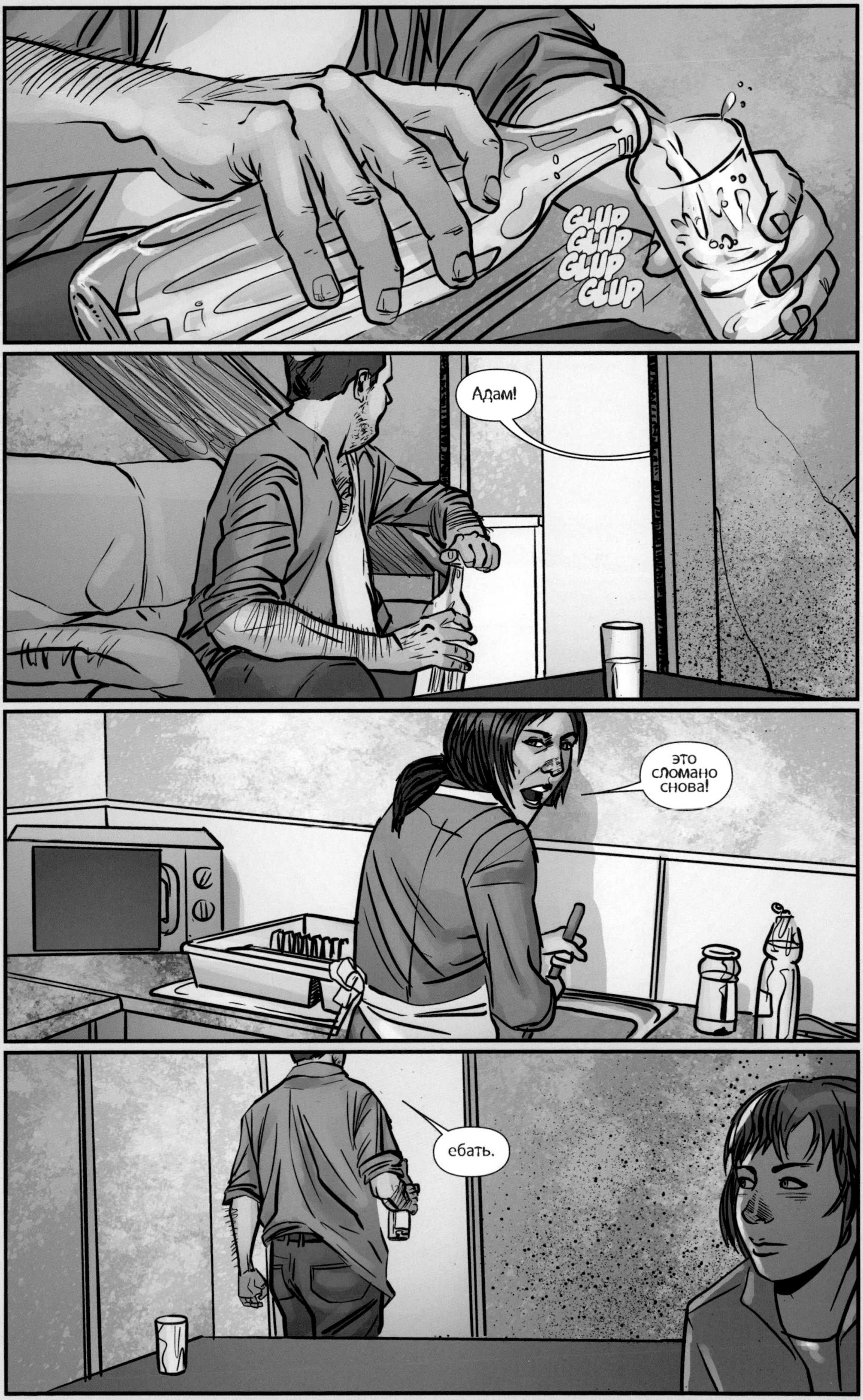
GLUP GLUP GLUP GLUP
Адам!
это сломано снова!
ебать.

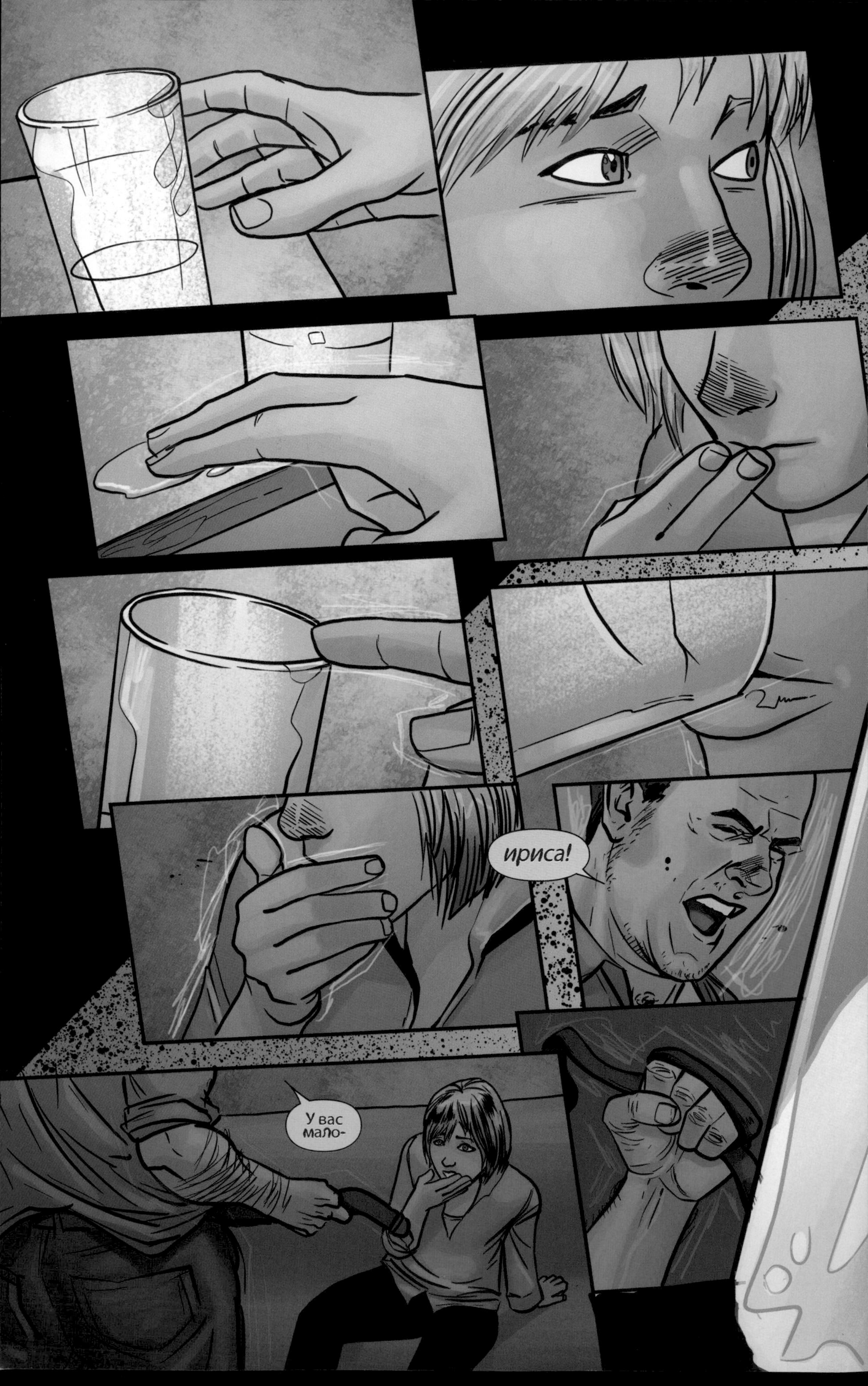
ириса!
У вас мало-

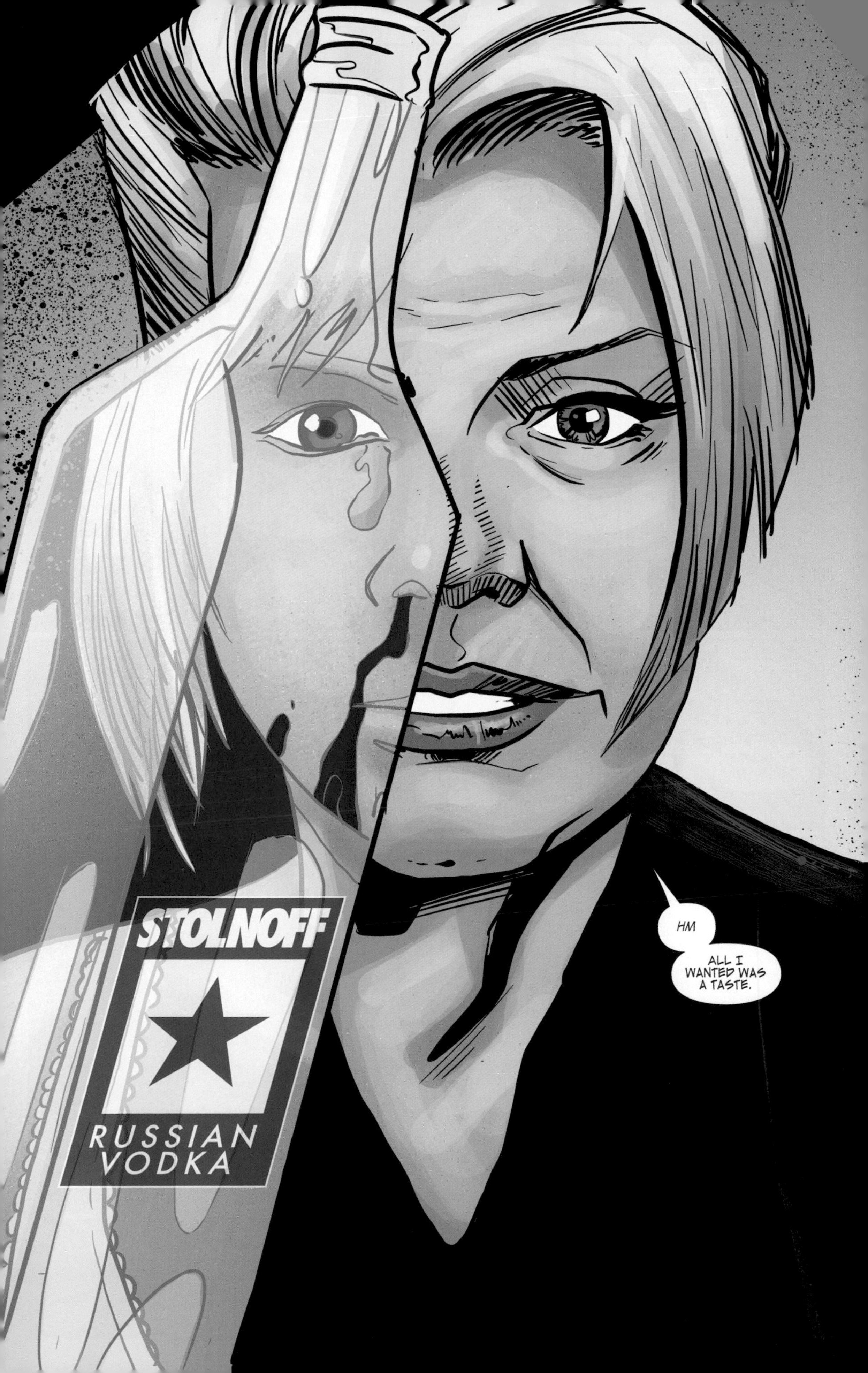
STOLNOFF
RUSSIAN VODKA
HM
ALL I WANTED WAS A TASTE.

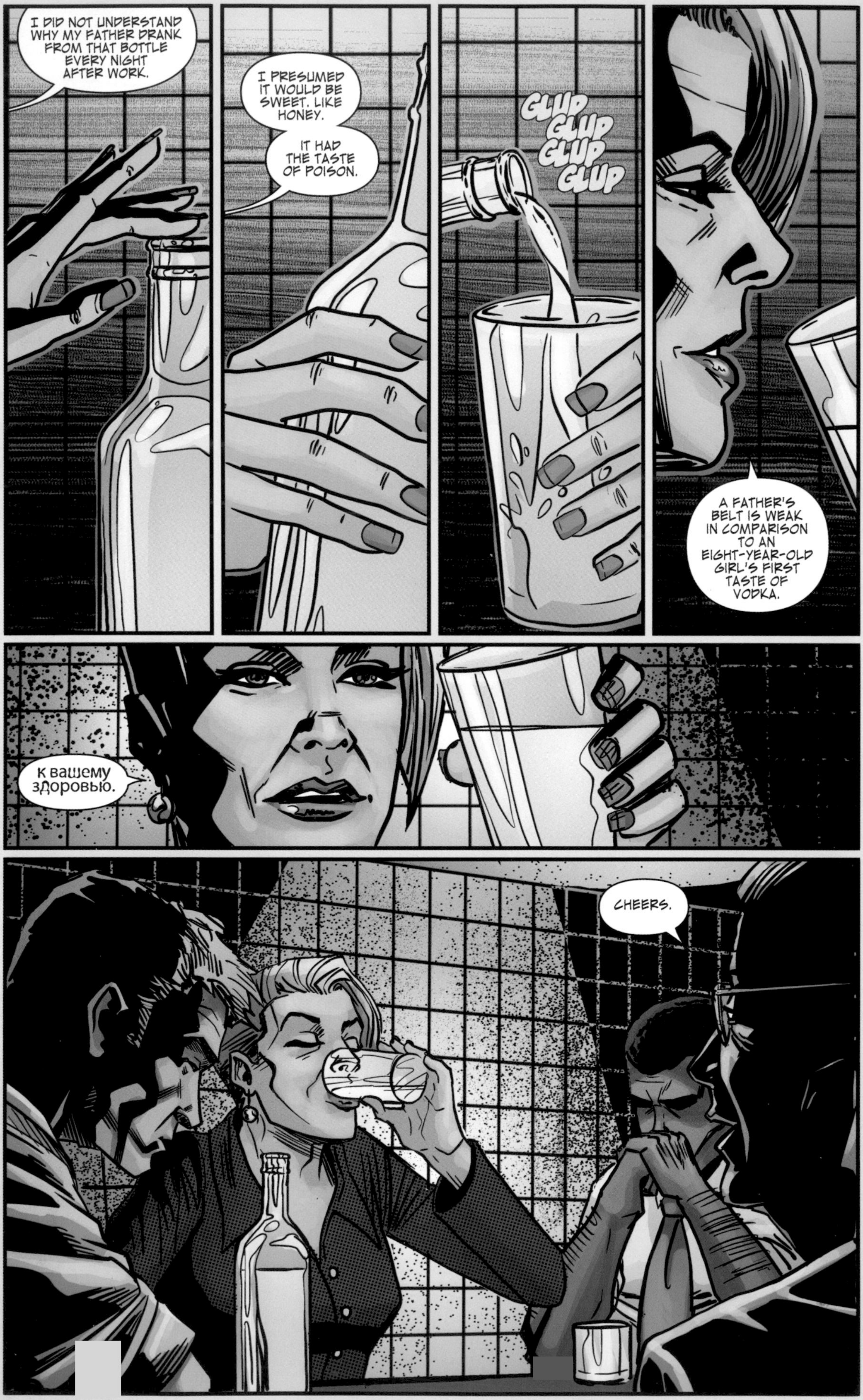
I DID NOT UNDERSTAND WHY MY FATHER DRANK FROM THAT BOTTLE EVERY NIGHT AFTER WORK.
I PRESUMED IT WOULD BE SWEET. LIKE HONEY.
IT HAD THE TASTE OF POISON.
GLUP GLUP GLUP GLUP
A FATHER'S BELT IS WEAK IN COMPARISON TO AN EIGHT-YEAR-OLD GIRL'S FIRST TASTE OF VODKA.
к вашему здоровью.
CHEERS.

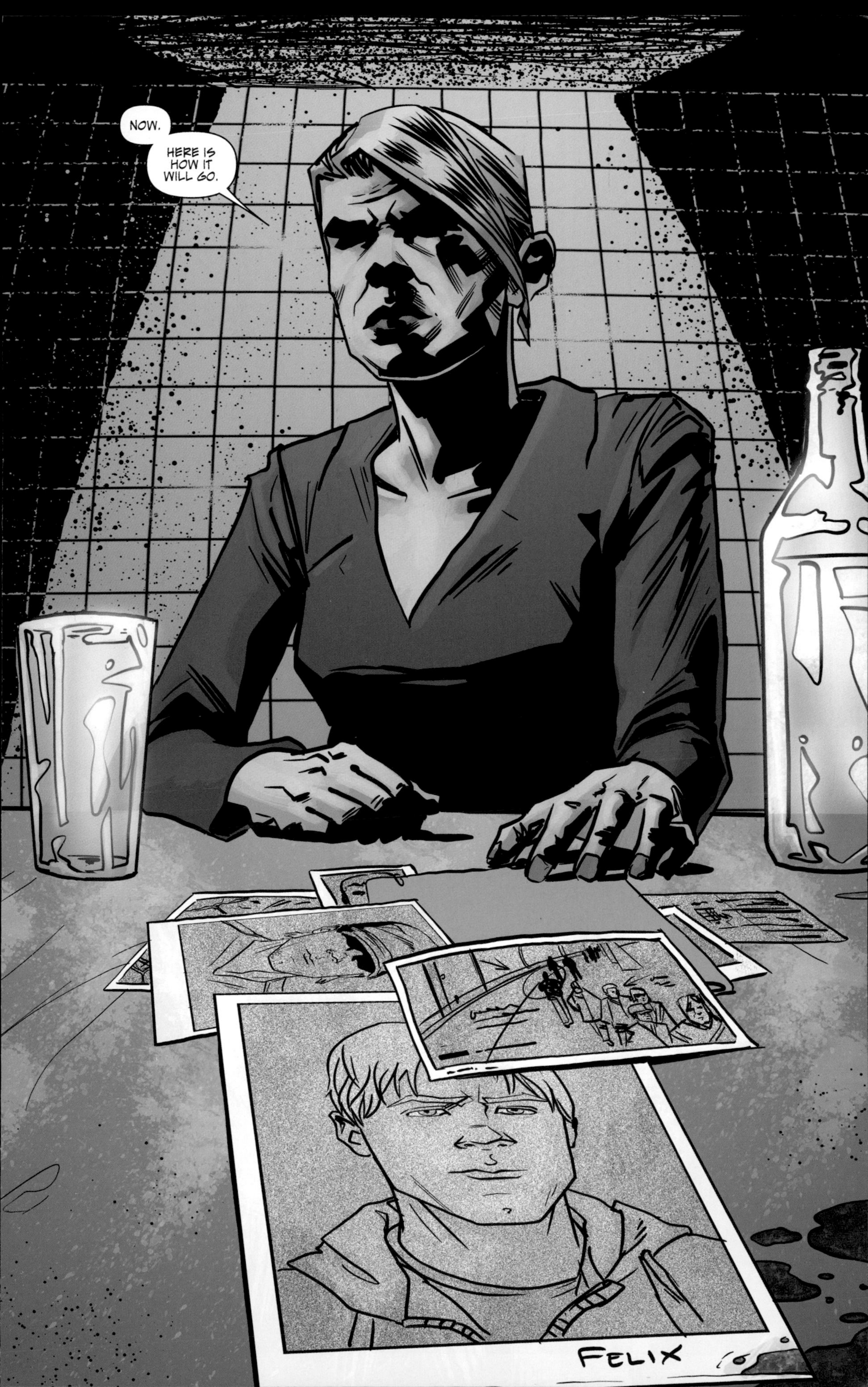

NOW.
HERE IS HOW IT WILL GO.
FELIX

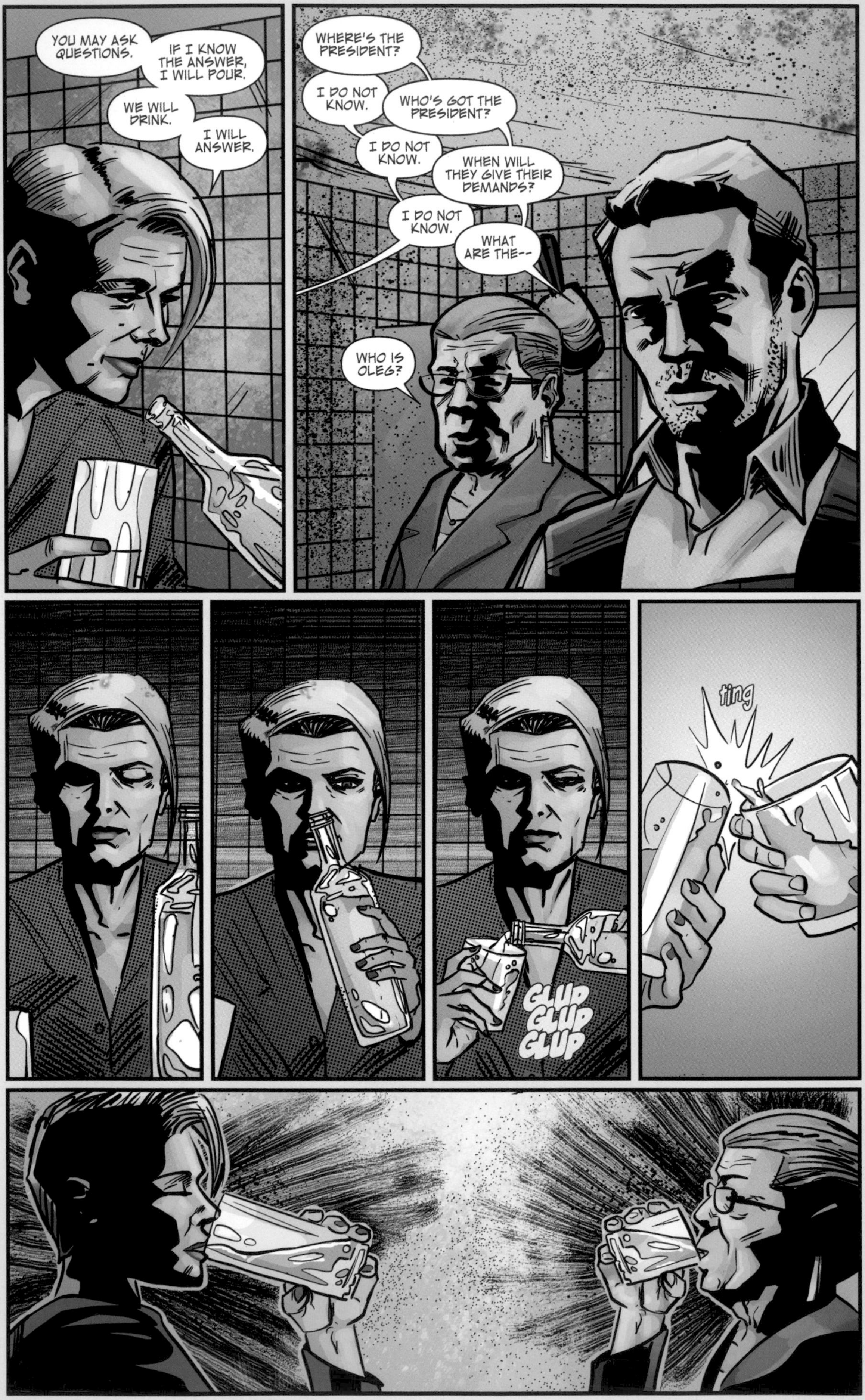
YOU MAY ASK QUESTIONS.
IF I KNOW THE ANSWER, I WILL POUR.
WE WILL DRINK.
I WILL ANSWER.
WHERE'S THE PRESIDENT?
I DO NOT KNOW.
WHO'S GOT THE PRESIDENT?
I DO NOT KNOW.
WHEN WILL THEY GIVE THEIR DEMANDS?
I DO NOT KNOW.
WHAT ARE THE--
WHO IS OLEG?
GLUP GLUP GLUP
ting

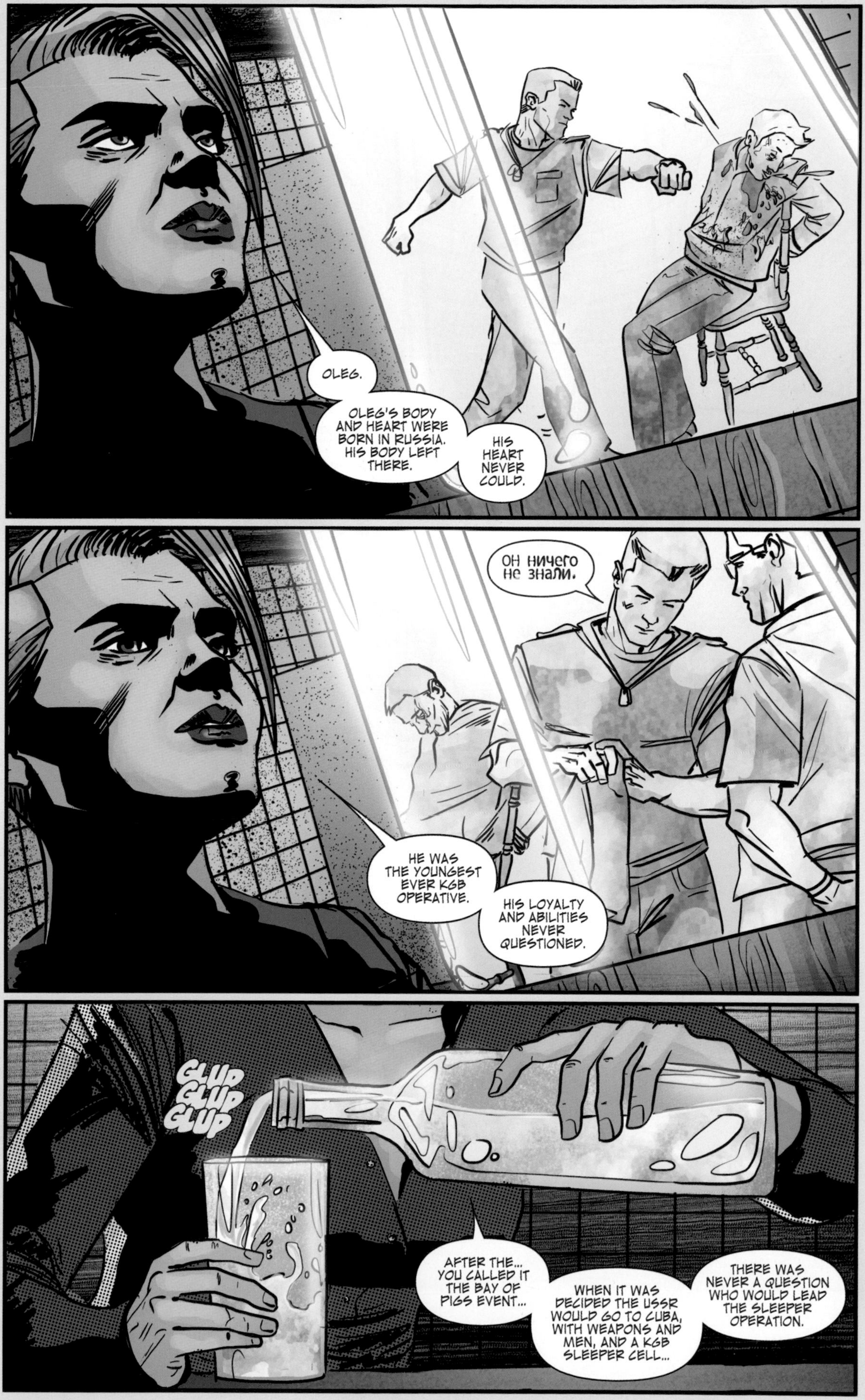
OLEG.
OLEG'S BODY AND HEART WERE BORN IN RUSSIA. HIS BODY LEFT THERE.
HIS HEART NEVER COULD.
Он ничего не знали.
HE WAS THE YOUNGEST EVER KGB OPERATIVE.
HIS LOYALTY AND ABILITIES NEVER QUESTIONED.
GLUP GLUP GLUP
AFTER THE... YOU CALLED IT THE BAY OF PIGS EVENT...
WHEN IT WAS DECIDED THE USSR WOULD GO TO CUBA, WITH WEAPONS AND MEN, AND A KGB SLEEPER CELL...
THERE WAS NEVER A QUESTION WHO WOULD LEAD THE SLEEPER OPERATION.

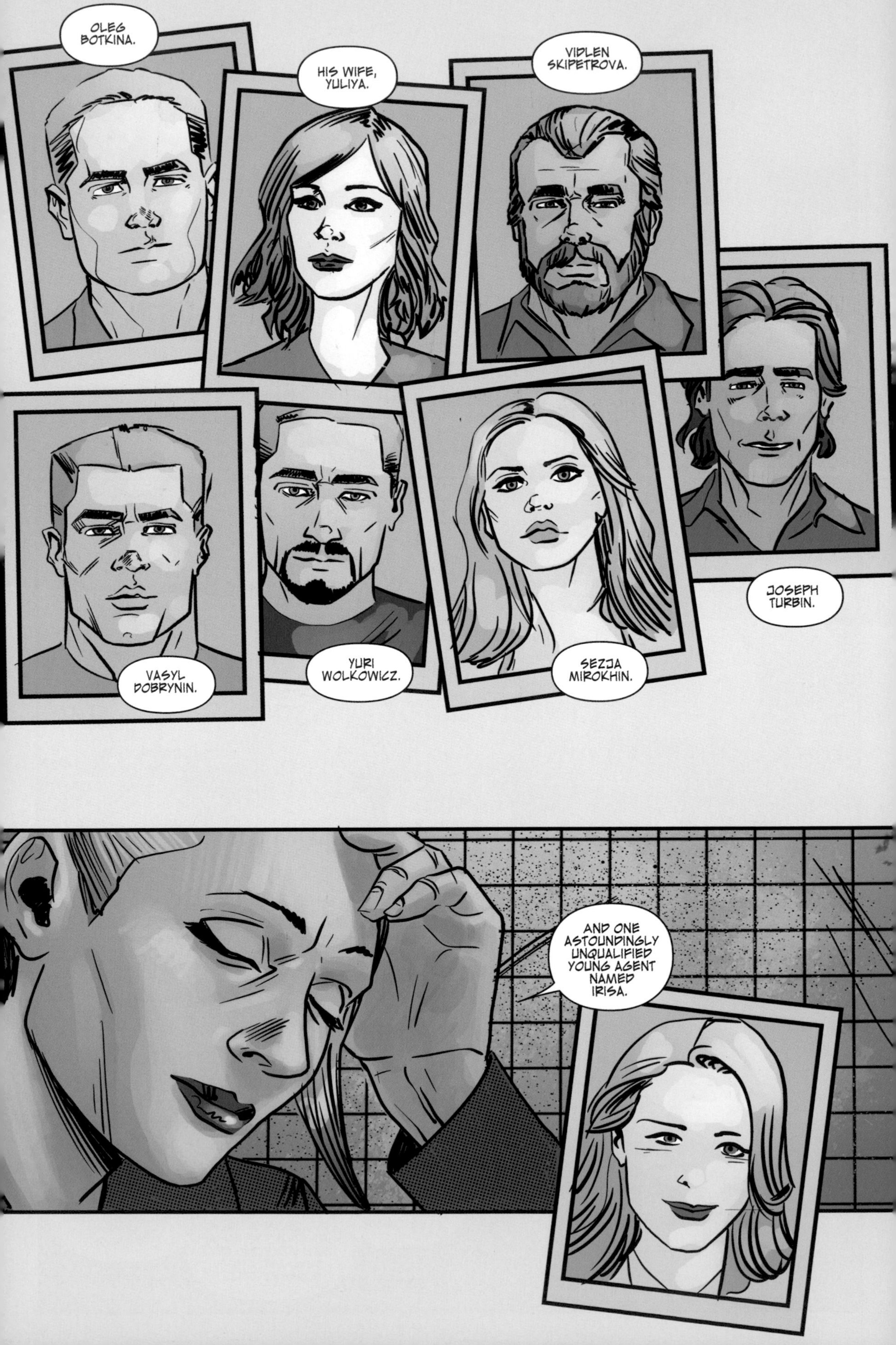
OLEG BOTKINA.
HIS WIFE, YULIYA.
VIDLEN SKIPETROVA.
JOSEPH TURBIN.
VASYL DOBRYNIN.
YURI WOLKOWICZ.
SEZJA MIROKHIN.
AND ONE ASTOUNDINGLY UNQUALIFIED YOUNG AGENT NAMED IRISA.

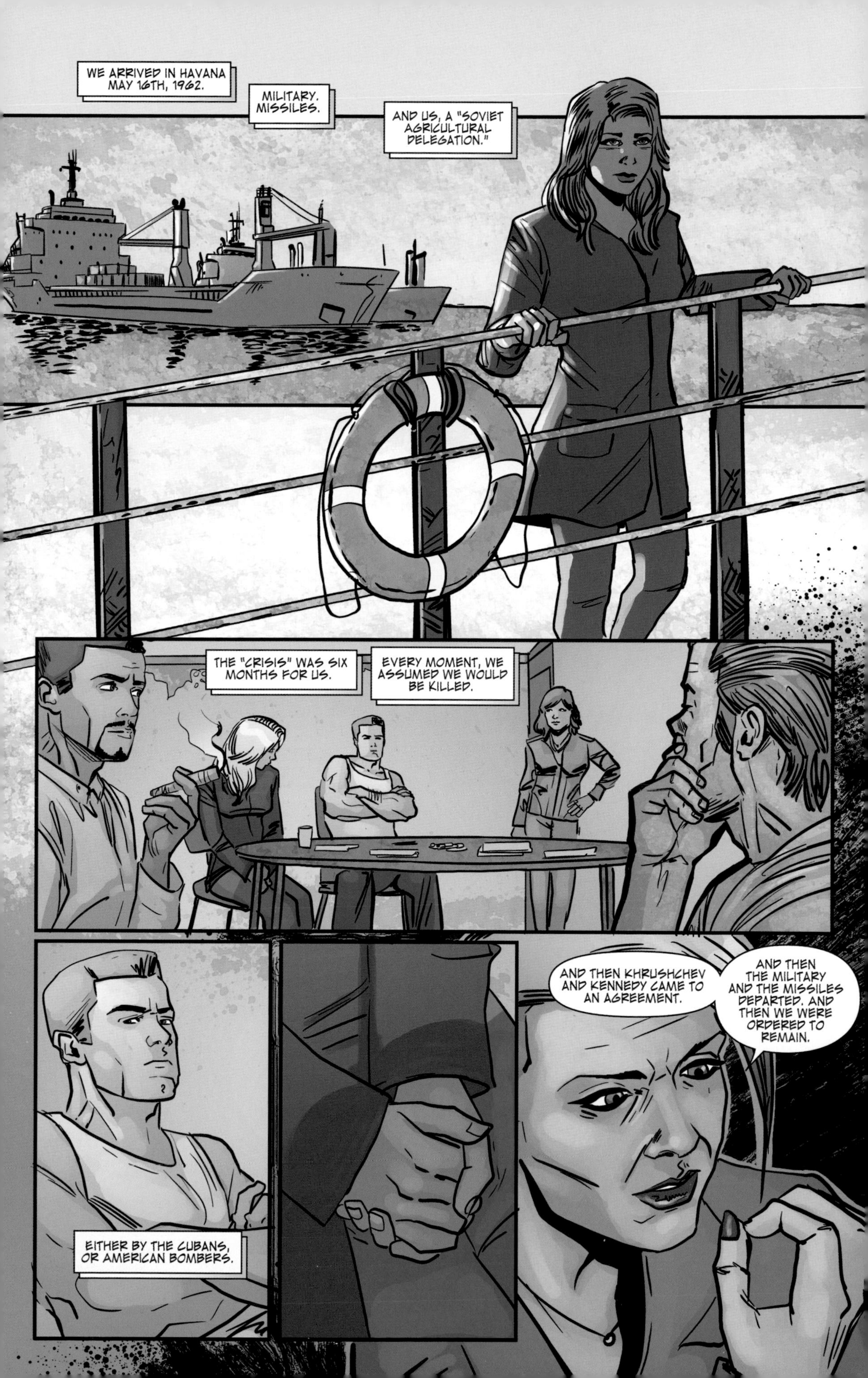

WE ARRIVED IN HAVANA MAY 16TH, 1962.
MILITARY. MISSILES.
AND US, A "SOVIET AGRICULTURAL DELEGATION."
THE "CRISIS" WAS SIX MONTHS FOR US.
EVERY MOMENT, WE ASSUMED WE WOULD BE KILLED.
EITHER BY THE CUBANS, OR AMERICAN BOMBERS.
AND THEN KHRUSHCHEV AND KENNEDY CAME TO AN AGREEMENT.
AND THEN THE MILITARY AND THE MISSILES DEPARTED. AND THEN WE WERE ORDERED TO REMAIN.

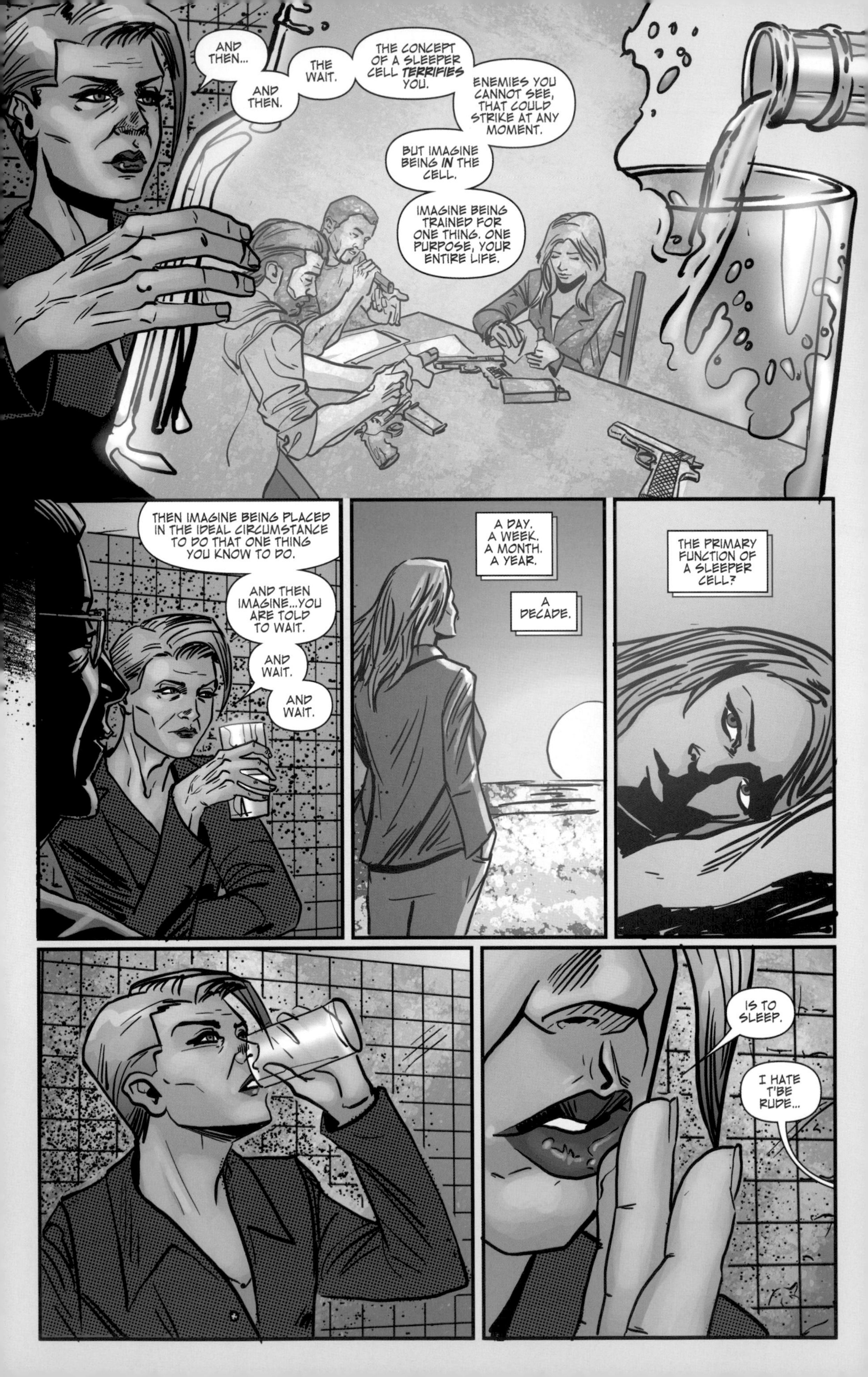
AND THEN...
AND THEN.
THE WAIT.
THE CONCEPT OF A SLEEPER CELL TERRIFIES YOU.
ENEMIES YOU CANNOT SEE, THAT COULD STRIKE AT ANY MOMENT.
BUT IMAGINE BEING IN THE CELL.
IMAGINE BEING TRAINED FOR ONE THING. ONE PURPOSE, YOUR ENTIRE LIFE.
THEN IMAGINE BEING PLACED IN THE IDEAL CIRCUMSTANCE TO DO THAT ONE THING YOU KNOW TO DO.
AND THEN IMAGINE...YOU ARE TOLD TO WAIT.
AND WAIT.
AND WAIT.
A DAY. A WEEK. A MONTH. A YEAR.
A DECADE.
THE PRIMARY FUNCTION OF A SLEEPER CELL?
IS TO SLEEP.
I HATE T'BE RUDE...

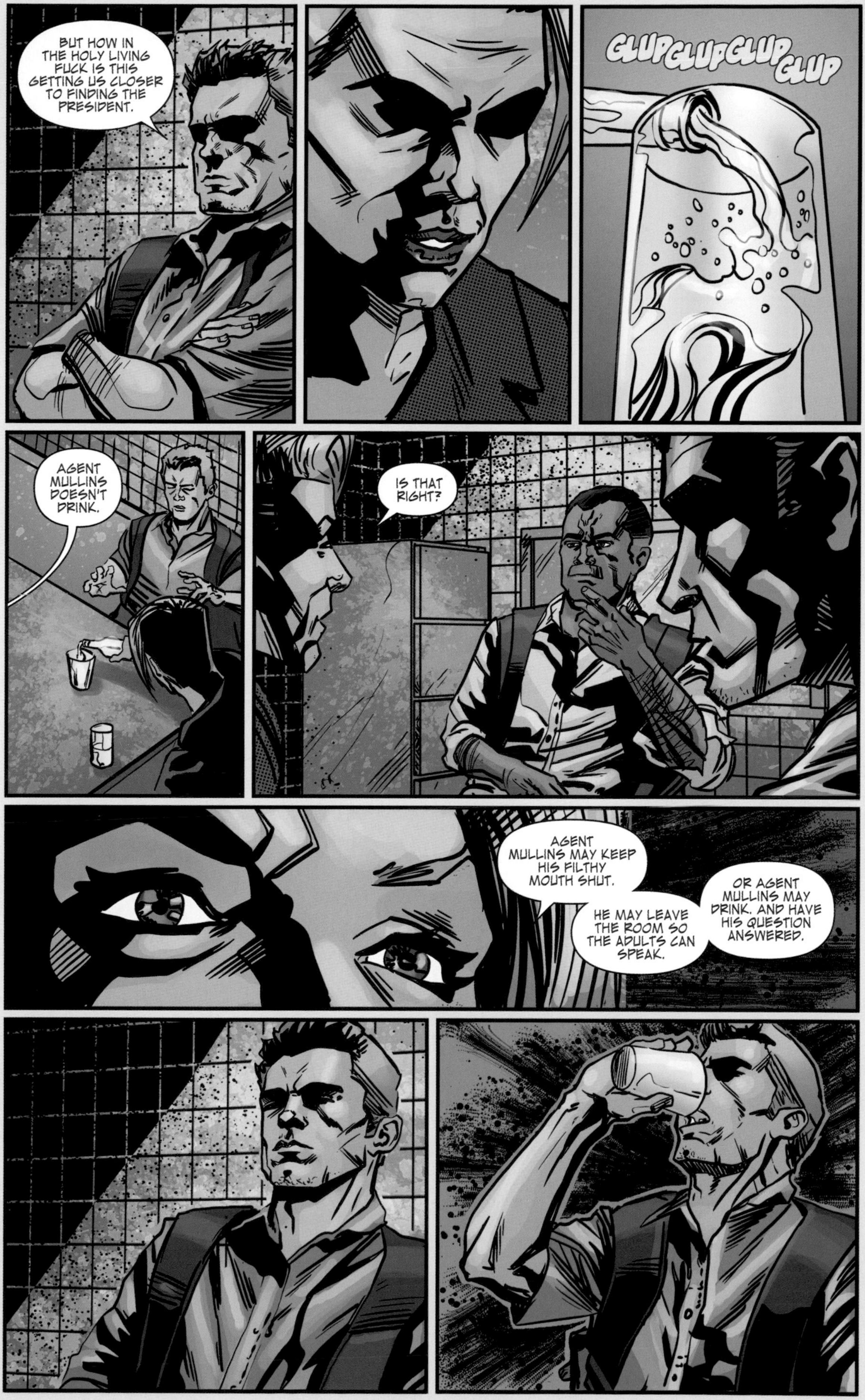
BUT HOW IN THE HOLY LIVING FUCK IS THIS GETTING US CLOSER TO FINDING THE PRESIDENT.
GLUPGLUPGLUPGLUP
AGENT MULLINS DOESN'T DRINK.
IS THAT RIGHT?
AGENT MULLINS MAY KEEP HIS FILTHY MOUTH SHUT.
HE MAY LEAVE THE ROOM SO THE ADULTS CAN SPEAK.
OR AGENT MULLINS MAY DRINK. AND HAVE HIS QUESTION ANSWERED.

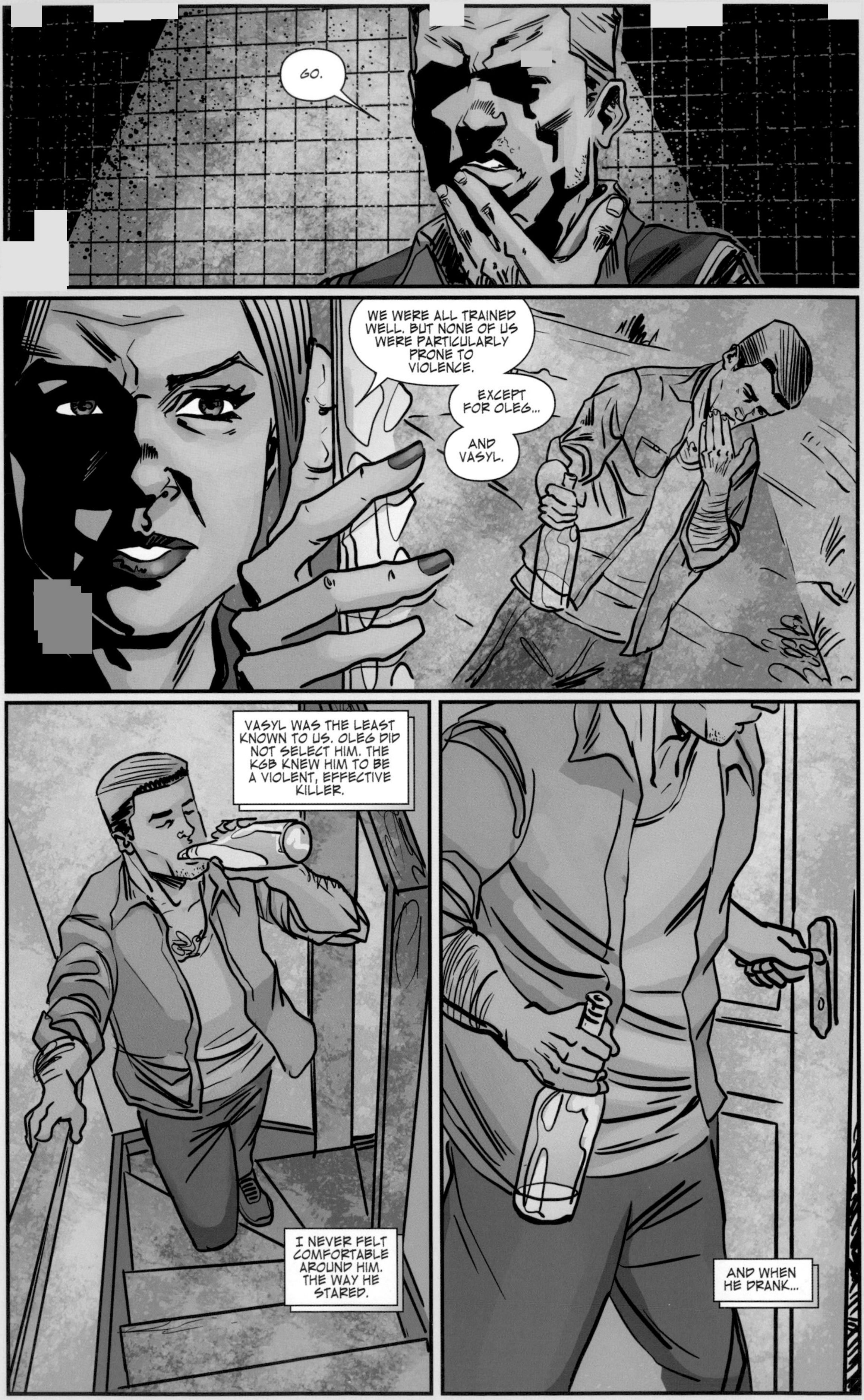
GO.
WE WERE ALL TRAINED WELL. BUT NONE OF US WERE PARTICULARLY PRONE TO VIOLENCE.
EXCEPT FOR OLEG...
AND VASYL.
VASYL WAS THE LEAST KNOWN TO US. OLEG DID NOT SELECT HIM. THE KGB KNEW HIM TO BE A VIOLENT, EFFECTIVE KILLER.
I NEVER FELT COMFORTABLE AROUND HIM. THE WAY HE STARED.
AND WHEN HE DRANK...

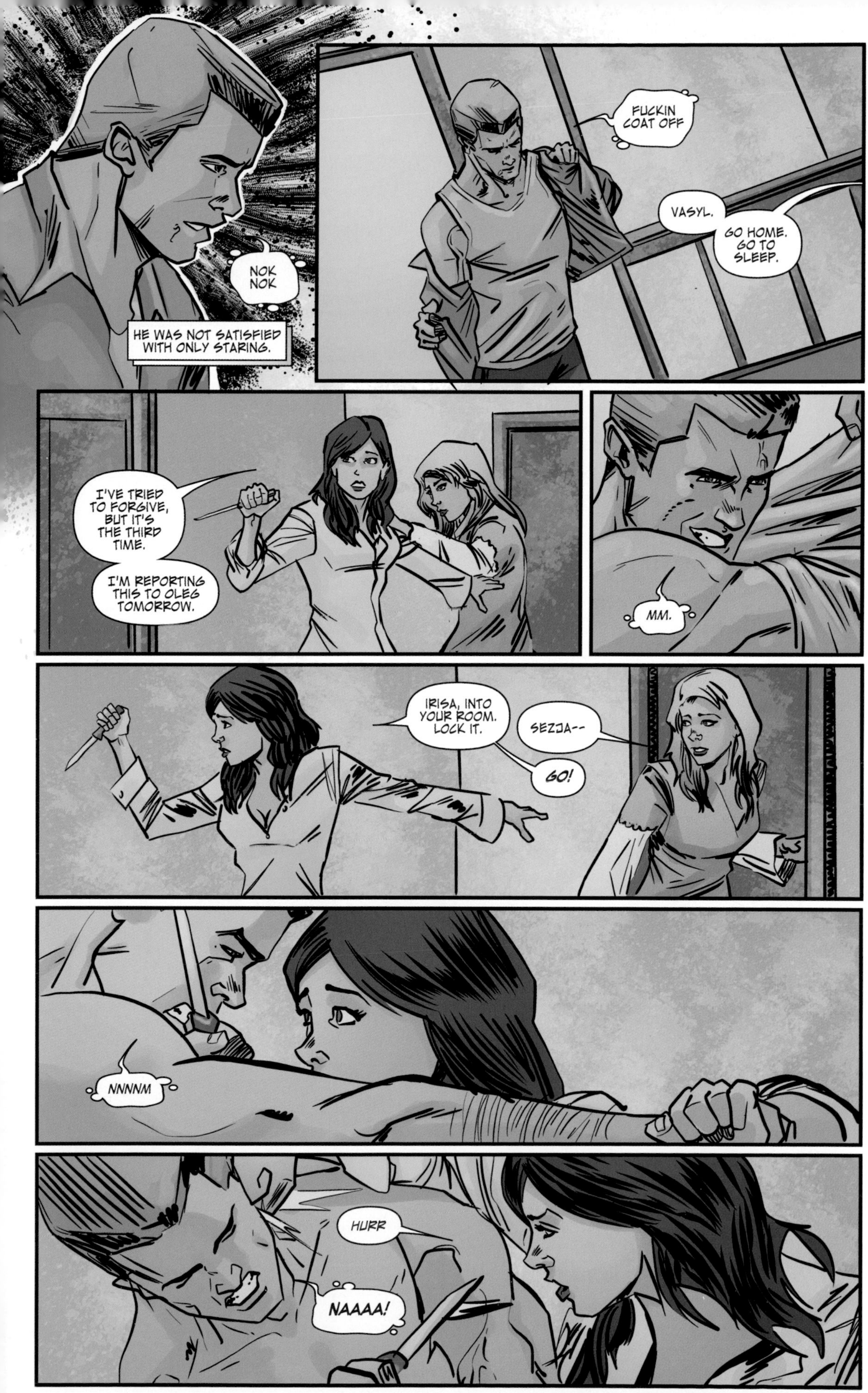
NOK NOK
HE WAS NOT SATISFIED WITH ONLY STARING.
FUCKIN COAT OFF
VASYL.
GO HOME. GO TO SLEEP.
I'VE TRIED TO FORGIVE, BUT IT'S THE THIRD TIME.
I'M REPORTING THIS TO OLEG TOMORROW.
MM.
IRISA, INTO YOUR ROOM. LOCK IT.
SEZJA--
GO!
NNNNM
HURR
NAAAA!

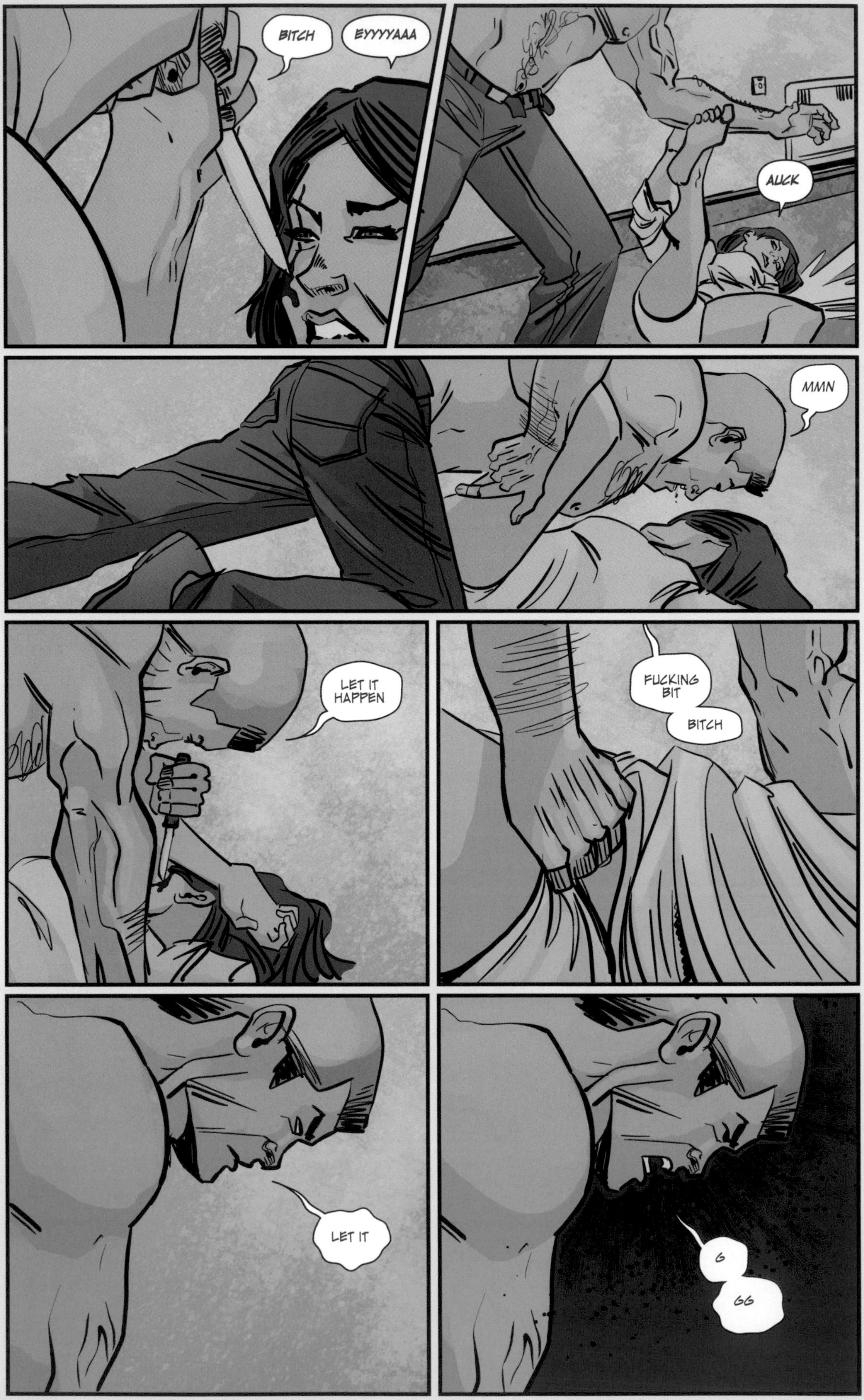
BITCH
EYYYYAAA
AUCK
MMN
LET IT HAPPEN
FUCKING BIT
BITCH
LET IT
G
GG

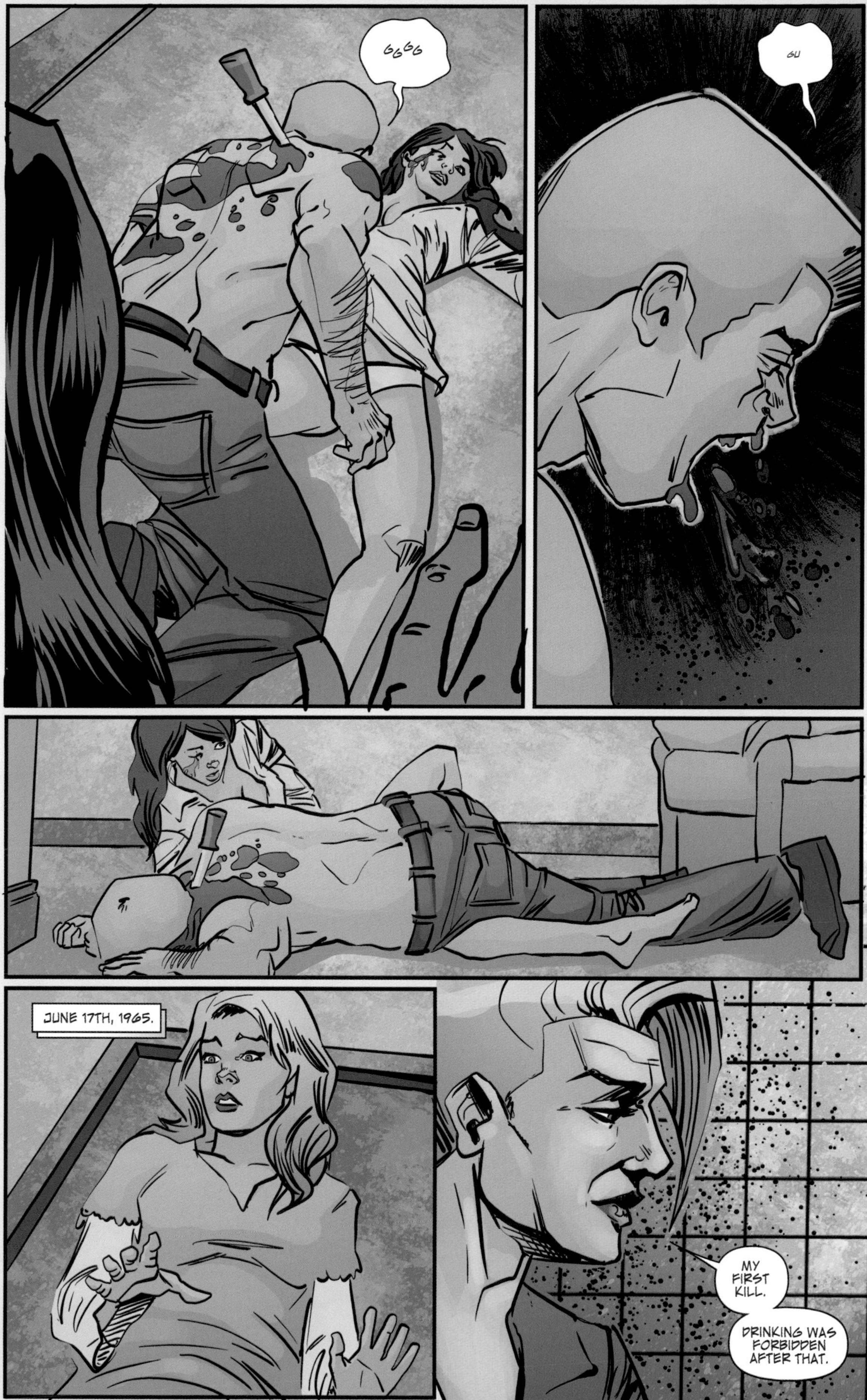
GGGG
GU
JUNE 17TH, 1965.
MY FIRST KILL.
DRINKING WAS FORBIDDEN AFTER THAT.

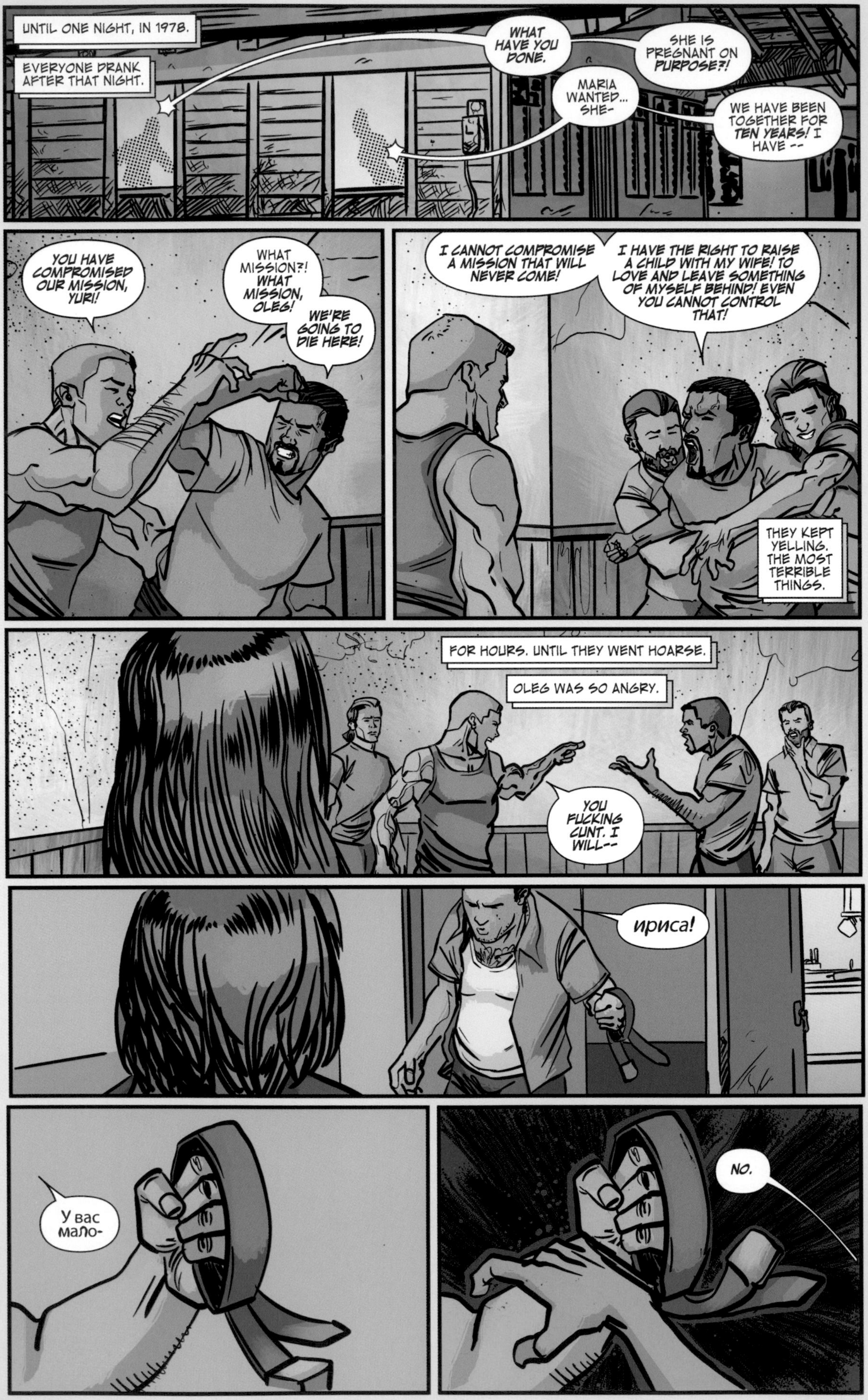
UNTIL ONE NIGHT, IN 1978.
EVERYONE DRANK AFTER THAT NIGHT.
WHAT HAVE YOU DONE.
SHE IS PREGNANT ON PURPOSE?!
MARIA WANTED... SHE-
WE HAVE BEEN TOGETHER FOR TEN YEARS! I HAVE --
YOU HAVE COMPROMISED OUR MISSION, YURI!
WHAT MISSION?! WHAT MISSION, OLEG!
WE'RE GOING TO DIE HERE!
I CANNOT COMPROMISE A MISSION THAT WILL NEVER COME!
I HAVE THE RIGHT TO RAISE A CHILD WITH MY WIFE! TO LOVE AND LEAVE SOMETHING OF MYSELF BEHIND! EVEN YOU CANNOT CONTROL THAT!
THEY KEPT YELLING. THE MOST TERRIBLE THINGS.
FOR HOURS. UNTIL THEY WENT HOARSE.
OLEG WAS SO ANGRY.
YOU FUCKING CUNT. I WILL--
ириса!
У вас мало-
NO.

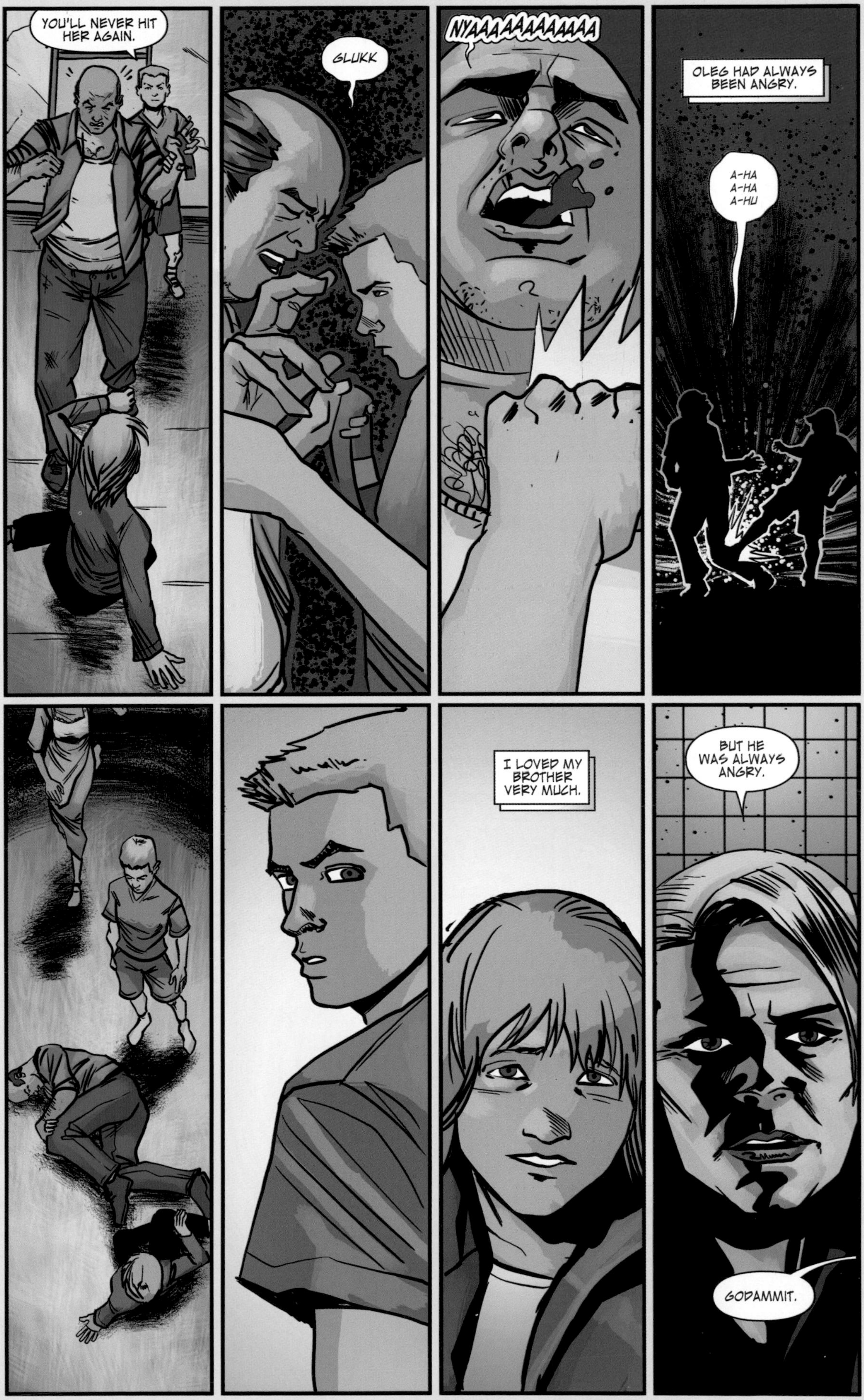
YOU'LL NEVER HIT HER AGAIN.
GLUKK
NYAAAAAAAAAAAA
OLEG HAD ALWAYS BEEN ANGRY.
A-HA A-HA A-HU
I LOVED MY BROTHER VERY MUCH.
BUT HE WAS ALWAYS ANGRY.
GODAMMIT.

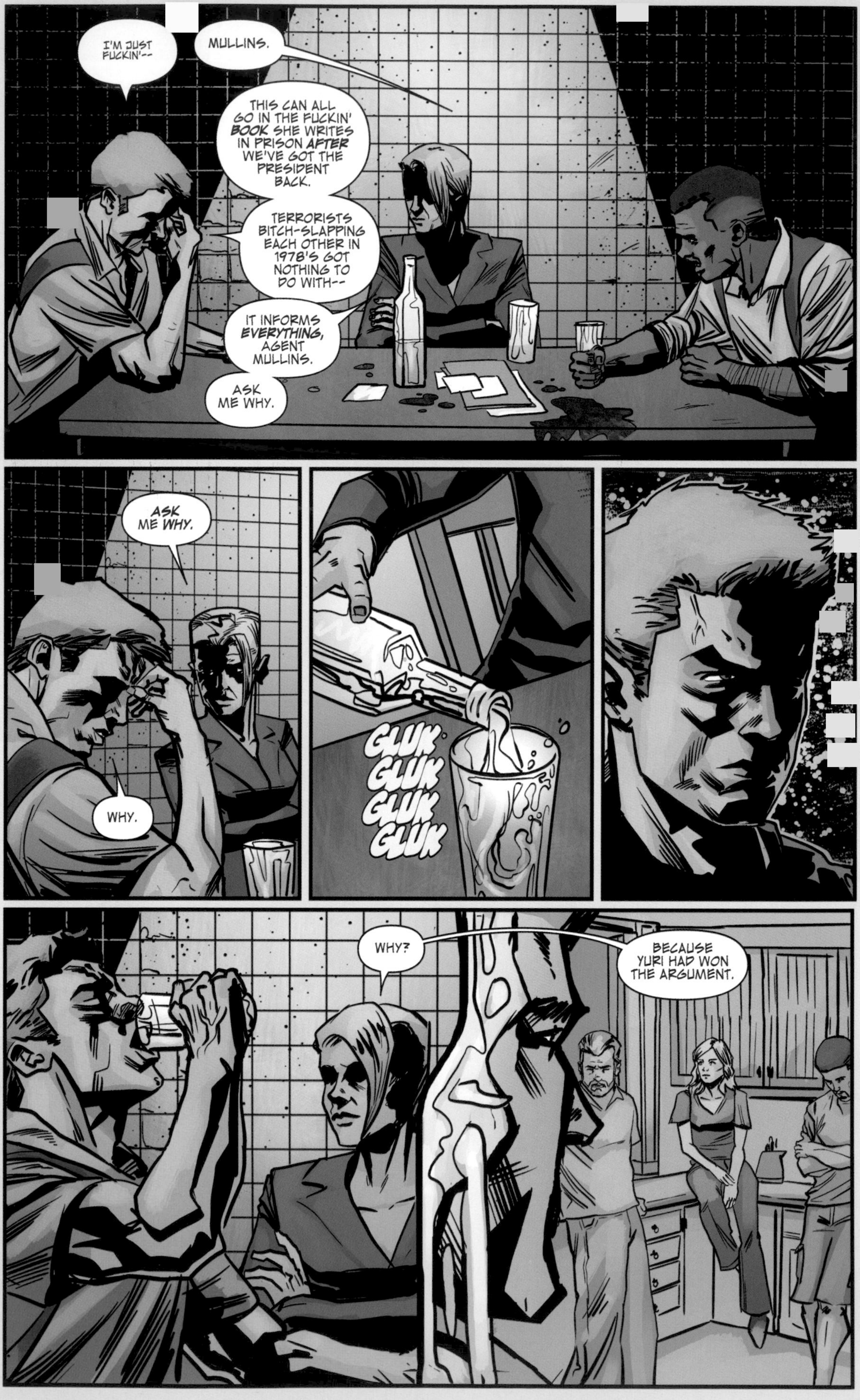
I'M JUST FUCKIN'--
MULLINS.
THIS CAN ALL GO IN THE FUCKIN' BOOK SHE WRITES IN PRISON AFTER WE'VE GOT THE PRESIDENT BACK.
TERRORISTS BITCH-SLAPPING EACH OTHER IN 1978'S GOT NOTHING TO DO WITH--
IT INFORMS EVERYTHING, AGENT MULLINS.
ASK ME WHY.
ASK ME WHY.
WHY.
GLUK GLUK GLUK GLUK
WHY?
BECAUSE YURI HAD WON THE ARGUMENT.

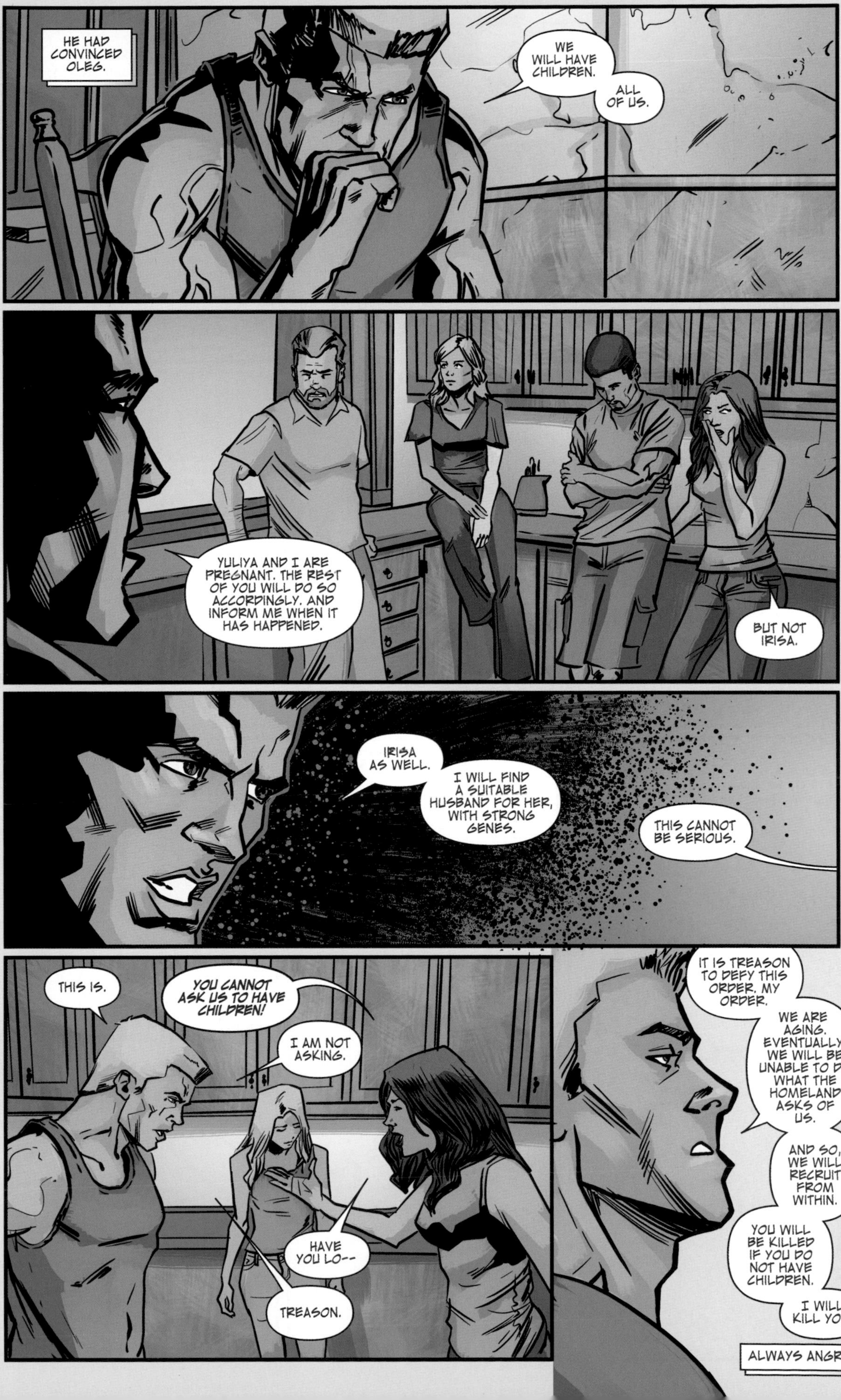
HE HAD CONVINCED OLEG.
WE WILL HAVE CHILDREN.
ALL OF US.
YULIYA AND I ARE PREGNANT. THE REST OF YOU WILL DO SO ACCORDINGLY. AND INFORM ME WHEN IT HAS HAPPENED.
BUT NOT IRISA.
IRISA AS WELL.
I WILL FIND A SUITABLE HUSBAND FOR HER, WITH STRONG GENES.
THIS CANNOT BE SERIOUS.
THIS IS.
YOU CANNOT ASK US TO HAVE CHILDREN!
I AM NOT ASKING.
HAVE YOU LO--
TREASON.
IT IS TREASON TO DEFY THIS ORDER. MY ORDER.
WE ARE AGING. EVENTUALLY, WE WILL BE UNABLE TO DO WHAT THE HOMELAND ASKS OF US.
AND SO, WE WILL RECRUIT FROM WITHIN.
YOU WILL BE KILLED IF YOU DO NOT HAVE CHILDREN.
I WILL KILL YOU.
ALWAYS ANGRY.

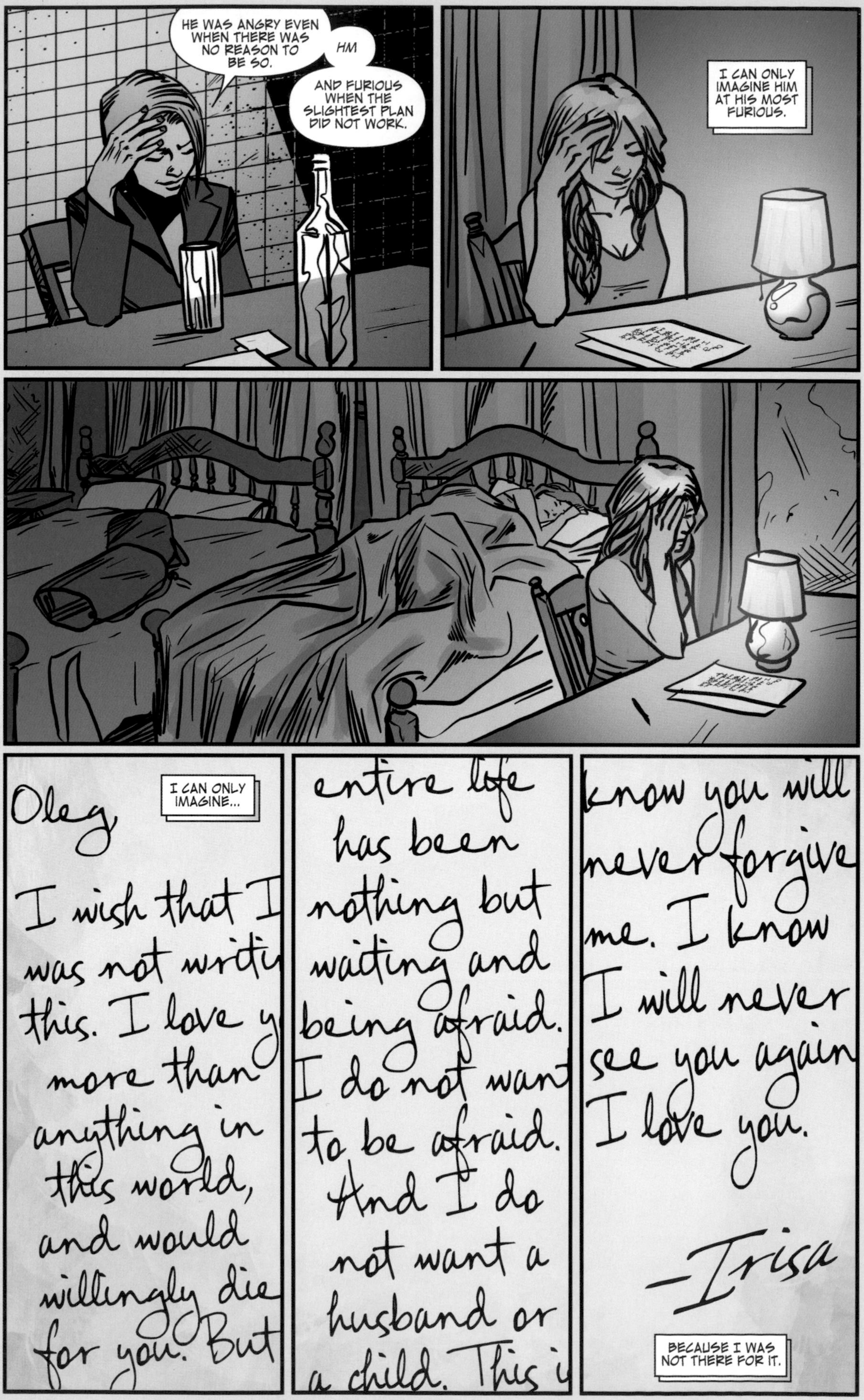
HE WAS ANGRY EVEN WHEN THERE WAS NO REASON TO BE SO.
HM
AND FURIOUS WHEN THE SLIGHTEST PLAN DID NOT WORK.
I CAN ONLY IMAGINE HIM AT HIS MOST FURIOUS.
I CAN ONLY IMAGINE...
Oleg
I wish that I was not writi this. I love y more than anything in this world, and would willingly die for you. But
entire life has been nothing but waiting and being afraid. I do not want to be afraid. And I do not want a husband or a child. This i
know you will never forgive me. I know I will never see you again I love you.
-Irisa
BECAUSE I WAS NOT THERE FOR IT.

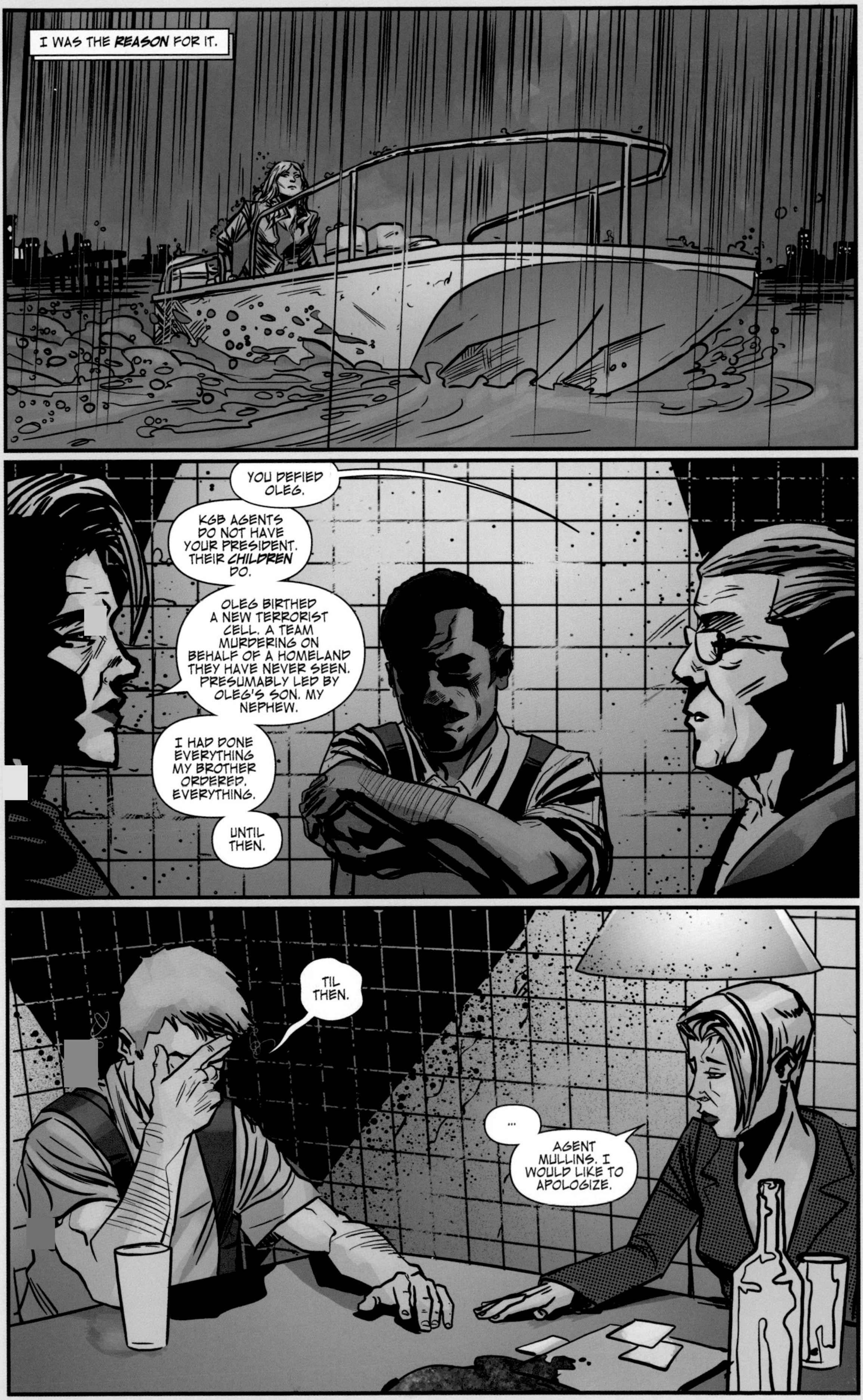
I WAS THE REASON FOR IT.
YOU DEFIED OLEG.
KGB AGENTS DO NOT HAVE YOUR PRESIDENT. THEIR CHILDREN DO.
OLEG BIRTHED A NEW TERRORIST CELL. A TEAM MURDERING ON BEHALF OF A HOMELAND THEY HAVE NEVER SEEN. PRESUMABLY LED BY OLEG'S SON. MY NEPHEW.
I HAD DONE EVERYTHING MY BROTHER ORDERED. EVERYTHING.
UNTIL THEN.
TIL THEN.
...
AGENT MULLINS. I WOULD LIKE TO APOLOGIZE.

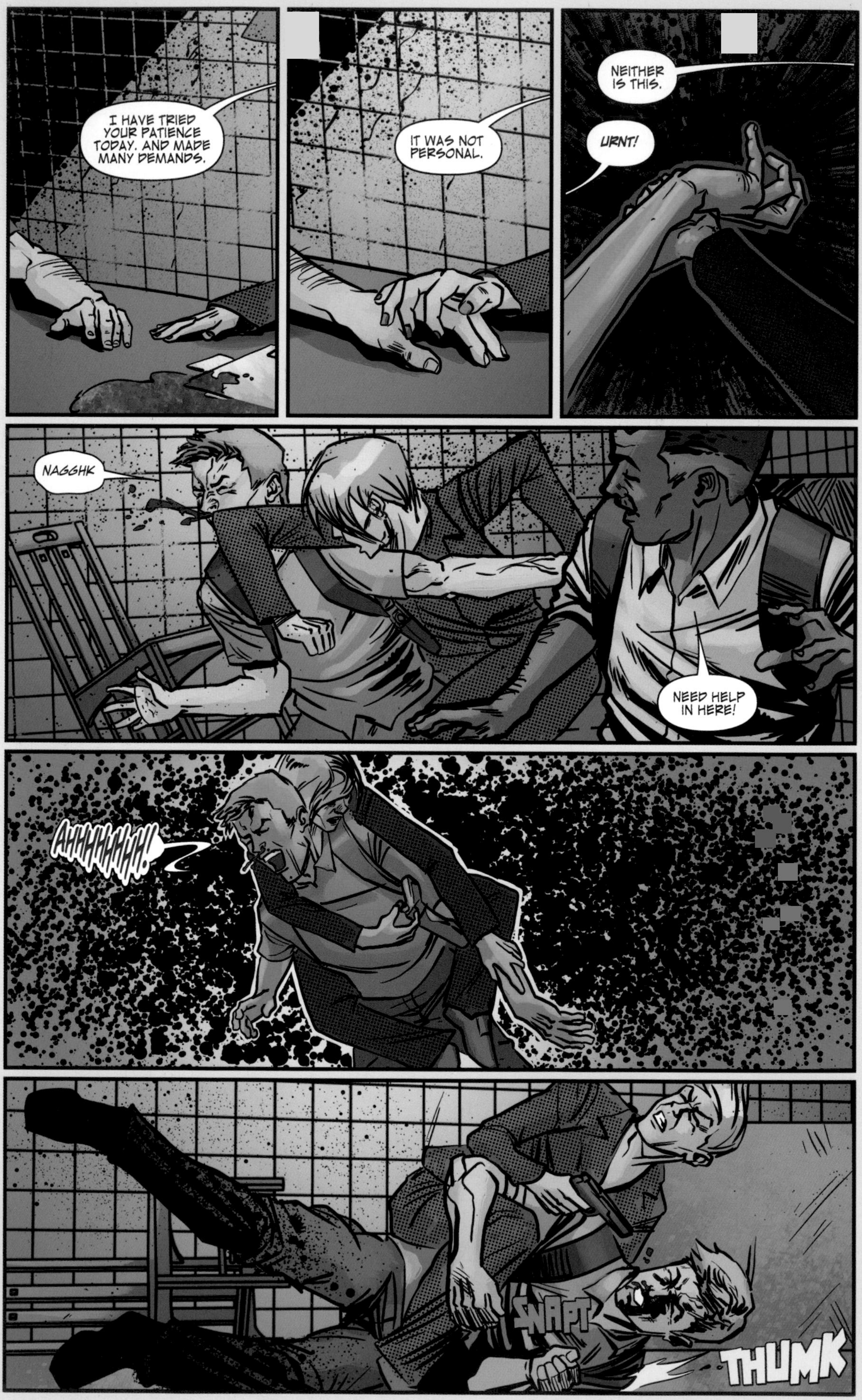
I HAVE TRIED YOUR PATIENCE TODAY. AND MADE MANY DEMANDS.
IT WAS NOT PERSONAL.
NEITHER IS THIS.
URNT!
NAGGHK
NEED HELP IN HERE!
AHHHHHHHH!
SNAPT
THUMK

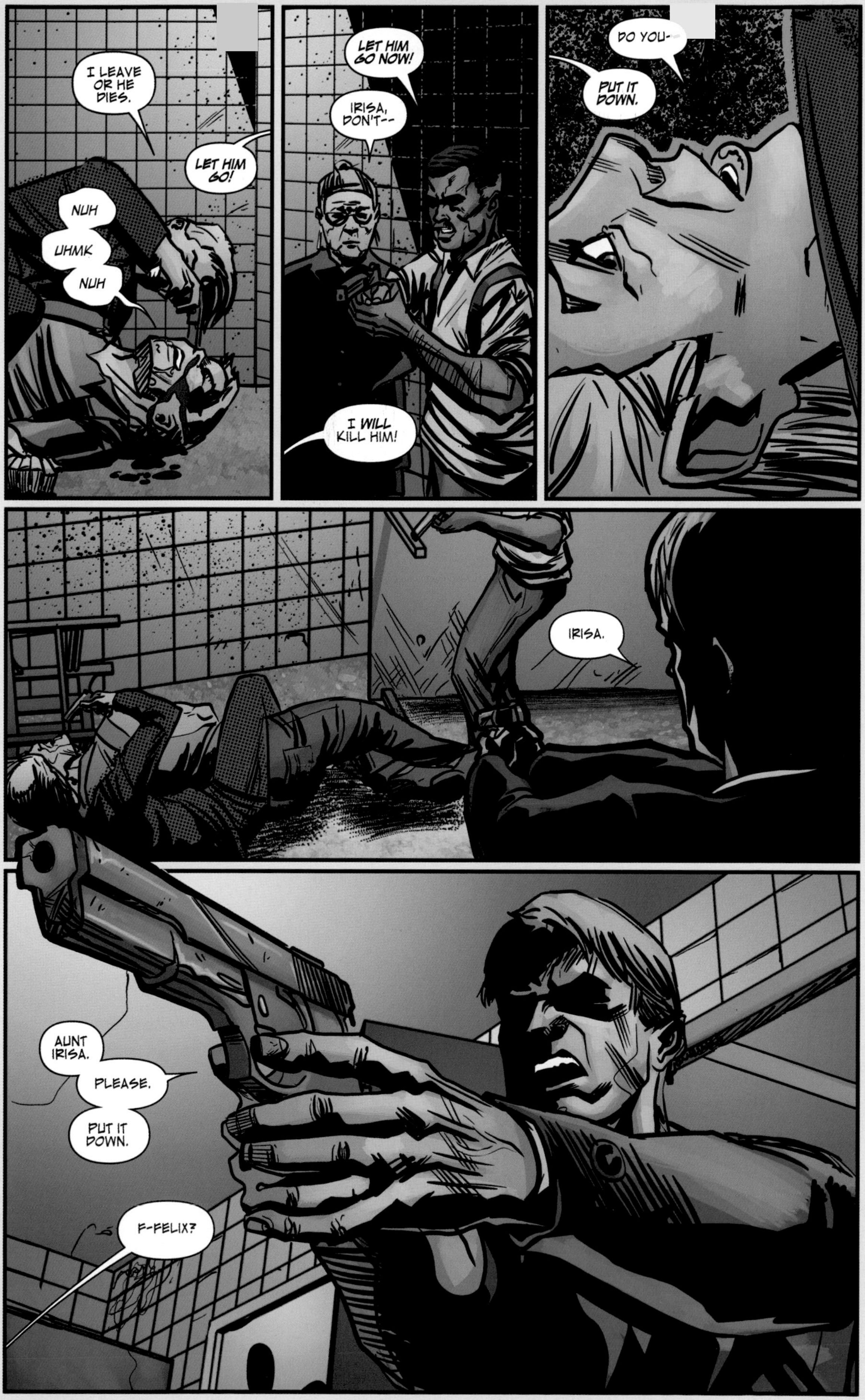
I LEAVE OR HE DIES.
LET HIM GO!
NUH
UHMK
NUH
LET HIM GO NOW!
IRISA, DON'T--
I WILL KILL HIM!
DO YOU-
PUT IT DOWN.
IRISA.
AUNT IRISA.
PLEASE.
PUT IT DOWN.
F-FELIX?

COVER GALLERY

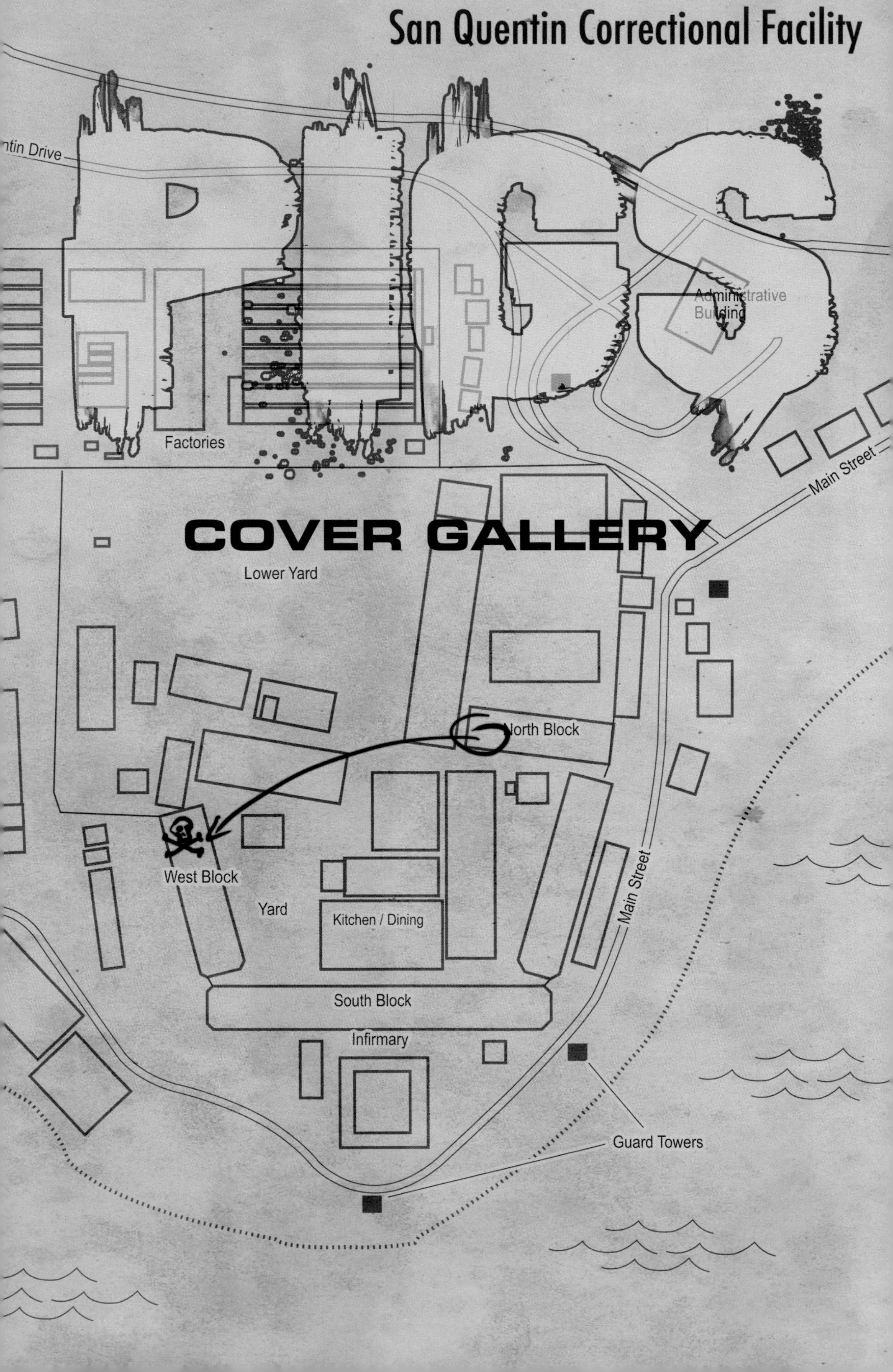
San Quentin Correctional Facility
ntin Drive
Administrative Building
Factories
Main Street
Lower Yard
North Block
West Block
Yard
Kitchen / Dining
Main Street
South Block
Infirmary
Guard Towers

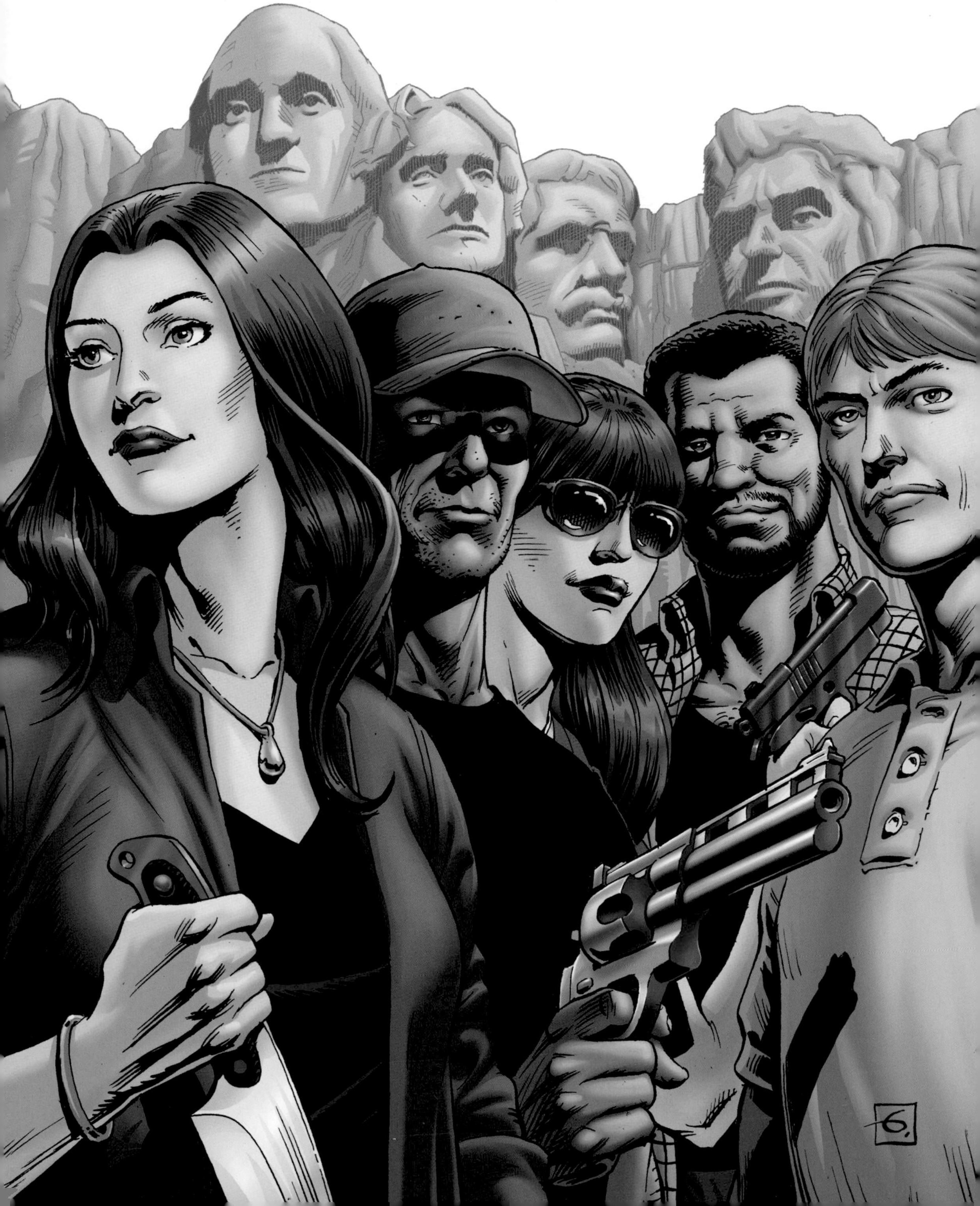

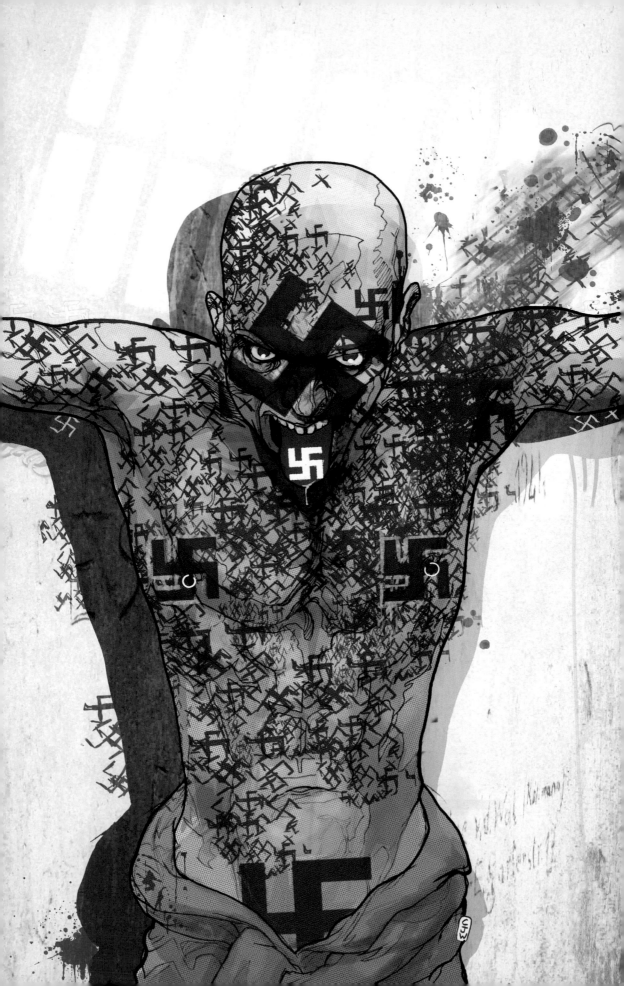

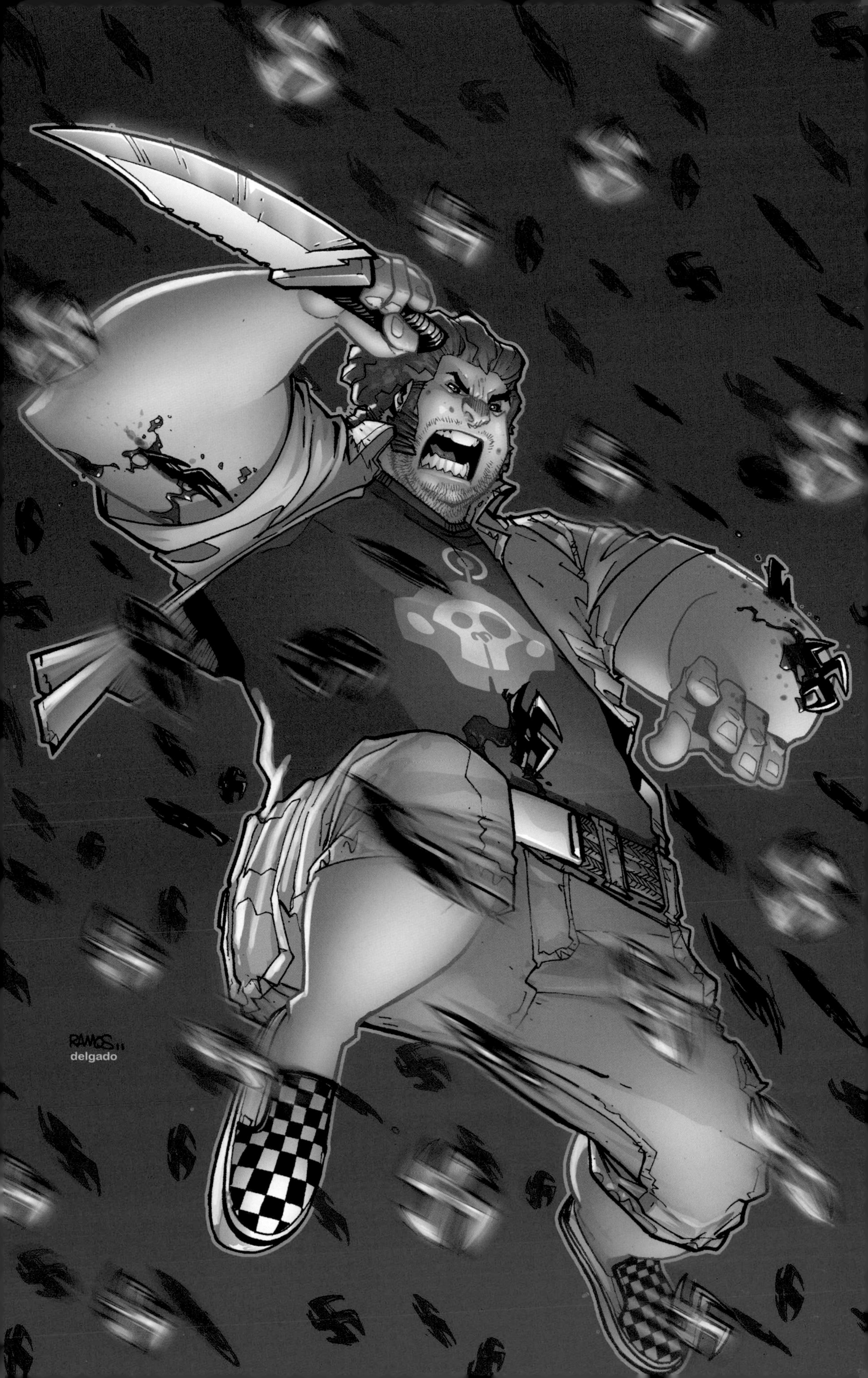
RAMOS
delgado

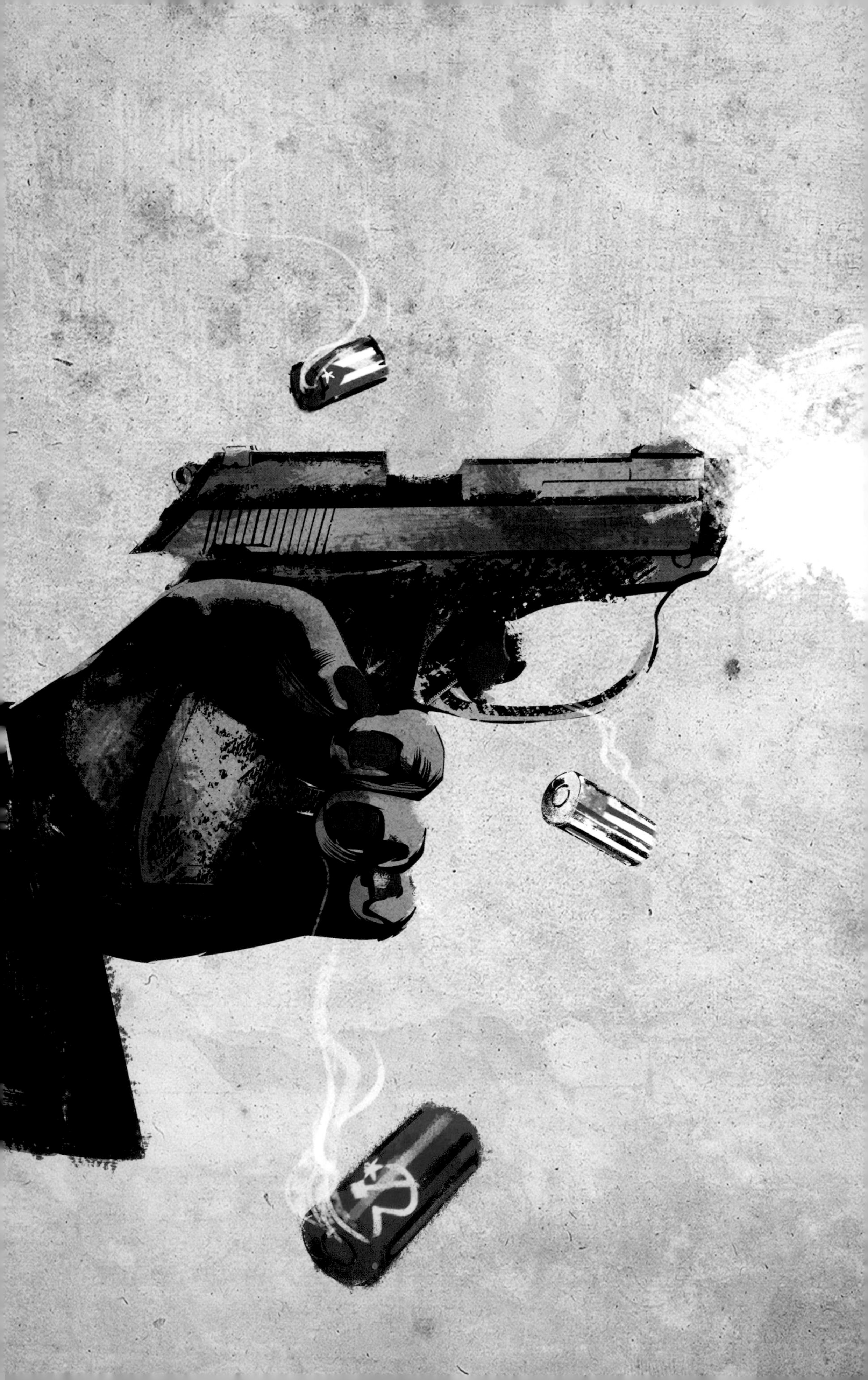

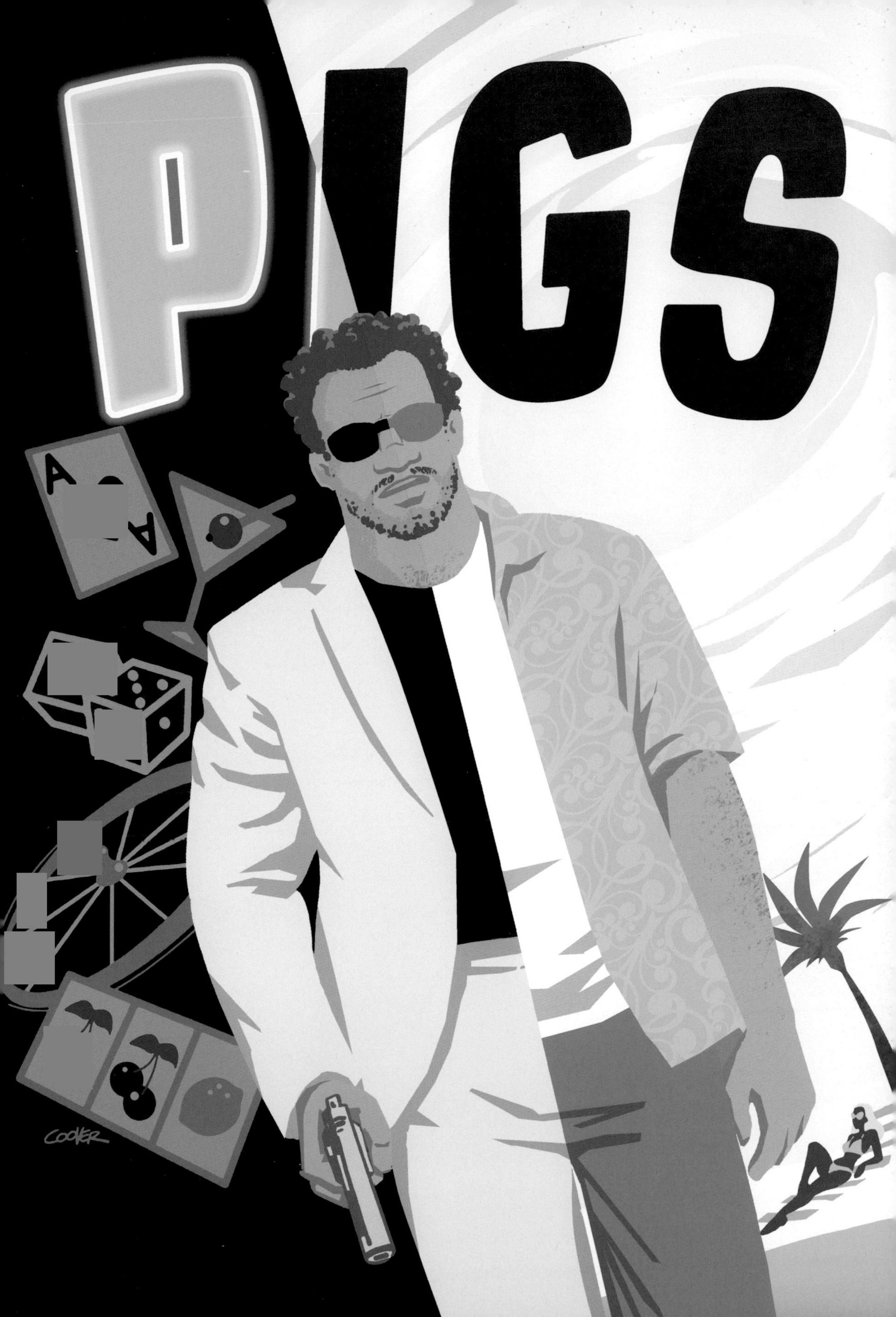
PIGS
COOVER

Art by: COLLEEN COOVER

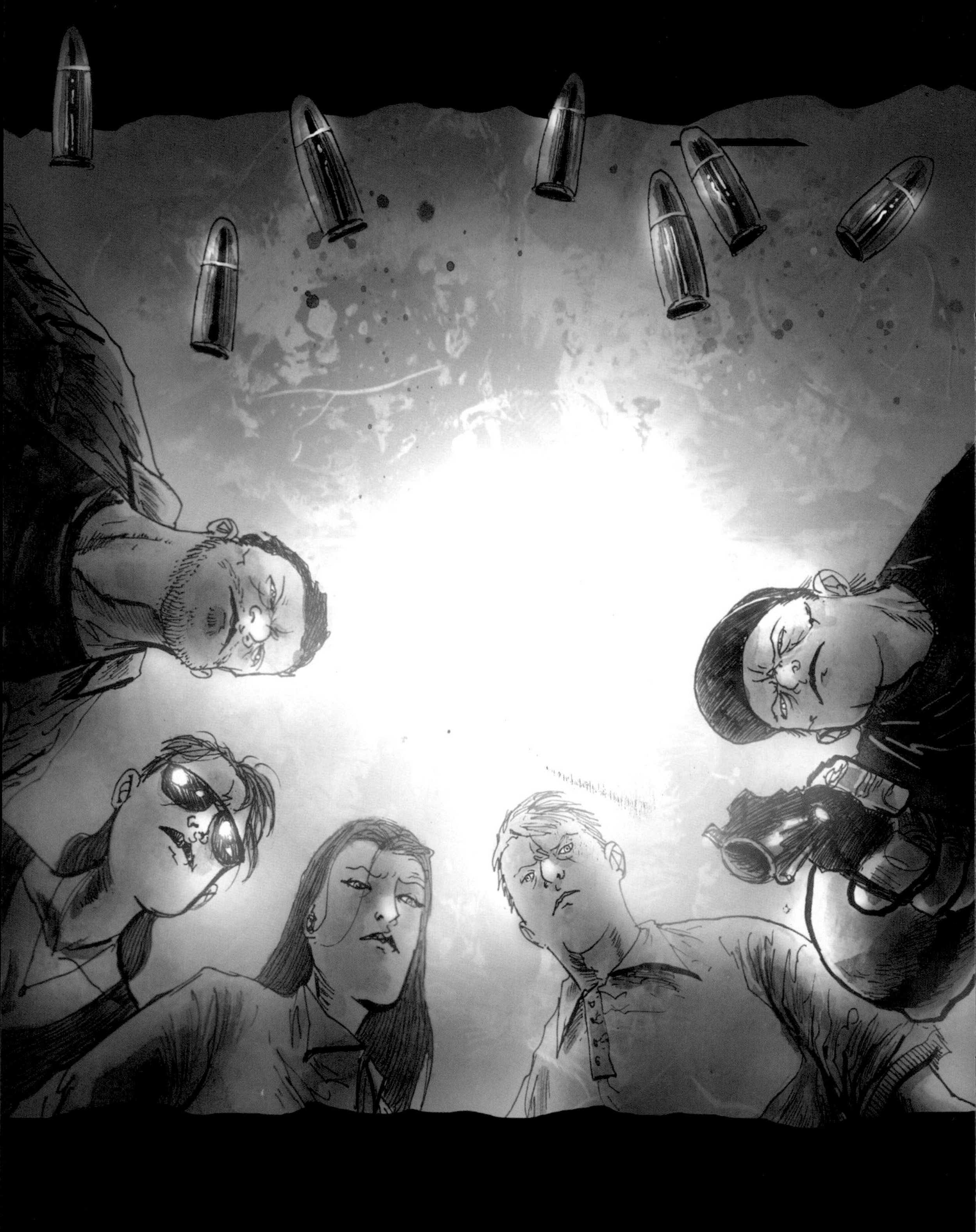

Art by: BEN TEMPLESMITH

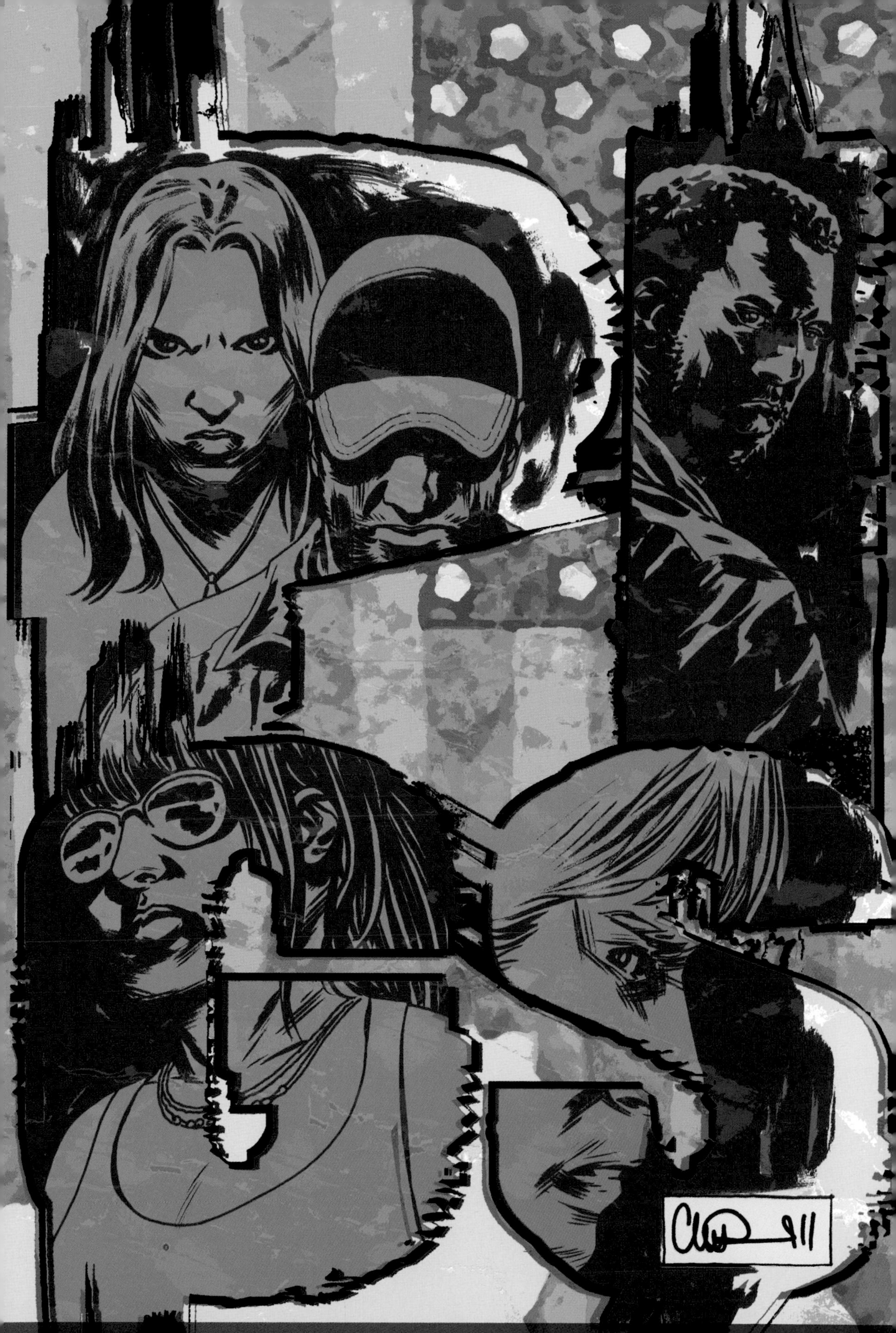

Art by: CHARLIE ADLARD

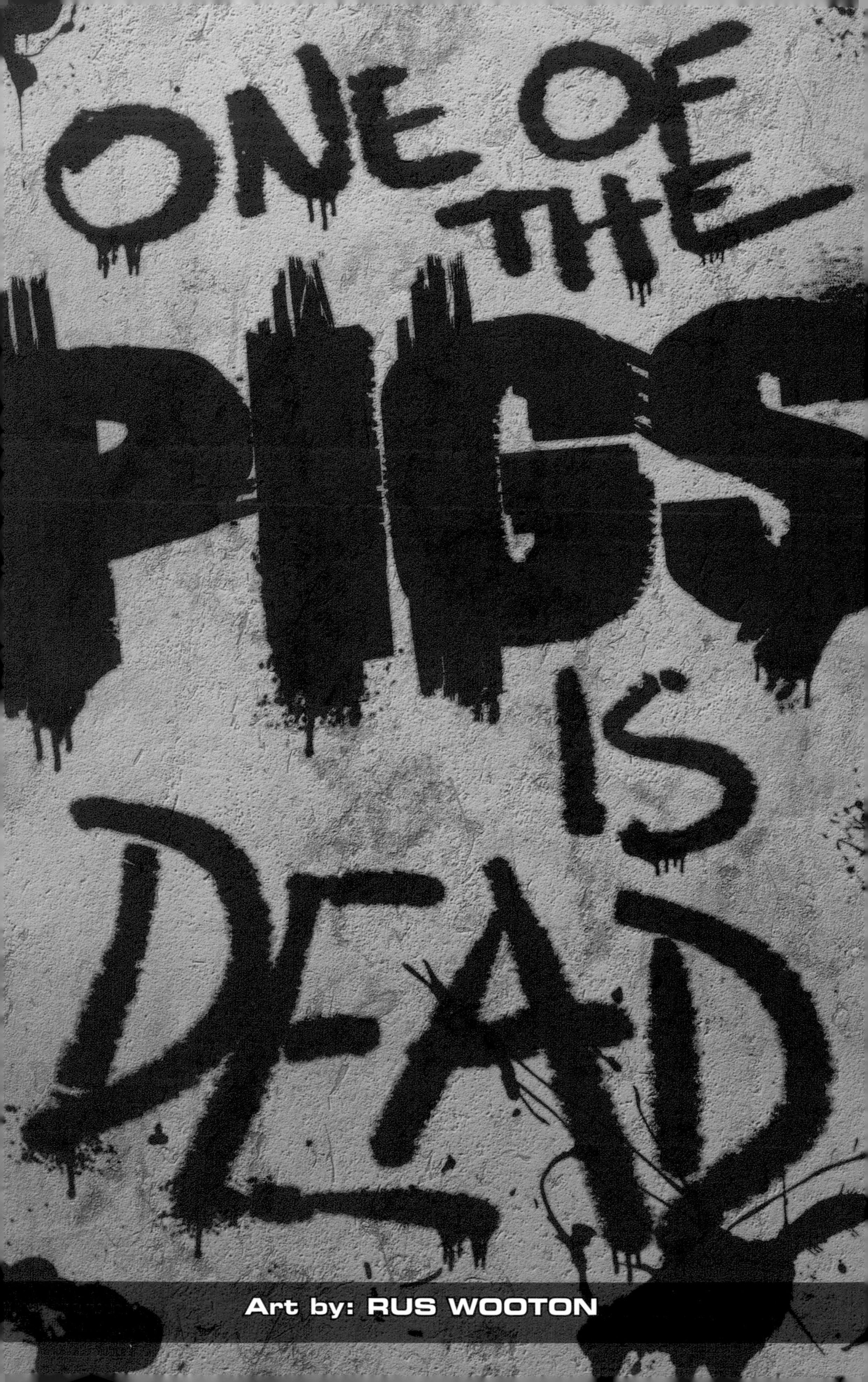
ONE OF THE
PIGS
IS
DEAD

Art by: RUS WOOTON

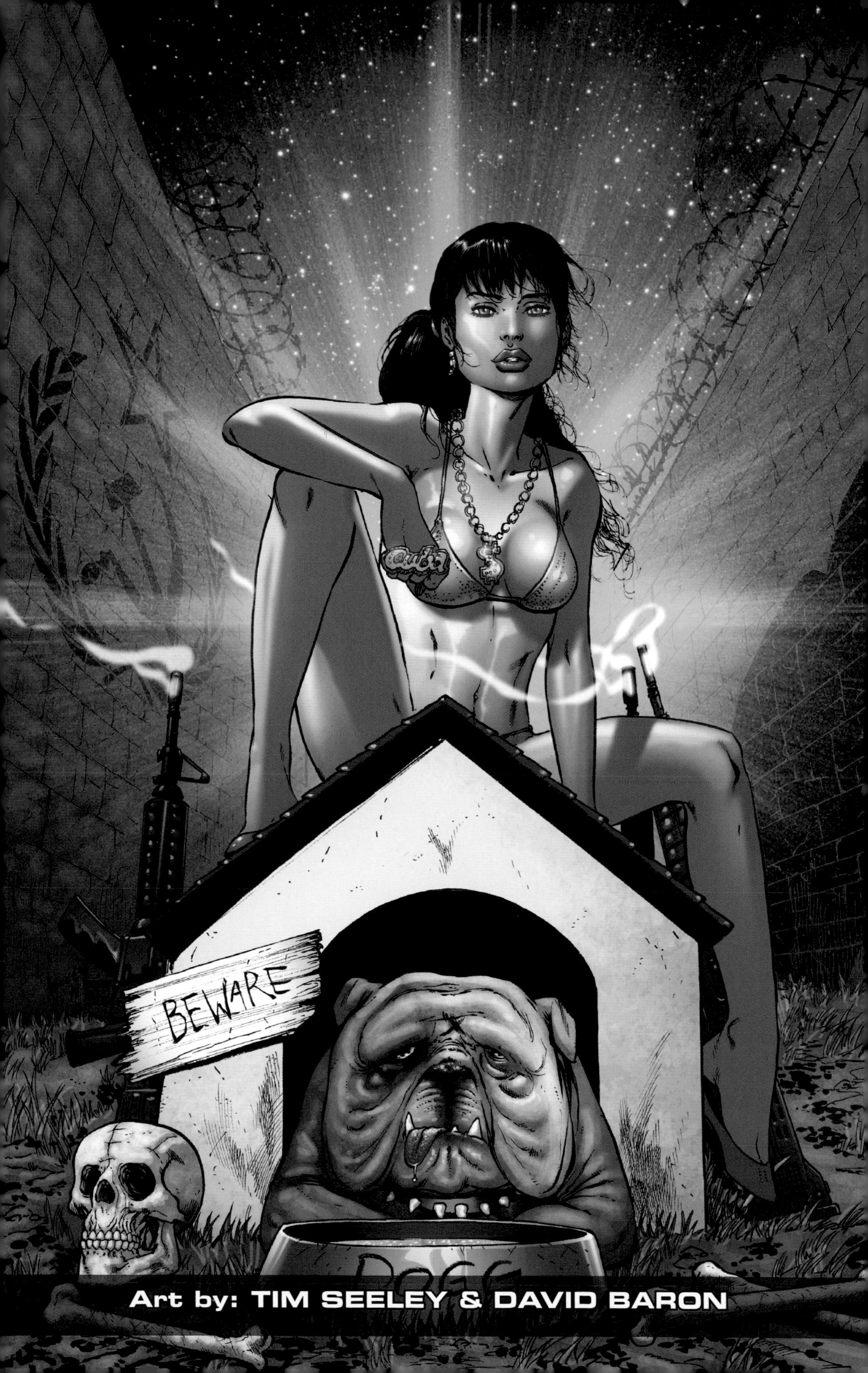
BEWARE

Art by: TIM SEELEY & DAVID BARON

CREATOR BIOS

NATE COSBY is a writer, editor and producer from Mississippi. He was a producer/writer for PBS' relaunched *THE ELECTRIC COMPANY*, where he developed animated properties. He was an editor at Marvel Entertainment, overseeing acclaimed series including the Harvey Award-winning *THOR THE MIGHTY AVENGER*, the Eisner Award-winning *WONDERFUL WIZARD OF OZ* and *MARVELOUS LAND OF OZ*, as well as *X-MEN FIRST CLASS*, *SPIDER-MAN*, *PRIDE & PREJUDICE*, *HULK*, *SPIDER-MAN LOVES MARY JANE* and many others. He co-wrote/edited the Harvey Award-nominated Jim Henson's *THE STORYTELLER* for Archaia Entertainment. He currently writes the acclaimed *COW BOY* for Archaia, *BUDDY COPS* for Dark Horse Entertainment, and co-writes *PIGS* for Image Comics.

BEN McCOOL is a British writer born in Birmingham, England. He has worked on characters such as *SUPERMAN* and the *JUSTICE LEAGUE* for DC Comics, and *CAPTAIN AMERICA* for Marvel Comics. Creator-owned projects such as *CHOKER* (with artist Ben Templesmith) and *MEMOIR* (with artist Nikki Cook) have been published by Image Comics. Other works include *THE FIVE-DIMENSIONAL ADVENTURES OF DIRK DAVIES* (with Emmy award-winning artist Dean Haspiel) for video game giants Namco Bandai; *NEVSKY*, a contemporary retelling of Sergei Eisenstein's classic 1938 film *ALEXANDER NEVSKY* (released by IDW Publishing); and *LOOKOUTS*, an all-new fantasy series based on the ultra-popular PENNY ARCADE property by Jerry Holkins and Mike Krahulik. When not writing (which isn't very often) Ben loves to watch strange films and read kooky books. Though he's afraid of ghosts, he'd very much like to meet another one. Ben lives and works in New York City.

San Quentin Correctional Facility

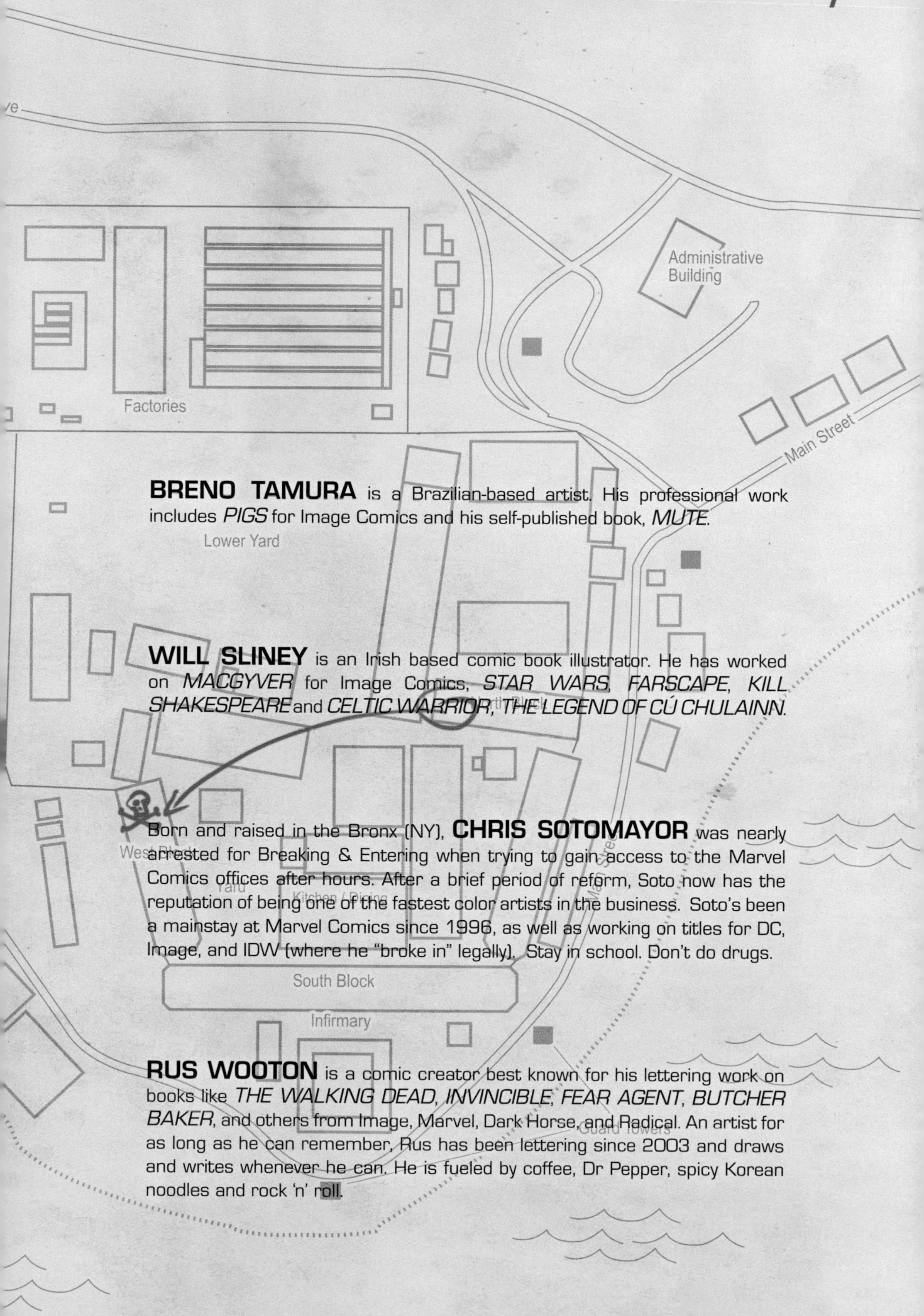

Administrative Building

Main Street

Factories

Lower Yard

BRENO TAMURA is a Brazilian-based artist. His professional work includes *PIGS* for Image Comics and his self-published book, *MUTE*.

WILL SLINEY is an Irish based comic book illustrator. He has worked on *MACGYVER* for Image Comics, *STAR WARS*, *FARSCAPE*, *KILL SHAKESPEARE* and *CELTIC WARRIOR, THE LEGEND OF CÚ CHULAINN*.

Born and raised in the Bronx (NY), **CHRIS SOTOMAYOR** was nearly arrested for Breaking & Entering when trying to gain access to the Marvel Comics offices after hours. After a brief period of reform, Soto now has the reputation of being one of the fastest color artists in the business. Soto's been a mainstay at Marvel Comics since 1996, as well as working on titles for DC, Image, and IDW (where he "broke in" legally). Stay in school. Don't do drugs.

West Yard

Kitchen / Dining

South Block

Infirmary

RUS WOOTON is a comic creator best known for his lettering work on books like *THE WALKING DEAD*, *INVINCIBLE*, *FEAR AGENT*, *BUTCHER BAKER*, and others from Image, Marvel, Dark Horse, and Radical. An artist for as long as he can remember, Rus has been lettering since 2003 and draws and writes whenever he can. He is fueled by coffee, Dr Pepper, spicy Korean noodles and rock 'n' roll.

Guard Towers